PEACEBUILDING in a FRACTIOUS WORLD

On Hoping against All Hope

Edited by
Richard Penaskovic
and Mustafa Şahin

PICKWICK *Publications* • Eugene, Oregon

PEACEBUILDING IN A FRACTIOUS WORLD
On Hoping against All Hope

Pickwick Publications
An Imprint of Wipf and Stock Publishers
199 W. 8th Ave., Suite 3
Eugene, OR 97401

www.wipfandstock.com

PAPERBACK ISBN: 978-1-5326-1648-8
HARDCOVER ISBN: 978-1-4982-4030-7
EBOOK ISBN: 978-1-4982-4029-1

Catloging-in-Publication data:

Names: Penaskovic, Richard, editor | Şahin, Mustafa, editor.

Title: Peacebuilding in a fractious world : on hoping against all hope / edited by Richard Penaskovic and Mustafa Sahin.

Description: Eugene, OR: Pickwick Publications, 2017 | Includes bibliographical references.

Identifiers: ISBN: 978-1-5326-1648-8 (paperback) | ISBN: 978-1-4982-4030-7 (hardcover) | ISBN: 978-1-4982-4029-1 (ebook).

Subjects: LCSH: Peace-building.

Classification: JZ5538 P374295 2017 (print) | JZ5538 (ebook).

Manufactured in the U.S.A. 10/20/17

We are particularly grateful to Dr. Franck Salameh, editor, who asked that we state the following: "Extracts previously published by Abdelwahab Hechiche, 'Jihad in Memory and History,' in *The Levantine Review* 4.2 (2016) 215–53. Copyright © *The Levantine Review* are all used with permission."

Richard Penaskovic—*For my wife, Nancy, family, and brothers, Frank, Bob, Tom, and, particularly, in memory of my dear brother Bill Penaskovic*

Mustafa G. Sahin—*For Altan, Gareth, Joe, Kemal B., Kemal K., Larry, Mansur, Richard, Roy, Scott, Terry, and Turan, in thanksgiving for their friendship and support.*

May Peace Be with You!

Contents

Acknowledgments

MOST OF THE CHAPTERS in this book were initially presented at the Peacebuilders Conference at Morehouse College in Atlanta, Georgia, sponsored by the Atlantic Institute in Atlanta, Georgia, and Martin Luther King Jr. International Chapel at Morehouse College from April 8–10, 2015. This Conference aimed at bringing together scholars and practitioners to foster dialogue in education, ethics, and nonviolent peacebuilding particularly in regard to global, social, and religious movements today. We wish to thank Lawrence E. Carter and Terry F. Walker Sr. and Gregory O. Hall, all from Morehouse College, in addition to Turan Kilic and Jennifer Gibbs from the Atlantic Institute in Atlanta, Georgia, for their work on the Organizing Committee for this Conference. We are indebted to the authors for their willingness to present their papers at this Conference and for their patience in seeing their work published in this volume. Special thanks to John Tures of La Grange College for his help with the Marketing Questionnaire.

We want to thank Pickwick Publications, an imprint of Wipf & Stock Publishers, particularly K. C. Hanson, editor in chief; Adam McInturf, reprint acquisitions; and Brian Palmer, editorial administrator, for their help in publishing this book. Finally, we owe a special debt of gratitude to Anne Maura English, without whose help as copyeditor, this volume would not have seen the light of day.

1

Introduction

Richard Penaskovic and Mustafa Şahin

This volume has three outstanding features that distinguish it from other books on peacebuilding. First, it approaches the theme of peacebuilding from both a macro and a micro perspective. The macro point of view is featured prominently, for example, in chapter 2, in which Dr. Carbaugh shows how the method of "cultural discourse analysis" sheds a bright light on peacebuilding among cultures and nations. The micro perspective may be seen most clearly in chapter 8 where Dr. Allen reflects on the symbolic power for peace in the encounter between St. Francis of Assisi and Sultan Al-Kamil in the thirteenth century.

Second, we address the theme of peacebuilding from an interdisciplinary perspective. Why so? Peacebuilding should be approached from different perspectives, just as a diamond must be viewed from many angles to see its full beauty. Peacebuilding involves questions dealing with history, communication theory, politics, society, religion, and social conditions. In sum, to do justice to the topic, complex questions like peacebuilding must be examined from many viewpoints, as we have done in this volume.

Third, the various contributors to this book have endeavored to transcend vague theories and generalities. Instead, they believe that their reflections have application to, and can solve, problems in the real world. For example, in chapter 6, Daisaku Ikeda, a Buddhist, argues that all nations must downsize their stockpile of nuclear weapons if we are to avoid a nuclear catastrophe.

This introduction consists of three parts. Part I outlines the many problem areas where war may break out suddenly and sets the context for this volume. Part II gives a rationale for the subtitle of our book, "On Hoping against All Hope." In other words, this part of our introduction shows why we have reason to be hopeful, despite the quandary we face in working for a peaceful world. The final section summarizes the various chapters of this volume.

THE PROBLEM

We live in a time of uncertainty with numerous hotspots around the world in which war can break out with the drop of a hat. Mikhail Gorbachev said, "It all looks as if the world is preparing for war."[1] He noted that the United States is sending more troops to Europe, thus sending a clear message to Russia that we are there to protect our NATO allies and the countries in the Baltics. Meanwhile, NATO and Russian forces that were ordinarily "deployed at a distance" are now closer together, "as if to shoot point blank."[2]

In Europe, we have Vladimir Putin's takeover of the Crimean region of the Ukraine with little resistance from Western powers. In the Middle East, ISIS has occupied areas of Syria and Iraq, thus forcing millions of Syrians to other European countries like Germany, Turkey, and Greece. Presently, there are over sixty-five million refugees worldwide, the largest number of them since WWII.[3]

The situation in the Middle East between Israel and the Palestinians in the Gaza Strip and the West Bank is a powder keg ready to explode. Israel has allowed Israeli settlers to take over land in the Gaza Strip and West Bank, in clear violation of UN Security Council Resolution 2334, made in 2016. If the Republicans under President Trump move the US embassy from Tel Aviv to Jerusalem, this would set off a crisis between Israel and the Palestinians. Jerusalem would become a huge magnet for violence and terrorism, and US embassies, including their personnel, would be greatly threatened.[4]

1. Gorbachev, "It All Looks."
2. Ibid.
3. Bennis, "Trump is Carpet-Bombing."
4. Haass, "Don't Make Any Sudden Moves," A19.

President Erdoğan in Turkey has killed 2,000 of his own citizens and displaced 355,000 others in the southeastern part of Turkey. He has declared martial law to throw in jail all who dare oppose him, particularly academics and journalists, to the extent that Turkey is, effectively, no longer a true democracy.[5] The UN Human Rights Office noted that in Turkey as many as half a million people were displaced from July 2015 to December 2016, amid large scale destruction of residential neighborhoods in the Kurdish southeastern part of Turkey.[6] These are, indeed, difficult times for those who endeavor to bring about peace on earth.

Moreover, on March 7, 2017, North Korea, under its supreme leader, Kim Jong Un, fired five ballistic missiles, four of which landed in the Exclusive Economic Zone of Japan about 620 miles from the launch site in Tongchang-ri.[7] Additionally, North Korea threatens to test an intercontinental ballistic missile later this year, one that could potentially reach California. Per R. James Woolsey (Director of the CIA from 1993–95) and Peter Vincent Pry (who worked in the House Armed Services Committee and in the CIA) North Korea's nuclear weapons are probably more sophisticated and dangerous than many experts think. They argue that testing "is not necessary to develop nuclear weapons."[8] Many nations that have a nuclear arsenal, like the United States, France, Israel, South Africa, India, and Pakistan, have developed nuclear weapons without testing them.[9]

What is more worrisome about North Korea is this: The EMP Commission of Congress has concluded that North Korea may have "Super-EMP" weapons, that is, low-yield warheads that produce "gamma rays" rather than a big explosion. One of these warheads released over North America could kill 90 percent of the population by causing "starvation and societal collapse."[10]

Another bone of contention concerns the dispute over territory in the East and South China Sea that pits countries like the Philippines, Japan, Malaysia, Taiwan, and Vietnam against a superpower, namely, China. The area under dispute stretches from the Diaoyu/Senkaku Islands on the east of China to hundreds of islets in the archipelagos in the South China Sea.

5. Peker, "Turkey Sentences Officers," A7.
6. "UN Accused Turkey."
7. Cheng and Gale, "North Korea Missile," A7.
8. Woolsey and Fry, "Don't Underestimate."
9. Ibid.
10. Ibid.

This area has an abundance of both natural gas and hydrocarbons, and global trade flows through the nearby seas to the tune of trillions of dollars. China has recently dredged and claimed for itself thousands of lands in the South China Sea, built artificial islands, and constructed loading piers, runways, and satellite communication antennas.[11]

China's neighbors also claim some of this land and wonder if China wants this land for civilian or security reasons. Why so? China can use these constructed islands to base the S-400 missile defense systems and to deploy J-11 fighter jets and Y-8 patrol aircraft. The United States is wary of China's intentions and is monitoring the situation very closely since the United States may have to use military force to defend its allies, like the Philippines and Japan, because of its treaties with these nations.[12]

Both the United States and the entire world are now swimming in uncharted waters with the election of Donald Trump as President. "The most chilling concern about Donald Trump is the worldwide fear that he puts our very survival at risk," says The Science and Security Board of the Atomic Scientists, who monitor the Doomsday Clock. The Doomsday Clock goes back seventy years to a time when the United States and the USSR were engaged in a nuclear weapons race.[13] The experts who monitor the Doomsday Clock have recently announced that we are at "two and a half minutes to midnight," in which "midnight" refers to the end of civilization.[14]

Why does President Trump put our very survival at risk? In an interview with *The New York Times* in March 2016, Mr. Trump dialed back the United States' long-standing policy concerning nuclear proliferation. He stated that South Korea and Japan might have to have their own nuclear arsenals to protect themselves if the United States could not defend them. He also remarked that Japan and Korea might need to pay more money to the United States for their own defense.[15]

More unsettling is Mr. Trump's comment that "we have nuclear arsenals which are in a very terrible shape. They don't even know if they work."[16] One wonders if President Trump should suggest to the world that our nuclear arsenal is in "very terrible shape." Such a statement has sent

11. "China's Maritime Disputes," 1–15.
12. Ibid.
13. Sachs, "Trump and the Doomsday Clock."
14. Ibid.
15. "Transcript: Donald Trump."
16. Ibid.

chills down the backs of our allies, particularly our NATO allies in Europe, along with South Korea, Japan, the Baltic countries, and many others. Mr. Trump's remarks demonstrate that he is totally unfamiliar with what former President Obama did to modernize our nuclear capabilities.[17] Obama had set up a program to modernize our nuclear weapons, laboratories, and industrialized plants, many of which were built forty to sixty years ago. In regard to our nuclear weapons, "plastic parts degrade while metal parts corrode," hence the need for a modernization.[18] How are we able to have confidence in these systems, since the United States called a moratorium on actual nuclear testing in 1992? We have built "experimental facilities to study materials under extreme conditions, using computer software and hardware to pinpoint any major changes in our stockpile," notes Steven E. Koonin, a theoretical physicist and a former undersecretary for science at the US Department of Energy.[19] The total price tag for this modernization of weapons and facilities was $9.2 billion in 2016, $9.7 in 2017, and $1.3 billion annually for the years 2018 to 2023.[20]

We now have the Trump administration rolling back former President Obama's initiatives to lessen our dependence on fossil fuels that increase the carbon dioxide levels in the atmosphere. Scott Pruitt, the head of the EPA, has stated recently that carbon dioxide in the environment does not cause global warming, hence more research needs to be done about this matter. Pruitt's views run counter to that of the EPA itself, 97 percent of climate scientists, and the National Oceanic and Atmospheric Administration (NOAA).[21]

Climate scientists are worried about the rate of global climate change. In this connection climate change refers to a "statistically significant variation in the mean state of the climate or in its variability over a long period, e.g., decades or longer."[22] Scientists concur in stating that climate change is anthropogenic, i.e., the human species has changed or altered the composition of the earth's atmosphere."[23] The amount of carbon dioxide in the atmosphere has increased 200 time faster than in the past 650,000 years,

17. Bacevich, "Election 2016: New Nukes," 8.

18. Koonin, "Can We Trust," C3.

19. Ibid.

20. Ibid.

21. "EPA Chief," 5A. See also Barnett, "Saving the Seas," 66.

22. Dow, *The Atlas,* 15.

23. Ibid. See also Penaskovic, "Interreligious Dialogue," 35.

and carbon dioxide can remain in the atmosphere up to 200 years. Today our planet is the warmest it has been in some 1,000 years.[24]

Presently, we have a scarcity of water worldwide. In fact, the scarcity of water, not terrorism, may be the biggest problem facing the Arab world. The uprisings known as the Arab Spring were caused, in part, by rising prices for food, and these increases were due to the water crisis in the region.[25] Very high birth rates in the Arab world and the breaking down of natural ecosystems are all contributing factors to the water crisis. Almost fifty percent of Arabs are dependent on fresh water coming in from Turkey and the upstream nations on the Nile River, and, until recently, ISIS had taken over the upstream basins of the Tigris and Euphrates rivers in Syria.[26]

SOME HOPEFUL SIGNS

It would be hubris on our part and simplistic to suggest that we have a magic bullet that would solve the world's problems, since, realistically considered, they are largely intractable. However, this certainly does not mean we ought to put our heads in the sand like the proverbial ostrich. There are many hopeful signs that must be considered. That is exactly why the subtitle of this volume bears the title, "On Hoping against All Hope." Hope is not something an individual can achieve on his or her own, e.g., when we are at an airport we hope our flight will leave on time. However, passengers have no say whether the plane takes off as scheduled because, for one thing, mechanical problems will delay or even abort the flight. What can be done to address some of the problems enumerated in the above section?

We feel that not all the world's problems are problems in the same way. Three of them stand out, namely, the nuclear arms race (that we have spoken about at length in chapter 6), global climate change, and the presidency of Donald Trump. Global climate change resembles a runaway train heading toward a crash. Consider this: scientists tell us that only about 1 percent of the water on earth is fresh and renewable, and circa 70 percent finds itself frozen in ice. Aquifers or geological formations that contain water, particularly ones that supply water for springs or wells, are draining much faster than the "natural recharge rate."[27] Gas and oil firms have heavily pol-

24. "NASA, NOAA Data."

25. Chellaney, "Arab's biggest Problem."

26. Ibid.

27. Penaskovic, "Interreligious Dialogue," 35.

luted the Great Lakes that contain about 20 percent of the fresh water in the world. Meanwhile the funding of the EPA will be cut by 25 percent with three thousand workers let go, per President Trump's budget for 2018.[28]

However, there still exist signs of hope. Item: the world religions may be a force for the good. Why so? Collectively, the world religions bring a lot to the table: they have billions of followers, vast financial resources, the striking ability to build community, and the moral and spiritual power to shape world views.[29] There also exists a dialogue of action among religious leaders and their flocks who are pushing the notion of "sustainable living," that is, living in such a way that people today can meet their own needs without compromising the needs of future generations. The National Association of Evangelicals (NAE) has 45,000 churches and wants action on reducing global climate change, pollution, and habitat destruction.[30]

Also, in the 2017 presidential election the presidential candidate, Jill Stein, received about 1.2 million votes. This augurs well for the future of our country because the next presidential candidate must consider this voting bloc if he or she hopes to win the 2020 election. Moreover, the major world religions, with a total investment of about seven trillion dollars, are moving their investments into companies that are environmentally sustainable and socially responsible.[31]

Additionally, in the past two years, sustainable investing funds have grown 33 percent in the United States and have nine trillion dollars in assets under management. For example, big investors, such as Blue Harbour Group LP, the firm of Clifton S. Robbins, (that manages circa $3.5 billion dollars) wants companies to focus on environmental and social issues, including climate change, employee well-being, and diversity, since such a move "makes good investing sense."[32] Mr. Robbins argues that environmental, social, and governance issues should be on the same plane as financial considerations. Also, the world's biggest money manager, BlackRock Inc. presses companies to consider how climate change affects their businesses. This is a hopeful sign for the environment, when Wall Street starts doing the right thing, morally speaking. Another hopeful sign is the meeting of most of the world's nations at the United Nations headquarters in New York

28. Cole, "Dirty, Hot, Deadly."

29. Gardner, *Invoking the Spirit*, 11.

30. Penaskovic, "Interreligious Dialogue," 35.

31. O'Brien, *Atlas of Religion*, 76.

32. Benoit, "Activist Pushes Firms," B8.

on March 27, 2017. Their agenda calls for historic negotiations on a treaty designed to ban nuclear weapons.[33]

Although only two months since Barack Obama's term as president ended, President Donald Trump wants to privilege military might over diplomacy and soft power. The budget of the Defense Department is not only larger than that of "the next seven countries" combined, but its accounting systems are so inaccurate, that they are the only federal agencies that cannot pass an audit. We argue that nonviolent and "soft" power solutions must rule the day, rather than reliance on sheer military might. As General Jim Mattis remarked in 2013, "If you don't fund the State Department fully, then I need to buy more ammunition."[34]

In his World Day of Peace message on December 12, 2016, Pope Francis gave examples of individuals, such as Mahatma Gandhi, Mother Teresa, and Liberian activist, Leymah Ghowee (who worked on ending the Second Liberian Civil War in 2003), who used nonviolence as a tool to effect political change.[35]

Taking his cue from Gandhi, Martin Luther King Jr. also insisted on using "nonviolent resistance" to eliminate segregation in the 1960s. For Dr. King nonviolent resistance has redemption, reconciliation, and the building of *koinonia*, or communion and community, as its goals. In the 1960s, there were those in the black community, e.g., the Black Panthers, who wanted to retaliate against the white community by using violent methods to effect racial equality. Thankfully, M. L. King Jr. knew that this strategy of "fighting fire with fire" would be self-defeating for the black community and for America at large. Dr. King's main targets were sinful social structures, those institutions or structures that ignore injustice or cause it to happen.[36]

A sign of hope may be seen in the way our government is constituted with the separation of powers into the executive, the legislative, and the judicial. Although the present Congress has a Republican majority in both the House and the Senate, there exists sharp disagreement among Republicans about the repeal and replacement of the Affordable Care Act. Even if a Republican majority in Congress votes in favor of a new plan, they may win the war but lose the heart and soul of the estimated twenty-four million people who might well lose their coverage. And this oversight may cost the

33. *Bulletin of the Atomic Scientists.*

34. Ibid.

35. McElwee, "Francis calls on Christians," 3.

36. Martin Luther King Jr., "The Current Crisis," 85–90.

Republicans to lose both the midterm elections and the presidential election in 2020. Trump's health plan has failed, in part, because his inner circle of advisors are neophytes regarding the political process, as seen in the storm of controversy surrounding his first two executive orders banning Muslims and others from entering the United States. This inexperience of Trump and his team may come to haunt their efforts to overhaul the tax code and to create jobs.

Also, since we have a system of checks and balances, Mr. Trump may not achieve his goals as easily as he first thought. For example, President Trump's first two bans on immigration have been scrapped because federal judges have struck down these executive orders in such states as Washington, Hawaii, Minnesota, and New York. Moreover, these bans on refugees, undocumented immigrants, and migrants from Muslim-majority countries "violate international law requiring countries to provide refuge to those in desperate need," says Phyllis Bennis, an expert on the Middle East. Bennis notes that Trump's "order bans refugees from wars that in many cases the United States itself started."[37] The best thing we can do with the sixty-five million refugees in the world is to end the wars that created refugees and welcome millions more into our country.[38]

Historically, President Reagan's buildup of the military ratcheted up the tensions between the United States and the USSR, thus wasting money that could have benefitted millions of citizens who must survive by living from paycheck to paycheck. What is worse about putting more money into defense is this: the new Secretary of State, Rex Tillerson, either fired or asked for the resignation of four of the most senior people in the State Department. As Bennis observes in speaking about the State Department, "They've lost all the people who know how to make diplomacy happen, and you have a perfect storm of war winning out over diplomacy."[39]

Does it make good political sense to dismantle the international order in the West? President Trump has upset our allies by claiming that NATO is obsolete, angered the President of Mexico by suggesting that Mexico pay for the border wall that would separate Mexico from the United States, and criticized Angela Merkel because of her policy of allowing a million Syrian refugees to stay in Germany. Is this the way to treat our allies, particularly since they are our first line of defense against Russian aggression? As Jacek

37. Bennis, "Trump is Carpet-Bombing."

38. Ibid.

39. Ibid.

Rostowski, former Deputy Prime Minister of Poland, notes, "In conventional geostrategic terms, the EU is almost a costless extension of US political and military power."[40]

Is this in the best interest of the United States? Hopefully, the Trump administration will learn in a process of trial and error that "soft power" works, as we have seen in the Kyoto Climate agreement, the agreement among the United States and other countries with Iran's commitment to refrain from making nuclear weapons, and the benefits associated with burying the hatchet and trading with Cuba, initiated under President Obama.

Another hopeful sign is this: per Michael Bloomberg, cities, rather than the District of Columbia, will have the most effect on the future of our country. The action will shift from the center in Washington to the periphery, that is, to the local level. Bloomberg points out that creative mayors from New York to Seattle, working together with active citizens, are bringing about needed change. In New Orleans, for example, Mayor Mitch Landrieu has helped set up a program that provides students from low-income neighborhoods with learning skills so that they can find jobs in growing companies and businesses.[41]

Additionally, the cities of Detroit, Houston, Seattle, and Phoenix are extending their transit systems (for example, a high-speed rail system will connect the city of Dallas to Houston), while Chicago and New York are pushing for the reduction of drinks with high sugar content in hopes of reducing cases of diabetes.[42]

Also, mayors in large megacities and in small towns are reducing their carbon footprint by using alternative energy sources, bringing infrastructure up to date, attracting new industries, and lessening greenhouse gas emissions to create a healthy milieu for their citizens.[43] Although Congress has not even passed one bill dealing with climate change, the United States will continue to reduce the emission of carbon dioxide into the environment. In sum, all of us need to get involved locally to save our planet because that is where the action will be in the future. Thomas Berry once noted that "we humans are unable to make a single blade of grass, yet there may not be any more grass in the future unless it is protected by humans."[44]

40. Rostowski, "Feature, not Bug."

41. Bloomberg, "Where Washington Fails," 24.

42. Ibid.

43. Ibid.

44. Berry, *Evening Thoughts*, 21.

OVERVIEW OF THE VOLUME

We begin with chapter 2, "Three Dimensions for Reflective Dialogue," in which Donal Carbaugh reflects on three dimensions to bear in mind when dialogue breaks down. Using case studies, Carbaugh clarifies how: 1) interactional, 2) relational, and 3) informational needs function in dialogue. Carbaugh uses the method of "cultural discourse analysis" with a focus on cultural practices of dialogue to advance peacebuilding among cultures and nations. It seems that sincere and honest dialogue can break down the barriers between people who are extremely diverse but know how to listen carefully and with empathy.

In chapter 3, Ori Z. Soltes reflects on "Ethics and the Problem of Interpretation in Sacred Scripture." Most religious traditions hold that questions about morality are ultimately answered in revelation or a divine source as mediated by prophets or seers. In both the Abrahamic traditions and in Hinduism there is the revelation itself plus the interpretation of that revelation by scholars and pious believers. Hence revelation is simultaneously a divine word and a human word. In this process of interpretation—or hermeneutics—dialogue, discussion, and debate are essential. Why so? No one person, nor one religious tradition has a monopoly on the truth. We humans see through a glass darkly. Instead of demonizing others who do not share our vision, we must hold hands and work at peacebuilding, as Fethullah Gülen suggests.

In chapter 4, "The Importance of Interreligious Dialogue for Peacebuilding: A Muslim's Itinerary," Abdelwahab Hechiche invites us to accompany him on his journey to bring about peace through interreligious dialogue. The author discovered that without true diversity, dialogue becomes a "soliloquy" or a talking to oneself in front of a mirror. The author was asked to join the first American Jewish-Christian-Muslim delegation for a peace mission in the Middle East supported by President Jimmy Carter. In this capacity Hechiche became acquainted with Rabbi David Hartman and the Shalom Hartman Institute in Jerusalem where he studied the three holy scriptures of the Abrahamic religions. This raised his consciousness on the Islamic elements in Judaism and the Jewish components in Islam.

In chapter 5, John A. Tures, in "'Whirling Diversions' in Turkey," examines the domestic imbroglio in Turkey that brings in its wake problems on the international scene. Although Turkish President Recep Tayyip Erdoğan claims to usher in a "New Turkey," he seems to divide the nation internally, while simultaneously alienating its partners and neighbors externally. Instead of admitting the corruption in his own party, the AKP, President Erdoğan has accused the Hizmet movement led by Fethullah Gülen of organizing a parallel state. In this scenario Erdoğan sows public confusion as to who is the real enemy. Scholars call this the diversionary theory of conflict. Leaders use a diversionary tactic to distract citizens from domestic problems by initiating a crisis that focuses on an external threat. In the case of Turkey, the external threat is the Hizmet movement led by an expatriate, namely, Fethullah Gülen and his followers at home and abroad, who are then scapegoated as the real enemy of Turkey's problems. Such a strategy used by President Erdoğan may lead Turkey into war both at home and abroad.

In chapter 6, Richard Penaskovic, in "Peacebuilding according to Daisaku Ikeda and Sōka Gakkai International," argues that there exists no good reason to continue to update and stockpile nuclear weapons since there can never be a time when such weapons can be used, morally and humanely speaking. Penaskovic examines the history and genesis of Sōka Gakkai International with a focus on its second president, Daisaku Ikeda, and his efforts to bring about a more peaceful world.

In chapter 7, "The Israeli-Palestinian Peace Process and Nongovernmental Organizations," Jason Tatlock points out that in the postwar era nongovernmental organizations (NGOs) have a crucial role to play in peacebuilding efforts. He uses the Israeli-Palestinian crisis in the Gaza Strip in 2006 as a paradigm to support his thesis. Tatlock notes that the Secretary-General of the United Nations pointed to three areas, namely, mobilization, democratization, and assistance, in which NGOs had a significant part to play in the Israeli-Palestinian peace process. Tatlock also argues that the five permanent members of the UN Security Council have the power and ability to build peace by standing up for human rights. If that is the case one may ask why there has not been more progress regarding bringing about peace between Israel and the Palestinians. Tatlock makes the point that Israel and the Palestinians themselves, not the United Nations, bear ultimate responsibility for building peace.

In chapter 8, Wm. Loyd Allen, in "The Symbolic Power for Peace in the Encounter between St. Francis and Sultan Al-Kamil," notes that the encounter between St. Francis of Assisi and Sultan Al-Kamil has symbolic value for those involved in interreligious dialogue and peacebuilding in the twenty-first century, just as it did in the thirteenth century. Dr. Allen notes that St. Francis went to meet Sultan Al-Kamil as part of his desire to preach the gospel to every creature, in full knowledge of the fact that he could have become a martyr in the process. Rather than looking upon the sultan as an enemy of the church, St. Francis saw the sultan as a child of God to be respected and loved. Correspondingly, the sultan treated the saint with hospitality, appreciating the piety of St. Francis. The meeting between the two may serve as a paradigm for today. In the 2016 presidential election we had some candidates who stereotyped all Muslims as the evil enemy who should not be allowed entry into the United States. One wonders if these presidential candidates had any close friends who were Muslims. Peace-building through personal encounter builds bridges between religions, as opposed to building walls of separation.

In chapter 9, Robert N. Nash, in "Roger Williams, Religious Freedom, and the Path to Peace," examines the thought of Roger Williams in bringing about tolerance and peace among the Abrahamic religions and denominations. Roger Williams insists on treating members of other religions with respect and dignity based on their respective faith traditions. Williams bases his ideas on religious freedom and the separation of church and state theologically, namely, the absolute goodness and sovereignty of God and the absolute depravity and sinfulness of human nature. For Roger Williams, there could be no theocratic government and no true church until the parousia, the return of Christ at the end of time.

In chapter 10, James M. Dawsey and Adam Wells in their essay, "In the Steps of Pope John XXIII, the Reverend Doctor Martin Luther King Jr., and Archbishop Oscar Romero" suggest that a straight line connects the thought-worlds of Pope John XXIII, Martin Luther, John Wesley, M.L. King Jr., and Archbishop Oscar Romero. John XXIII remarked that peace comes about when individuals and states work synergistically to structure society as God intended. Martin Luther and John Wesley saw the demand for social justice grounded in the natural law that applies to every person. Martin Luther King Jr. outlined a specific and concrete program for bringing about peace by changing sinful and unjust social structures. Oscar Romero's death by assassination united him with Christ's crucifixion which brought about the salvation of the world. Finally, Emmanuel Lévinas reminds us that an encounter with God who is *totaliter aliter,* or totally other, forces us to recognize our responsibilities toward those who are "other" to us because of their race, religion, or gender.

In chapter 11, Paul Harris and William E. Baker, in their essay on "Reflections on Refugee and Asylum Policy in the United States and Germany:

Bringing Peace to a Fractious World," point out that the United States has served as an asylum for the world's oppressed in line with the famous sonnet of Emma Lazarus' "The New Colossus" with the phrase "Give me your tired, your poor, your huddled masses yearning to breathe free." However, since 9/11 the refugee and asylum policy of the United States resembles law enforcement as opposed to a policy of humane treatment. Presently, asylum seekers who are not criminals must wear an electronic anklet to monitor their whereabouts. Per the Real ID Act, asylum seekers can be denied asylum if they lack corroborating documents and "suspicious demeanor" can be grounds for denial. These policies make the United States look foolish in the eyes of other countries, particularly Muslim countries, Russia, and China where most of the people there do not trust the United States. Our bombing of innocent people in Iraq and Syria, plus our refusal to take refugees from these countries, does not establish goodwill but encourages individuals in Muslim countries to join terrorist organizations.

BIBLIOGRAPHY

Associated Press. "North Korea Warns of Potential Nuclear Disaster." *Opelika-Auburn News,* March 7, 2017, 7A.

Bacevich, Andrew J. "Election 2016: New Nukes? Turning Away from Disarmament." *Commonweal* 143 (2016) 8–10.

Barnett, Cynthia. "Saving the Seas." *National Geographic* 231 (2017) 54–75.

Bennis, Phyllis. "Trump Is Carpet-Bombing . . . U.S. Foreign Policy." *Informed Comment: Thoughts on the Middle East, History and Religion,* January 2017. https://www.juancole /2017/01/carpet-bombing-foreign.html.

Benoit, David. "Activist Pushes Firms to do the Right Thing." *The Wall Street Journal,* March 20, 2017, B8.

Berry, Thomas. *Evening Thoughts: Reflecting on Earth as Sacred Community.* San Francisco: Sierra Club, 2006.

Bloomberg, Michael. "Where Washington Fails to Drive Progress, Cities Will Act." *Time,* December 26, 2016/January 2, 2017, 24.

Bulletin of the Atomic Scientists. March 24, 2017. www.icontact-archive.com/xNLOqQCSSU61TQnl.ZB3dCuX4u15_mN?w=4#.

Chellaney, Brahma. "Arab World's Biggest Problem Not Terrorism or Fundamentalism but Water!" *Informed Comment: Thoughts on the Middle East, History and Religion,* July 27, 2016. http://www.juancole.com/2016/07/biggest-terrorism-fundamentalism.html.

Cheng, Jonathan, and Alastair Gale. "North Korea Missile Test Stirs ICBM Fears." *The Wall Street Journal,* March 7, 2017, A7.

Cole, Juan. "Dirty, Hot, Deadly: The Real Trump Scandal is What He's Done to the Environment." *Informed Comment: Thoughts on the Middle East, History and Religion,*

March 6, 2017. https:www.juancole.com/2017/03/deadly-scandal-environnment.html.

Council on Foreign Relations. "China's Maritime Disputes: A CFR InfoGuide Presentation," February 2016, 1–16. http://www.cfr.org/asia/and-pacific/chinas-maritime-disputes/p31345#!/.

Dow, Kirstin, and Thomas E. Downing. *The Atlas of Climate Change: Mapping the World's Greatest Challenge*. Berkeley: University of California Press, 2007.

"EPA Chief: Carbon Dioxide not Primary Cause of Warning." *Opelika-Auburn News*, March 10, 5A.

Gardner, Gary. *Invoking the Spirit: Religion and Spirituality in the Quest for a Sustainable World*. Worldwatch Paper #164. Washington, DC: Worldwatch Institute, 2002.

Gorbachev, Mikhail. "It All Looks as if the World Is Preparing for War." *Time*, January 26, 2017. Time.com/464542/gorbachev-putin-trump/.

Gray, Bryce. "Proposed EPS Cuts Spark Concerns about Local Impacts." *St. Louis Post-Dispatch*, March 16, 2017. www.stltoday.com. . .proposal-epa-cuts-spark-concens. . . /article_5b2f45c4-799c-54.

Haass, Richard. "Don't Make Any Sudden Moves, Mr. Trump." *The Wall Street Journal*, January 19, 2017, A19.

King, Martin Luther. Jr. "The Current Crisis." In *A Testament of Hope: The Essential Writings and Speeches of Martin Luther King, Jr.*, edited by James M. Washington, 85–90. New York: Harper, 1986.

Koonin, Steven E. "Can We Trust Our Aging Nukes?" *The Wall Street Journal*, October 15–16, 2017, C3.

Lee, Carol E., and Alastair Gale. "U.S. Reviews North Korea Options." *The Wall Street Journal*, March 2, 2017, A7.

McElwee, Joshua. "Francis Calls on Christians to Embrace Non-violence in World Day of Peace Message." *National Catholic Reporter*, December 12, 2016.

National Aeronautics and Space Administration: Goddard Institute for Space Studies. "NASA, NOAA Data Show 2016 Warmest Year on Record Globally," January 18, 2017. https://www.giss.nasa.gov/research/news/20170118/.

O'Brien, Joanne, and Martin Palmer. *The Atlas of Religion*. Berkeley: University of California Press, 2007.

Peker, Emre. "Turkish Court Sentences Two Military Officers to Life in Prison for Coup Role." *The Wall Street Journal*, January 5, 2017, A7.

Pemberton, Miriam. "Making Us Less Safe: Trump Bloating Pentagon Budget, Cutting Diplomacy, Science." *Informed Comment: Thoughts on the Middle East, History and Religion*, March 12, 2017. https://www.juancole/2017/03/bloating-pentagon-diplomacy .html.

Penaskovic, Richard. "Interreligious Dialogue in a Polarized World." In *Pathways for Interreligious Dialogue in the Twenty-First Century*, edited by Vladimir Latinovic, Gerard Mannion, and Peter C. Phan, 29–40. New York: Palgrave Macmillan, 2016.

Rostkowski, Jacek. "Feature, not Bug: Trump's Chaos Theory of Government." *Informed Comment*, February 7, 2017. http://www.juancole/2017/02/feature-trumps-government .html.

Sachs, Jeffrey. D. "Trump and the Doomsday Clock." *The Boston Globe*, February 12, 2017. https://www.bostonglobe.com/opinion/2017/02/12/trump-and-doomsday.

"Transcript: Donald Trump Expounds on His Foreign Policy Views." *The New York Times,* March 26, 2017. https: //www.nytimes.com/2016/03/27/uspolitical/donald/trump-transcripts .html.

"UN Accuses Turkey of 'Serious' Human Rights Violations Against Its Kurdish South-East Region," *Euro News,* March 10, 2017. www.euronews.com.

Walt, Stephen. M. "ISIS as Revolutionary State: New Twist on an Old Story." *Foreign Affairs* 94 (November/December 2015) 42–51.

Woolsey, R. James, and Peter Vincent Pry. "Don't Underestimate North Korea's Nuclear Arsenal." *The Wall Street Journal*, February 27, 2017. https://www.dont-underestimate-north-korea's-nuclear-arsenal-1488239693.

2

Three Dimensions for Reflective Dialogue

Donal Carbaugh

ABSTRACT

Intercultural dialogue and its many variants such as interfaith, interethnic, and interracial dialogue set global scenes with some sort of differences at play. This paper examines difference by proposing ways to develop a reflective capacity relative to specific dialogic practices and goals which are typical in peacebuilding. The chapter is organized into two parts. In the first part, three dimensions of peacebuilding praxis are introduced which focus on interactional needs, relational needs, and informational needs or truth-value. Each is explored in specific cases. The second part of the paper elaborates how these very practical matters can be valued differently in different religious, intellectual, and cultural traditions. The differences can be productively engaged, however, as we deepen our understanding of the ways dialogic peacebuilding encounters activate different models of personhood, means of relating, vocabularies of emotion, and ways of dwelling in the nature of things.

INTRODUCTION

A common stance for dialogue in prominent western cultural scenes is that one should speak directly to others; that one should do so in a way that maintains social relationships; and that one should speak truthfully. This stance for dialogic practice has served many well as a mutual way of addressing important local and global matters from economical, indigenous, political, religious, and racial inequalities to ecological injustices, to mention only a few. However, this stance, as any stance, has its limitations and an ability to reflect upon those limitations, upon dimensions of this dialogic stance, especially as it comes to the fore in practice among different peoples, is essential at times for productive dialogue to occur and to be sustained.

This paper proposes a reflective capacity along three dimensions which are essential when dialogue—as some people believe it should be—gets frustrated or reaches its limits. The reflective capacity is discussed as follows. After presenting some background for the reflections, I introduce three cases of dialogue among people who differ from one another. The cases demonstrate deep differences in what is deemed to be proper practice by each when interacting with the others. A summary of the cases highlights different interactional, relational, and informational needs, respectively, as basic elements in what is deemed proper as dialogue. The point is made explicit with the cases: an ability to reflect upon these dimensions, as they occur in practice, can enhance dialogic practice. The second part of the paper discusses how these dimensions of difference are associated with deep cultural models for being a person, for acting properly, for feeling in various ways, and for dwelling in the nature of things.

BACKGROUND[1]

The discussion that follows is designed within a long-standing program of inquiry in the study of communication codes generally, and intercultural communication in particular.[2] The methodology is a version of cultural

1. This section is a slightly revised excerpt from one of our published articles on the communication codes of dialogue (see Carbaugh et al., "Cultural Discourses," 89–90).

2. See Carbaugh, *Cultural Communication*; Katriel, *Dialogic Moments*; Philipsen et al., "Speech Codes Theory."

discourse analysis[3] with a special focus on cultural practices of dialogue.[4] The approach, as a way of building culturally sensitive practices, has been advanced explicitly with regard to peacebuilding—including in security issues—with special emphasis on initiatives of the United Nations.[5] Specifically, peacebuilding in these ways can not only honor local cultures but also forge better, longer-term, more satisfying plans for future actions.

Regarding our focus on dialogue, our research projects have been implemented as follows: 1) we identified in a language a term, if one is—or more are—available, which has some significant semantic overlap with the English term "dialogue"; 2) we described and investigated uses of that term in specific social contexts; 3) we analyzed the acts, events, and/or styles of communication being referred to with that term, or those terms; and 4) we interpreted the deeper cultural meanings of these terms concerning dialogue itself, as well as presumptions the terms carry about personhood, feelings, and social relations. Eventually, the latter phases of analysis interpreted persons, social identities, relationships, and institutions, in addition to the explicit meanings about what is preferred as dialogic communication itself.

Our procedures follow a specific theoretical model,[6] which has been used in varying degrees in earlier studies of such phenomena, including Leslie Baxter's study of the differences in an English speech community between "talking things through" and "putting it in writing";[7] Mary Garrett's study of Chinese "pure talk";[8] Brad Hall's and Mutsumi Noguchi's study of the Japanese ritual of *kenson*;[9] Tamar Katriel's study of Hebrew "dialogic moments," including *dugri* speech and "soul talks";[10] Richard Wilkins' study of the Finnish *asiallinen* (or matter-of-fact) style of talk;[11] and Makato Saito's study of the silencing of gay identity in Japanese.[12] This

3. Carbaugh, *Situating Selves*; *Cultures in Conversation*; and "Cultural Discourse Analysis." Carbaugh et al., "A View of Communication."

4. See, for example, Carbaugh et al., "Cultural Discourses."

5. Miller and Rudnick, "Case for Situated Theory."

6. Carbaugh, "Fifty Terms"; and Carbaugh, ed., *Handbook of Communication.*

7. Baxter, "Talking Things Through."

8. Garrett, "Wit, Power and Oppositional Groups."

9. Hall and Noguchi, "Engaging in 'Kenson.'"

10. Katriel, *Dialogic Moments.*

11. Wilkins, "Optimal Form."

12. Saito, *Silencing Identity.*

program of work has now explored, and is now exploring, over 100 such terms for communication practices in several different languages—and varieties within languages—including American Sign Language, Arabic, Blackfoot, Chinese, Danish, English, Finnish, German, Hebrew, Hungarian, Japanese, Ojibwe, Russian, Sakapultec, and Spanish.[13]

THREE CASES: DIALOGUE AND ITS INTERACTIONAL, RELATIONAL, AND INFORMATIONAL DIMENSIONS

Discussion of the following cases is built partly upon these earlier and ongoing studies of Wierzbicka.[14] Some of our earlier research reports have explored "dialogue" in Carl Rogers' and Martin Buber's exchange,[15] in various languages,[16] and the field of Dialogue Studies generally.[17] By the end, and building upon our prior works, we look across our cases to identify the large discursive landscape being charted through "dialogue," its considerable crosslinguistic and cultural domains, in order to enhance our dialogic capacities especially when deep differences are at play. On the bases of these studies, I have selected the following cases which demonstrate differences in dialogue which invite deeper modes of dialogue, that is, those dialogic forms which can embrace such differences and hopefully derail monologic assertions, violence, or other destructive forms of behavior.

Case of Dialogue Without Speaking: Reflecting upon Stances for Interaction

For many Native American peoples, places in one's natural environment are deemed sacred. Such places as the Badger-Two Medicine area or the Sweet Grass Hills on the Blackfeet reservation are set aside for ceremonial use and meditation, just as a building of worship is for others. As the Blackfeet man, Rising Wolf, has said to me: "The land that you walk upon is your church." Similarly, for members of the San Carlos Apache of Arizona, Mount Graham is considered such a place. When this place, Mount

13. Carbaugh, *Handbook of Communication.*

14. Wierzbicka, "Concept of 'Dialogue.'"

15. Anderson and Cissna, *Buber-Rogers Dialogue*; Carbaugh, "Cultural Terms."

16. Carbaugh et al., "Dialogue in Cross-cultural Perspective."

17. Carbaugh, "On Dialogue Studies."

Graham, was proposed as a site for an astronomical observatory, support for the proposal was given by the University of Arizona, Germany's Max Planck Institute of Radio Astronomy, and the Vatican Observatory among others. In the wake of the proposal, resistance was expressed, and the San Carlos Apache were asked to respond. The supporters of the observatory proposal, in other words, sought a dialogue with those Apache people who opposed it.

As is typical in the United States, the social stage of a public hearing was set with the expectation that one speak about the issue of concern. This expectation goes back at least as far as the colonial tradition of the New England Town Hall Meeting. The belief is that speaking to the issue is the main reason not only to bring differing parties together but also the means whereby the differences are addressed and mediated. In other words, it is through talking that differences are expressed and can be overcome. This belief about talk is prevalent and prominent in popular American culture and deep in its political tradition.

There are, however, other traditions deeply woven into the fabric of the country. Among Apache people, for example, a reverence and respect for a sacred place like Mount Graham becomes known by being there in that very place, by using it in traditional ways, and by being guided by what it "says" to you. This, the place's spiritual guidance, is much deeper than any one person and each is expected to be properly respectful of that grand power. Given this power, it is best that any one person not try to speak about the place's spiritual power or use its voice, for any one effort by any one person risks diminishing, even desecrating, the sacred spirit that dwells there and all that it is. This severe reluctance to speak on behalf of the sacred mountain obtains among some traditional Apache people. The dynamic is further magnified when Apache people are with others who know nothing about Mount Graham, who know little of treating such a place as sacred, and even less about the specific ceremonies occasioned in this sacred place as well as the traditional Apache ways cultivated there.[18] In such a situation, how could one speak of all of this? It is best to witness the power of the place nonverbally.

The case invites both deep and broad reflection upon what stance is best for dialogic interaction. Is speaking the only stance or are other stances deeply at play? Does verbal interaction interfere with or violate cultural or spiritual principles that are active? What alternate means of communication

18. Helfrich, "Cultural Survival"; Wilkins et al., "Situating Rhetoric."

may be needed or necessary to proceed? If people feel forced to participate, then to do so in ways that violate their beliefs, the results will hardly be of enduring value. Reflection upon stances for speaking or not—what is presumably good or best—for participants is warranted.

A Case of Dialogue That Targets Harmony: Reflecting upon Relationships as the Top Priority

Chinese scholar of communication, Guo Ming Chen, has written that "Chinese culture treats harmony (*he xie*) as the cardinal value. Only through harmony can a conflict free network of human relationships be achieved. Competence—social and moral—is measured by one's ability to maintain harmony, with harmony lubricating the wheels of interaction."[19] Chen makes it clear that the top interactional goal when addressing difficulties from a Chinese view is maintaining harmonious human relationships. When differences risk rising to the fore or dissolving into social conflict, it is best to do what one can to defer to others so relations with them can remain strong, cordial, and productive.

Similarly, Chinese scholar Shi-xu has written: Proper Chinese communication

> is guided by the overarching neo-Confucian principle of being and doing: to bring, maintain and enlarge worldly harmony. That is, relational in nature and holistic in worldview, [Chinese communication] strives to achieve power-balanced harmony, or equilibrium, in society (平天下, peace of humanity under the heaven) as the ultimate moral principle and it does so by conflict avoidance, empathy with others, self-sacrifice, conviviality, etc. in speaking and understanding."[20]

Such a stance and focus can result in a "deep distrust of language in relation to meaning."[21] In other words, from a Chinese point of view, it is best to make positive social relationships the main interactional concern or the targeted goal of dialogue, especially when conflict, difference of opinion, tension, or stress is possible.

19. Chen, "Harmony."

20. Shi-xu, "Chinese Assumptions," 79.

21. Ibid.

Scholars like Guo Ming Chen and Shi-xu characterize a preferred Chinese style for dialogue which involves—relative to the subject matter of concern—being indirect, subtle, and adaptive. In this way, one can address and construct positive social relationships. This sort of deeply cultural value in harmonious relations can stand uneasily beside others. For example, a prominent and preferred style of speaking in Finland is the style of being direct, of the *asiallainen*. When speaking this way, it is highly preferable that one speak directly about the facts of "the matter at hand." The Finnish preference is for a relatively sparse use of words which address the subject matter frankly with less focus on the "face" of participants or relational matters. In fact to speak in a way "simply to give face" to others, or to focus primarily on relational matters without proper regard to the topical issue at hand would violate this preferred Finnish, *asia*-style.

Let's explore this matter more deeply.

A Conflicting Case of Dialogue with Different Targets: Speaking Facts about Flaws or about the Virtues of the Good Life

A group of Russian professors were invited to visit an American university in order to become familiar with its academic programs. The Russians had travelled to the United States in order to learn on-site how American universities were organized, how specific curricula were designed, and how university personnel were arranged. The professors in the United States were brought together to discuss with the Russians how academic life was conducted in each respective country's universities. Once the professors arrived on campus, a series of rather informal meetings among them was called in order for each to become acquainted. After some short hours together, the American professors began expressing frustration in not knowing what the Russians wanted and needed to know. At the same time, the Russian professors were expressing frustration because they were not getting the information they wanted or needed. Why was this happening?

The communication dynamics in these gatherings provides a possible explanation. When the Russian professors discussed their home university and its programs, they displayed consistently and relentlessly its corporate identity, via themes of solidarity, a view that was publicly agreeable to them. The view presented in their presentations was of a united and collective persona, focused on the virtues of their university, its programs, and personnel. Further, the Russians did not ask explicitly for information and guidance, as such questions might have suggested a fault with their system, thus presenting a risk of disloyalty and a threat to the solidarity of those gathered. The proper Russian face and stance for dialogue did not foreground disclosures of limitations and problems as both risked impropriety from their view.

The other half of this interactional occasion involved American professors who approached the gathering differently. As they listened to the Russians, they struggled to identify what the Russians most needed to know and wanted to hear from them. After hearing about the virtues of the Russian university, the Americans perhaps unwittingly invoked a reciprocity norm by talking about the problems and pitfalls with their home university, its programs, and other matters. They discussed in some detail the problems with their university—faulty facilities and sparse funding—in the United States. Displayed at the meeting, then, was a rather typical American problem orientation, self-focus, and recounted individual experiences relative, in this case, to a higher educational institution.

The dynamics between the modes of interaction at play here are worth making explicit. By targeting a corporate virtue, the Russian stance made it impossible to discover what information was most needed by them. By targeting a problem focus, the American stance eagerly made known what was least needed to the Russians. In a nutshell, the Russian stance foregrounded collective virtue, as the American stance foregrounded the facts of suboptimal problems. The resulting confusions and misalignments that resulted in this intercultural dialogue were difficult for all parties.

DEEP ROOTS OF DIALOGUE: DIFFERENT MODELS FOR CONDUCT, FEELING, AND PERSONHOOD

The three cases above demonstrate in particular ways how people in peacebuilding can approach their situations of dialogue quite differently. In doing so, we step often unknowingly into a stance concerning interactional needs, relational views, with presumed priorities pertaining to what is properly informational, whether factual disclosures or expressions of virtue are most desirable. An Apache speaker, equipped with a deeply traditional spiritual view, may find it not only difficult, but lacking virtue, to speak about a sacred landscape. A Chinese participant may find expressions geared toward relational harmony much better than an expression of fact or truth which risks arousing conflict and intense differences of opinion. Russian speakers may at times in public prefer expressing what is good and virtuous to them rather than problems about their institutions or social systems. In this latter case, I have heard Russians reflect further that Americans at times can seem to be without moral fiber or virtue; then Americans reflect that Russians refuse to speak candidly or factually about their work conditions. And the dramas of dialogue go on!

We may find it difficult to reflect upon these matters; but for peacefully enhanced action, reflect upon them we must. The difficulty may seem impenetrable as it is often housed in customs we take deeply for granted, in beliefs that run deep. The advantages, however, are considerable if we develop the capacity to scrutinize not only the issues but our preferred dialogic means for understanding them. Such reflection, active along the dimensions discussed above, may open new ways to achieve our objectives peacefully. As a result, such reflections can run deeply into our cultural ways and means. This can be difficult, but it also can be highly productive and preferable to running roughshod or violently over others' ways, rendering their ways ineffectual—if they're not going to speak to us we can't help them—and as a result, rendering them helpless. One needs only a reminder of Rollo May's central insight: the seeds of violence are rooted in the soils of helplessness; or alternately, if we can embrace diversity in dialogic ways, we may serve the objective of nonviolent action.[22]

The above cases have been arranged to invite reflection upon three key dimensions in the conduct of dialogic exchanges, especially when differences among people are at play. Before each is elaborated a bit, a central point needs to be made. Dialogue always occurs in a highly particular context; that context is socially occasioned by participants for their purposes; it is also deeply informed by specific, typically unquestioned cultural traditions. Participants to dialogue are best equipped to deal in dialogue when they take the time to know the specificity of that context, the social situation, the cultural traditions at play, as these will be active in the exchange. And as important as it is to develop a reflective capacity along the dimensions only outlined here, that capacity is powerful when applied generally to all means and meanings of dialogic practice.

When difference comes into play, the proposal here suggests asking three basic questions: what is the interactional stance of the participants (and in turn, what interactional stance is being presumed by you)? One key feature in a response is whether one should speak or not; another involves

22. May, *Power and Innocence.*

explicitly how to speak (or not) and in what ways? This is a key interactional dimension as conceived and enacted in dialogue.

The second question for reflection is: how, if at all, are social relationships being targeted in this dialogue? And in what ways? The question invites one to think about connections (or divisions) being forged among people and in what ways this is being done. Some participants approach dialogue with the primary goal to forge relations; others with the goal of exchanging information, as we see next. This is a key relational dimension of dialogue.

The third question asks: what information and/or ideas must be exchanged and in what ways? How do these effect participants? It may be, for some, that information should be at best implied rather than directly stated, especially when face-threats are related to that information. It may be for others that the truth must never be harnessed by any other objective. For still others, what should be expressed is housed in statements of virtue and visions of the "good life." None of these of course are mutually exclusive, yet each can appear where another is expected, thereby seeming somehow out of place to one, about the other. This is a key informational dimension(s) of dialogue.

Reflection upon these dimensions of dialogue can help inform how people work together and enhance their effectiveness in doing so, that is, by acknowledging a range of stances and objectives at play, scrutinizing each, then working in an integrative way to advance the range of stances and ideas at play.

Applying this point to the cases above results in several more specific reflections:

1. Dialogue might involve a nonverbal stance that pays witness through silence.
2. Dialogue might involve massaging interpersonal relationships so people feel comfortable together, being related harmoniously, even at the expense of the information or facts being exchanged. In fact, the information exchanged might not quite be true, or may even be misleading, but the goal of harmonious relations is being served and this can be good.
3. Dialogue might involve, even when asked a question of fact (what actually happened?), a lengthy response about the good, virtuous life (this is the way we think people should live)!

4. A dialogic stance oriented to speaking directly and honestly to the facts of the matter may be least effectual, even harmful.

Typically, elements like those discussed here are beyond the realm of the discussable. They are unknowing or unreflective aspects of discursive preferences and habits. As such, they often serve as unwitting bases for negative judgments, stereotypes, and misunderstanding. By capably bringing these dimensions up for reflection, by reflecting upon these elements in the dialogic practice, participants can scrutinize each, making the process work better for both, and the outcomes more fitting and enduring to the occasion. This task is of course not simple. Why not?

These reflections can and often are tied to deep cultural, religious, and/or political orientations. This is of course demonstrated above as the Apache stance, through its traditional ways, as it is adopted as part of the ancient wisdom of a people. Similarly, the Chinese view, through basic Confucian principles, carries with it a deep cultural tradition. In a different way, basic dynamics of political life can make a tradition of speaking truthfully in public difficult, as in many post-Soviet societies, not to mention a host of others where minority voices are prohibited. This of course runs counter to other traditions where speaking out in public, freely, even if discreditable as George Washington did, is held as a sacred value. The various trajectories for proper conduct bring deeply different stances to dialogue. Reflecting upon them, endeavoring to recombine them in practices toward goals of social betterment, all is required for humane and peaceful advances to be made.

So in closing, recall from the Tao Te Ching: "The Tao that can be spoken is not the eternal Tao." Keep in mind the "ineffable Tao," for it reminds us that the truth at times or perhaps never can be spoken. But also be mindful of John 1:1, "In the beginning was the word, and the word was with God, and the word was God."[23] Through sharing our words, and our different worlds, we can create not only the hope but a practical procedure for moving forward together. Reflecting upon, then using better, diverse dimensions in dialogue can provide for productive moves in many directions.

23. Biblical reference from Oxford English.

BIBLIOGRAPHY

Anderson, Rob, and Kenneth Cissna. *The Martin Buber–Carl Rogers Dialogue: A New Transcript with Commentary*. Albany: State University of New York Press, 1997.

Baxter, L. "'Talking Things Through'" and 'Putting It in Writing': Two Codes of Communication in an Academic Institution." *Journal of Applied Communication Research* 21 (1993) 313–26.

Carbaugh, Donal, ed. *Cultural Communication and Intercultural Contact*. Hillsdale, NJ: Lawrence Erlbaum, 1990.

———. "Cultural Discourse Analysis: The Investigation of Communication Practices with Special Attention to Intercultural Encounters." *Journal of Intercultural Communication Research* 36 (2007)167–82.

———. Cultural Terms for Talk: Dialogue among them. Paper presented at the International Communication Association's Pre-conference on A Dialogue on Dialogue: Exploring Normative and Descriptive Traditions, New York, NY, May 26, 2005.

———. *Cultures in Conversation*. LEA's Communication Series. Mahwah, NJ: Erlbaum, 2005.

———. "Fifty Terms for Talk: A Cross-cultural Study." *International and Intercultural Communication Annual* 13 (1989) 93–120.

———, ed. *The Handbook of Communication in Cross-cultural Perspective*. International Communication Association Series. London: Routledge, 2016.

———. "On Dialogue Studies." *Journal of Dialogue Studies* 1 (2013) 9–28.

———. *Situating Selves: The Communication of Social Identity in American Scenes*. Albany: State University of New York Press, 1996.

Carbaugh, Donal et al. "Cultural Discourses of 'Dialogue': The Cases of Japanese, Korean and Russian." *Journal of International and Intercultural Communication* 4 (2011) 87–108.

———. "Dialogue in Cross-cultural Perspective." In *Aspects of Intercultural Dialogue*, edited by Nancy Aalto and Ewald Reuter, 27–46. Cologne: Saxa, 2006.

———. "A View of Communication and Culture: Scenes in an Ethnic Cultural Center and Private College." In *Emerging Theories of Human Communication*, edited by Branislav Kovacic, 1–24. SUNY Series in Human Communication Processes. Albany: State University of New York Press, 1997.

Chen, Guo Ming. "Harmony: Key Concept #52." Center for Intercultural Dialogue Website. 2005. http://centerforinterculturaldialogue.org/2015/02/24/key-concept-52-harmony-by-guo-ming-chen/.

Garrett, M. "Wit, Power, and Oppositional Groups: A Case Study of 'Pure Talk.'" *Quarterly Journal of Speech* 79 (1993) 303–18.

Hall, Bradford J., and Mutsumi Noguchi. "Engaging in 'Kenson': An Extended Case Study of One Form of Common Sense." *Human Relations* 48 (1995) 1129–47.

Helfrich, Joel T. "Cultural Survival in Action: Ola Cassadore Davis and the Struggle for *dzil nchaa si'an* (Mount Graham)." *Journal of the Native American and Indigenous Studies Association* 1.2 (2014) 151–75.

Katriel, Tamar. *Dialogic Moments: From Soul Talks to Talk Radio in Israeli Culture*. Detroit: Wayne State University Press, 2004.

May, Rollo. *Power and Innocence: A Search for the Sources of Violence*. New York: Norton, 1972.

Miller, Derek, and Lisa Rudnick. "The Case for Situated Theory in Modern Peacebuilding Practice." *Journal of Peacebuilding and Development* 5.2 (2010) 62–74.

Philipsen, Gerry et al. "Speech Codes Theory: Restatement, Revisions, and a Response to Criticisms." In *Theorizing about Intercultural Communication*, edited by William B. Gundykunst, 355–79. Thousand Oaks, CA: Sage, 2005.

Saito, Max. *Silencing Identity through Communication: Situated Enactments of Sexual Identity and Emotion in Japan*. Saarbrücken: VDM, 2009.

Shi-xu. "Chinese Assumptions of Chinese Communication." In *Handbook of Communication in Cross-cultural Perspective*, edited by Donal Carbaugh, 76–85. International Communication Association Handbook Series. London: Routledge, 2017.

Wierzbicka, Anna. "The Concept of 'Dialogue' in Cross-linguistic and Cross-cultural Perspective." *Discourse Studies* 8 (2006) 675–703.

Wilkins, Richard. "The Optimal Form: Inadequacies and Excessiveness within the 'Asiallinen' [Matter-of-fact] Nonverbal Style in Public and Civic Settings in Finland." *Journal of Communication* 55 (2005) 383–401.

Wilkins, Richard et al. "Situating Rhetoric in Cultural Discourses." In *Culture in Rhetoric*, by Richard Wilkins and Karen Wolf, 12–21. Language in Action 19. New York: Lang, 2014.

3

Ethics and the Problem of Interpretation in Sacred Scriptures

Ori Z. Soltes

The source for answering ultimate questions, including how to define good and evil and how to shape an ethical and moral code, is found in most if not all religious traditions in texts (both oral and written) that are believed to have come from a divine source and revealed through sacerdotal intermediaries called "prophets." Throughout the first few millennia of human written history, ethics and morality were defined according to what a given society understood to be the will and the wishes of a divine source conveyed through those intermediaries. The Laws of Hammurabi and the Laws of Moses, for example, were understood by the Babylonians and Israelites respectively to offer instructions for proper behavior for which Hammurabi and Moses were merely conduits: divinity was understood to be the ultimate starting point for both of these legislative structures.

It is a given for traditional Jewish, Christian, and Muslim understanding that Moses returned from a forty-day-and-night encounter with the God of Israel bearing in his arms at the very least ten essential commandments and at the very most the entire Torah/Tawrat with its 613 commandments. (That specific aspects of these commandments are later superseded for Christians and Muslims through subsequent revelations is a separate matter, as we shall see).

We may not only understand this idea of divine transmission through revelation by way of sacerdotal intermediaries conceptually but also observe it graphically expressed on monuments like the Stele of Hammurabi. There we see the image of the king receiving the imprimatur for the code of laws inscribed below the image—from the hand of the god, Shamash, who sits majestically, as a king would sit, extending his scepter-holding right hand to touch the king, while Hammurabi stands, as a courtier would stand, one hand touched to his lips in praise and obeisance, as the laws are approved in being passed from the god to the king to us.

THE INTERPRETATIONAL PROBLEM OF REVELATION

That the guide for ethical and moral behavior is a reality beyond ourselves—that religion and law, morality, ethics, and justice cannot be disentangled from each other—raises important questions. What are the complications that attend the process of understanding the revealed instructions, so that our ancestors and we may be certain that we are fulfilling and not abrogating God's will and wishes—from the problem of the language of divinity (what do "will" and "wishes" mean in a divine context? what do "good" and "evil" mean in God's terms, as opposed to our own?) to the writing down of those instructions? For there is a significant difference between revelation and the legislation of what constitutes proper, moral behavior, for legislation is a consequence of the interpretive process to which the revelation has been subject, that is, what is decreed by God is construed by humans.

Consider one among many instances of these complications. The Sixth Commandment elaborated in the Torah's Exodus Chapter 20, forbids us to commit murder. But what does "murder" mean? If I swat a mosquito, or if I kill a man in self-defense, or in defense of a woman or child from being badly beaten—have I committed murder? If I execute a mass murderer, am I a murderer? It would seem that "kill" and "murder" (and "execute") are not synonyms. It would seem that the revealed words of God connected to any sacred text, whether here or in any number of other circumstances, require human interpretation in order to see the divine commandments properly carried out—and "properly" would mean, "in accordance with divine will."[1]

1. This matter is further complicated if one follows the King James English-language

We might ask how we humans arrive at an understanding of what the divine will is—in the matter of killing or any number of other matters. The short answer is that every religious tradition, not surprisingly, offers overtly interpretive literature sooner or later as, with the passing of the original prophetic individual(s) from the scene to whom and through whom God speaks directly, the burden of guiding the community to fulfill God's will falls more heavily on the shoulders of nonprophetic community leaders.

However, that process is a slippery slope (not necessarily in the negative manner in which that phrase is typically used). For it leads to a second question: when and how do humans begin to strike out on their own, shaping legal, judicial, and moral codes that are understood to derive altogether from human thought and not from divine prescription—and how can we, if we can at all, be fully free of that divine prescription in shaping ethical and moral societies? Questions proliferate: Do we have free will? Why and how do we assume so? If we do, when does the process of asserting it toward the articulation of ethics and morality begin—and can it ever end with an absolute code like those prescribed through Hammurabi and Moses?

When Plato, a Greek who believed in myriad pagan gods, sought to shape a community that would be guided by moral principles and conform to the dictates of justice, he posited an ideal leadership: the philosopher-king. This individual would not be a prophet and would therefore not be guided by the gods, per se, but by his own extremely well-trained instincts. He would be a lover of wisdom (in Greek: *philosophos*), a seeker after truth, and a pursuer of justice—who in fact, would rule only reluctantly as king, because of his conviction that he was best-equipped to lead his community. Plato had one opportunity to put this theoretical model into use, but his philosopher-king-in-training, Dionysius the Younger of Syracuse, failed to become what Plato had hoped he would. In despair at the realization that the shaping of such an individual through even the most rigorous of educational programs might not ever come to pass, Plato in his old age wrote his treatise, *Laws*, an exhaustive discussion of what he hoped would present every conceivable issue and circumstance that might arise in a community that would require adjudication in order to yield justice. In contrast to Moses and Hammurabi, then, Plato offered an approach to justice and morality that was derived from his own thought processes, not the gods.

translation of the Sixth Commandment, where the Hebrew term has been rendered as "kill" instead of "murder." The translator as interpreter seems to have left us defenseless against mosquitoes and against the person who attacks others with a knife.

But for Judaism, Christianity, Islam, and Hinduism (among others) the ultimate source of ethical guidance comes from a concept of God very different from that of Plato. These four faiths share, in common, belief in an absolute deity, all-powerful, all-knowing, all-good, and interested in intervening periodically in human affairs. In turn, each of these world religions offers its own particular sense of both revealed text and patterns of interpretive literature. Whereas, for Judaism, divinely revealed words are contained in the Hebrew Bible, with its three components (Torah, Prophets, and Sacred Writings), for Christianity, the same material constitutes a prelude—delineating the details of an Old Covenant (Old Testament)—to the more consummate articulation of God's word contained in the New Covenant (New Testament), with its Gospels, Acts of the Apostles, Epistles, and Book of Revelation. Moreover, whereas Catholic and Orthodox Christians embrace intertestamental books such as First and Second Maccabees, Ecclesiasticus, and Judith as part of their Bible, the Protestant denominations that develop from the sixteenth century onward reject these books as Apocrypha.[2] When Islam steps onto the stage of history in the seventh century, it views all of these works as flawed preludes to the consummate text, the Qur'an, articulated by the consummate prophet, Muhammad.

Someone outside these faiths would recognize the obvious: that the very question of what constitutes the most important revelation is a matter of interpretation (why not Judith in the Hebrew Bible? Why the Gospel according to Mark but not according to Thomas in the Christian Bible?)—even as, for any believer, it is equally obvious, based on faith, that the text that s/he understands to be absolute is absolute: precisely because it is absolute. Moreover, each of these traditions develops its own body of formal interpretative literature—or put otherwise: their literatures come in two primary forms, that which constitutes the revelation and that which interprets the revelation directly or indirectly.

INTERPRETING THE REVELATION IN THE ABRAHAMIC TRADITIONS

In Judaism—for which the Hebrew Bible (the totality of revealed literature) was canonized by 140 CE—the rabbinic literature of interpretation falls into two categories: that which is a direct discussion of passages in

2. The Ethiopian Church also embraces the Book of Enoch, which is not found within the canon of any of the other denominations.

the Torah and other biblical books (*midrash*, from the Hebrew root *d-r-sh*, meaning to dig beneath the surface) and that which deals with an endless variety of everyday problems, ranging from the possession of property to how properly to celebrate a given festival to what the obligations of a husband to his wife might be and how that might differ for, say, a husband who is a bricklayer as opposed to one who is a rabbi. This second body of literature, that often alludes to but doesn't always directly reference God's word, is broadly called *Talmud* (learning) and the compendium of rabbinic literature, as it continues to evolve in written form from the third century to our own time is called *halakhah*, meaning "the way to go."

Halakhah has its parallel in the Christian tradition—for which the definitive biblical canon was agreed upon by the Council of Bishops at Hippo, North Africa, between 393 and 397 CE. The scores of commentators from Ignatius of Antioch in the first century to commentators at the end of the eighth century CE are referred to as Church Fathers, and their writings are thus called patristic literature. The intellectual and spiritual leaders in the generations that follow, during which time the first European schools and universities were taking shape, largely under the umbrella of the Church, are referred to as "schoolmen" and their writings are called scholastic literature. They cover territory that ranges from biblical commentary to the address of specific ethical questions to theoretical arguments for the very existence of God, as, for example, in St. Anselm of Canterbury. These arguments, in particular Anselm's ontological argument, are circular, since they are shaped by and for believers in God's existence as a Perfect Being who, simply put, would not be perfect if He did not exist; there could be a more perfect being if it possessed all of God's attributes and actually did exist.

Over the course of the centuries following the advent of Islam and the canonization of the Qur'an—organized by the Caliph Uthman by 654–55—one notes the rapid development of *hadith*. These either quote words of the Prophet Muhammad in his own right (as opposed to in his role as a conduit through which God speaks) or elaborate accounts about Muhammad, sometimes in order to decipher a laconic passage in the Qur'an.[3] Beyond these beginnings, however, the far-flung Muslim community, divided between Sunnis and Shi'is, (who most obviously differ in their respective interpretations of who among the Prophet's inner circle was most qualified

3. Consider, for instance, the *hadiths* that elaborate the minimalist account of the *'isra*—the miraculous night-ride from Makka to "the farthest gathering place" and back again, found in Q 17:1.

to assume the leadership of the faith after his death), begins to elaborate distinct theological perspectives—*mu'tazilite* and *asha'rite*—that address questions, for example, regarding human free will and its relationship to divine absoluteness, or whether one can "see" the invisible God in the afterlife.

So too, an increasingly diverse series of schools of jurisprudence emerge and evolve over the five centuries after Muhammad's death in 632. These schools, called as a compendium *shar'ia*—the term is derived from the Arabic word, *shar*, referring to the sort of path that leads one, in the wilderness, to water—offer diverse understandings and interpretations of the myriad issues raised in the Qur'an and the *hadith*, the point and purpose of which, (as with the rabbinic literature and the patristic and scholastic literature), is to guide believers in a direction marked out by God.

The fact that there are diverse schools of *shari'a* (thus there is no such thing as *shari'a*, per se, but rather different *shari'as*), underscores the fact that all of this interpretive literature, in all three traditions, derives from human thought, human understanding, human attempts to engage, explore, and explain God and God's will. In theory, at least, no individual leader in any of these traditions can or should presume to equate his interpretation with God's word and God's unequivocal will. Alas, this self-abasing principle has been repeatedly abrogated across history, as human ego has often intervened to cause interpreters to confuse their conclusions with—or present them to their followers as—divinely revealed words.

The historical upshot of this somewhat complex framework in the Abrahamic traditions is that they are refracted into ongoing patterns of explicit and implicit debate (all too often leading to violent sectarian partisanship) regarding what God's word means and how what is revealed legislates proper human conduct. The debates reflected directly or indirectly in these literatures of interpretation include both the overall questions and the many specific and particular details or instances of what might be called morality. Thus, to repeat: the prescription found in the Bible in Exodus chapter 20 and repeated in Deuteronomy chapter 5, "Thou shall not commit murder" immediately provokes the question of what constitutes murder.

More subtly: what of the passage in Genesis 1:26 that humans shall "have dominion over" the other animals? Does dominion imply the right to do with other species as one sees fit, in terms of one's own needs and desires, or does it imply responsibility for taking care of them? How ought one to understand the passage in Qur'an 2:29 that parallels this verse in

Genesis, in which God declares His intention to create the first human, in order that he might be "a vice-regent—a *khalifa*—in/on the earth"?

Both of these statements are offered in the context of the narrative of Adam and Eve. Their subsequent act, of eating from the tree from which Adam was directly told by God not to eat, leads in three directions with regard to morality. First, Adam and Eve are exiled from the Garden of Eden. Second, their act is viewed as sinful in all three traditions, but in Christianity, that sin, labeled original sin, is deemed so egregious, as interpreted in the writings of St. Augustine (354–428 CE), a key patristic thinker, and St. Anselm (1033–1109), a key scholastic thinker, that only the extraordinary intervention of God in human form (as Jesus) can lead to salvation for humans who are the descendants of Adam and Eve and bear the ineradicable imprint of that first sin on their souls.

Judaism's interpretation is far less extreme (Adam and Eve made a very bad choice, abused the divine gift of free will in abrogating God's direct command, but their act is not an absolute and unique sort of sin, inherently affecting every subsequent human being); and the punishment is not as dire as in Christian thought—there is, in fact, no proper word for hell in Hebrew—and thus there is no need or expectation of an extraordinary act of salvation. Islam reads the story through the narrative in the Qur'an, not the Bible, and in the Qur'an the statement is explicit (Q 17:15) that one's sins are one's own and not those inherited from others—including ancestors like Adam and Eve. Moreover, Islam traditionally teaches that all humans at birth automatically become Muslims, hence Christian baptism or circumcision in Judaism are superfluous.

The third direction toward which the biblical narrative of Adam and Eve leads is directly to the story of Noah; for at the beginning of Genesis chapter 6, when we are introduced to Noah, we are informed that virtually everybody else in the world (besides him) is evil and that therefore God has decided to destroy them all. What is intriguing in this is that there is absolutely no explanation of what it is that they have done that makes them evil. Surely they are not being punished for the act of Adam and Eve, who were themselves punished generations earlier with exile and, arguably, the murder of one of their sons at the hands of the other. The only other divine commandment in the first five chapters of Genesis, (i.e., besides the commandment not to eat from a particular tree), has been to be fruitful and multiply—clearly a commandment that had been followed, not abrogated, by Adam and Eve and their descendants, or there would not have been so many people by the time of Noah to be swallowed up by a flood as recompense for their evil ways.

Thus we realize that what constitutes evil, and what we might understand as the basis for thinking ethically or unethically, morally or immorally, is not simple or clear in the revelation of Genesis. Jews, Christians, and Muslims are necessarily required to interpret God's revelation. Moreover, anytime we humans engage in that hermeneutical act, we are most likely to disagree as to what constitutes the "correct" interpretation.

DEFINING REVELATION AND INTERPRETATION IN "HINDUISM": THE BHAGAVAD GITA

The question of revelation and interpretation is no more simple if one turns outside the Abrahamic tradition to Hinduism. This term, "Hinduism," is a misnomer, since it simply means "India-ism," and implies a common form of faith. On the contrary, what we call Hinduism is extremely diverse with respect (among other things) to its understanding of God. As a convenience, one may (and I shall) use the term, but we must realize the following: Hinduism is complexly monotheistic, for it understands the One God, or Brahman, to be manifest through a large number of articulations or incarnations that go by various names. Thus Brahma, Vishnu, and Shiva are the three primary male expressions—one might even say, aspects—of the godhead; to articulate this in an oversimplified way, Brahma is understood as the creative aspect of God, Vishnu preserves the creation, and Shiva is associated with its destruction (a destruction, however, that yields further creation in an eternal cycle of creation-destruction-creation). To a Brahmanite, Brahma is the consummate expression of God; to a Vaishnite, Vishnu is; and to a Shaivite, Shiva is, but no Hindu denies the legitimate reality of the other expressions.

Nor is it that simple. Thus Vishnu, for instance, has many different avatars—he has taken different forms at different times—in order to intervene in the world of humans. One of those avatars is as a blue/black-skinned human, Krishna—and Krishna develops his own devotees, who see him as the consummate expression of God. Thus what for Vaishnites is one among many avatars of Vishnu is for Kraishnites the expression of the Absolute. Hinduism, furthermore, distinguishes between two sorts of fundamental literatures: revealed literature (called in Sanskrit, *shruti*, literally meaning "heard") and *smirti* (literally, "remembered") literature.

Texts like the Vedas are understood to be *shruti*, and epic poems like the *Mahabharata* are understood to be *smirti*. However, embedded within the *Mahabharata* is a chapter that takes on its own life, called the Bhagavad Gita—a phrase that means "the Divine Song." The divinity in question is Krishna. For Kraishnaites, the Gita is the consummate textual revelation of the views of the consummate expression of God, Krishna, whereas for non-Kraishnaites it is merely an important chapter of a vast *smirti* battle epic.

The content of the Bhagavad Gita, briefly, is this: the warrior (*kshatriya*), Arjuna, leads his troops against his blind uncle and cousins, because his uncle, who had raised Arjuna from childhood after Arjuna's father's death, had usurped the throne that should have passed to Arjuna when he reached manhood. Arjuna is privileged to have Krishna himself as his charioteer, and when the young prince begins to doubt whether he should in fact begin the battle against his uncle's army—distressed that he will, win or lose, kill people, including those who are near and dear to him—Krishna's response to this concern becomes an extended instruction (*dharma*) on how and what one should do to achieve the moral perfection that can lead to *moksha* (release from the ongoing cycle of life-death-life-death) and to a condition of *nirvana*—a term referring to a state (not a location, like Paradise in the Abrahamic traditions) of being one with Krishna, a state where the individual, as a droplet from the great sea of Being personified by Krishna, returns to that sea.

Specifically, Krishna tells Arjuna that what he is doing is attempting to restore the proper order (*dharma*) of things since he, Krishna, God Himself, was the one who established that order. Arjuna's blind uncle, who upset that order by usurping the throne, should not be king. He further instructs Arjuna that the very concern that the prince has expressed regarding family and community underscores why he must fight: he is a *kshatriya*, a warrior in a fourfold God-ordained caste system in which each segment of society has its God-appointed role. Were he not to fight, he would be abrogating the implied divine command for him to do so (and in this text, the command becomes explicit, not implicit), making him complicit in upsetting the proper order of things and pulling him further from the possibility of *moksha* and *nirvana*.

Additionally, Krishna argues that, in any case, he cannot kill those whom he fights. All he can destroy is their bodies, which are a physical carapace, a temporary housing for the soul (*atman*), a housing that is ultimately pure illusion (*maya*). The real individual is the *atman* of that individual, which is indestructible—and it could be the case that someone whom he "kills" has a soul ready for *moksha*, and so that individual's "death" on the battlefield may serve as a mechanism for gaining *nirvana*.

There is more to the story, of course, but for our purposes this part of the discussion will suffice, for it brings us full circle to the problem posed in Exodus chapter 20 and the question of what it means to kill and how that differs from the notion of committing murder. A member of the Abrahamic tradition (or for that matter, of Hammurabi's community or that of Plato) might not feel comfortable with the Kraishnaite promise that, if one's soul has achieved sufficient perfection to merit *moksha* and *nirvana*, the outcome will be a complete dissolution of the individual soul, which becomes subsumed into Being—in this case, (to repeat), understood to be personified as Krishna—itself. Members of these other traditions put too much stress on the notion of individuality.[4]

In the end, on the other hand, what the Babylonian, Abrahamic, and Hindu traditions share in common is the conviction that there is a divine Other that is ultimately responsible for human existence and can extend or terminate it. Each in its own way struggles to understand what divinity requires so that we are extended rather than terminated—whether in the here and now sense or with regard to a world beyond our world to which our souls accede after death—and each understands that the key to that understanding is found in texts through which the divinity reveals itself, through prophets (and priests, and kings), which necessitate detailed interpretive explorations in order for us to correctly follow their precepts. Each struggles to interpret the revealed word of divinity toward a viable and coherent guide for how to be in the world—and reflects that struggle in diverse further texts and traditions that reflect our diversely shaped human initiative.

4. The very important exception to this is found within the mystical traditions within the Abrahamic faiths, in which being subsumed entirely into God is a *desideratum*. In order to accomplish this, then, minimally one must empty one's self of self, so that one may be filled with God—and thus one's individual state is suspended. But this is a temporary condition: one must return to reality in order to improve the world through what one has gained by virtue of one's mystical experience. Not to desire to return and assist in that betterment process is selfish—and if one is selfish, then one cannot be filled with God, by definition, so the mystical process will fail. In Hinduism, by contrast, the condition, once achieved, is a permanent one.

DIALOGUE, INTERPRETATION, AND IMPROVING THE WORLD—FROM SOCRATES TO HIZMET

The implications of all this are enormous as one looks across human history and geography. They include the theoretical underpinnings of the Crusades that pitted Christians against Muslims for two centuries, beginning with Pope Urban II's call in 1095 to "wrest the Holy Sites from the control of the infidel" as an act of fulfilling divine will—which perspective would be questioned during the seventh Crusade by its very leader, the French King, Louis IX, who asked: if God wants us to do this because God is with us Christians, then why are we not consistently victorious over the Muslims?

The implications include the long age of religious wars between Catholics and Protestants, fought between (ca.) 1550 and 1715, in which political and spiritual hegemony over Western Europe wove a colorful tapestry of blood and gore; and the struggles between Shi'is and Sunnis, from the Battle of Karbala in 680 to the shaping of ISIS in the aftermath of the American dismantling of Iraq. The implications thus extend to our own time, to suicide bombers who believe that the slaughter of others and themselves follows a divinely ordained course of action or of groups like Boko Haram who swallow up communities in their bloody jaws, asserting that this is the kind of struggle for spiritual perfection that God enjoins.

More than two hundred years ago, in the aftermath of the Age of Religious Wars, Immanuel Kant wrote a work on Ethics and Morality, in 1785—he called it a *Groundwork of the Metaphysics of Morals*—in which he sought to shape an absolute moral code in the absence of a metaphysical superstructure, i.e., God. He arrived at his "Categorical Imperative," which he articulated this way: I conclude that I would, under any and all circumstances, do or not do some act (say, for example, "I would never kill a baby") and I arrive at that conclusion entirely from within myself, uninfluenced by others or by a sense of God looking over my shoulder. So certain am I that this is a moral absolute, that I would make it a universal law (not to kill babies) if I had the power to do so.

The problem, which Kant would himself eventually recognize, is this: Can I ever know for sure that my formulation came entirely from within myself, uninfluenced, say, by my parents' ideas, absorbed when I was a small child? More importantly, suppose I find myself in a situation that I did not and perhaps could not have predicted? For example, (let us shift his calendar forward one hundred fifty years or so), I find myself the leader of a group of a dozen Jews who have hidden in a trench in the woods during the

Nazi period, and among that dozen is a (very colicky) baby. We hear a Nazi patrol approaching; the baby begins to cry and he has enormous lungs; it is virtually certain that we will be found and that the Nazis will slaughter all of us, using the baby, no doubt, for bayonet practice. What then? Am I to smother the baby? Order his mother to do so? Risk the lives of a dozen people for the sake of one? This is a dilemma for which there exists no tidy solution.

In short, this question has no answer because my eyesight, as a human, is limited to the present: I cannot see the future. (I can barely remember the past clearly). I don't know and cannot know whether the patrol, whose members are busily and loudly talking among themselves, might veer off before they come within earshot of the baby. Or perhaps we are found, but the captain of the patrol has a baby himself whom he has not seen in six months and, remembering his own child, is so compassionately moved by the baby among us, that he whispers: "The border is a mile that way! We never saw you! Go!"—and the baby proves to have been our salvation.

The lesson from Kant is that in the end we cannot arrive at absolute morality and ethics on our own, since as a species we are relativists by definition. On the other hand, following the guidance of an absolute deity is only as reliable as our own relative ability to understand that guidance—and of our ability to recognize the limitations of our ability and not to mistake our relative wisdom for something absolute. Plato and his master, Socrates, whose sense of divinity was very different from that found in the Abrahamic and Hindu traditions (or even in Hammurabi's) argued that we can never stop asking questions regarding what piety and justice are, what ethics and morality are—viz., What is the Good, *hic et nunc*? It is when we think we know so certainly that we cease to be, in the fullest and best sense, "human," for to be human is to keep asking.

In this, Plato and Socrates stand on ground similar to that on which practitioners of Judaism, Christianity, Islam, Hinduism, and other faiths stand, who, through the ages, in shaping their moral codes, have continued to wrestle with the revealed word and its message. Such practitioners understand that the gift of free will embedded within us through the unfathomable generosity of God merely underscores our obligation to attempt to make the correct decision through ongoing discussion and dialogue.

Schools of thought and—literally—schools can teach about morality and can even presume to teach morality, but the best ones follow a Socratic (not by any means necessarily religious, per se) path: that of dialogue and discussion, review and rethinking. The best schools and the most important schools of thought recognize the significance of training students and adherents to think critically about questions of morality and ethics.

To be fully human, Socrates and Plato said, is to be engaged constantly in thinking: in cross-examining one's own and others' thoughts and conclusions, in discussing and debating—and, as such, to recognize that revelation is not the end of the process of operating as a species in league with the God (or gods) who made us. Revelation is the beginning; it is our constant attention to, exploration of, debating about the meaning of the revelation, not only in the abstract but with regard to living our lives in the concrete everyday world—all of which are components of the process of interpretation—that turn God's word into laws by which we can and should live.

This is what these four religious traditions in their interpretive literatures do at their best when they engage in the process of seeking to understand by engaging others, sometimes across centuries. This is what is present in the contemporary world in groups such as the Turkish *Hizmet*—service—movement, resonating from the writings of Fethullah Gülen, whose preaching and teaching have inspired the movement. The *Hizmet* movement reminds us that we connect to God and to God's love when we connect to each other and act lovingly toward each other. Members of this movement have established hundreds of schools across the world whose point and purpose is in large part to help solve the problem of human conflict by training students from elementary to university level to think, to cross-examine their own and each other's thoughts, to recognize the essential role that humans must play in shaping an ethical and moral world.

We play this role when we push ourselves to engage revelation in dialogues of interpretation in which, in shunning egotism, we also recognize the limits of each of our abilities to know the answers absolutely and so open ourselves to the sharing of our diverse understandings in an effort to approach moral truth.

Individuals and groups who promote ongoing and open-minded dialogue—genuine dialogue that has as its goal a level-grounded comparison of different modes and conclusions regarding truth, rather than discussions that have a hidden conversionary agenda derived from an ego-bound certainty—most emphatically fulfill a divine prescription found variously articulated in all of these traditions. That prescription is for us humans to be part of the process of ethical and moral ordering in which we partner with God (even those among us who are not certain that God exists) so that the world might someday be perfected. In an era devoid of kings and prophets the responsibility for helping that process along rests fully and freely on our ordinary shoulders.

BIBLIOGRAPHY

Anselm. *Cur Deus Homo,* in *Basic Writings.* Translated by S. N. Deane. LaSalle, IL: Open Court, 1966.

The Bhagavad Gita. Translated and edited by Franklin Edgerton. New York: Harper Torchbooks, 1944.

"The Code of Hammurabi." Translated by Theophile J. Meek. In *The Ancient Near East: An Anthology of Texts and Pictures,* edited by James B. Pritchard, 138–67. Princeton, NJ: Princeton University Press, 1958.

Gimard, Daniel. *La Doctrine d'al-Ash'ari.* Patrimoines. Islam. Paris: Cerf, 1990.

The Holy Scriptures according to the Masoretic Text. Philadelphia: Jewish Publication Society of America, 1966.

Kant, Immanuel. *Fundamental Principles of the Metaphysic of Morals.* Translated by Thomas K. Abbott. New York: Bobbs-Merrill, 1949.

Nader, A. N. *Le Systeme philosophique des Mu'tazila.* Beirut: Dar el-Machreq, 1984.

The New English Bible: New Testament. 18th ed. Oxford: Oxford University Press, 1968.

Plato. *Euthyphro.* In *The Last Days of Socrates.* Translated by Hugh Tredennick, 19–41. Baltimore: Penguin, 1969.

———. *Laws.* Translated by Trevor Saunders. Baltimore: Penguin, 2005.

The Qur'an: A New Translation by Tarif Khalidi. New York: Penguin, 2008.

Soltes, Ori Z. *Embracing the World: Fethullah Gülen's Thought and Its Relationship to Jalaluddin Rumi and Others.* Clifton, NJ: Tughra, 2013.

Zaehner, R. C. *Hinduism.* Oxford: Oxford University Press, 1970.

4

The Importance of Interreligious Dialogue for Peacebuilding

A Muslim's Itinerary[1]

Abdelwahab Hechiche

INTRODUCTION

I begin with a few critical moments about my journey of discovery to see the importance of interreligious dialogue for peacebuilding and, concomitantly, my awareness of "otherness." My public commitment to peace and to interreligious dialogue started in the early 1960s during my graduate studies at the University of Paris. This coincided with the war for Algeria's independence. Later on, I had the opportunity to intern at the United Nations in New York and became a young Fulbright Scholar at Virginia

1. This paper uses elements of previous research projects including my critique of "Israelis and the Jewish Tradition: An Ancient People Debating its Future" requested by its author, Rabbi David Hartman, Founder of the Shalom Hartman Institute in Jerusalem; the Oxford Roundtable on Terrorism; and the Oxford Kellogg College Seminar of September 2014: "The Event and the Idea." Some thoughts on *jihad* were used in Hechiche, "The Roots of Jihad."

Polytechnic University and the University of South Florida. This experience offered me critical intellectual and spiritual challenges during the time of the June 1967 Arab-Israeli War. The most significant turning point came with a special invitation from the US Inter-Religious Committee for Peace in the Middle East to join the first American Jewish-Christian-Muslim Delegation for peace talks in the Middle East, supported by former President Jimmy Carter.

That turn of fortune became a golden opportunity for me to be introduced to the Shalom Hartman Institute in Jerusalem, led by its founder the late Rabbi David Hartman. About the same time, in the fall of 1993, a Conference on Tolerance organized by the Euro-Arab University, (with some support from UNESCO), the University of Marmara, and the University of Istanbul crystallized and enhanced my academic and vocational commitment to peace through education and through interreligious dialogue. A catalyst of my engagement was attendance at the World Congress of Imams and Rabbis for Peace organized by the Hommes de Parole Foundation (2005) in Brussels and in Seville, under the cosponsorship of the kings of Morocco, Belgium, and Spain. I am also indebted to the Istanbul Cultural Center of Tampa Bay for having included me in several events: their frequent interreligious activities during their annual banquet "Know Your Neighbor" and their courses in the Turkish language and, in particular, for offering the University of South Florida faculty and administrators unique opportunities to discover and enjoy Turkish hospitality in various Turkish cities.

THE MOVE TOWARD DIALOGUE

From Dialogue to Trialogue

According to Richard John Neuhaus, shortly before his death André Malraux stated that "the twenty-first century will be religious or it will not be at all."[2] Should that be the case, it would be imperative to establish and institutionalize a dialogue between religions. Although Jewish-Christian dialogue had already started with Vatican II, Jewish-Muslim dialogue was still in its early stages. Paul F. Knitter explained how in urging a pluralistic, liberative dialogue, he came to prefer

2. André Malraux, as quoted in Richard John Neuhaus "The Approaching Century of Religion," 1.

> a correlational dialogue of religions [that] affirms the plurality of religions, not because it is a fact of life and the stuff of relationships. Rather, a correlational model seeks to promote authentic, truly mutual dialogical relationships among the religious communities of the world, analogous to the kind of human relationships we seek to nurture with our friends . . . These are relationships in which persons speak honestly with each other and listen attentively . . . Without genuine diversity, dialogue becomes talking to oneself in a mirror . . . In a true dialogue, people will be truly, courageously open to the witness to truth that others make. This is a mutual, back and forth co-relationship, of speaking and listening, teaching and learning, witnessing and being witnessed to.[3]

For John D'Arcy May, the theological debate or the dialogue of religions "has tended to take as its point of reference understandings of pluralism which originated in the European Enlightenment. It is beginning to dawn on Western theologians that there may be alternative models of pluralism with roots in other cultures and religions."[4]

When Fethullah Gülen was asked his opinion about Huntington's "Clash of Civilizations" thesis, he answered as follows. "If some people are planning such a thing based on their current dreams and making claims on this subject, and if such a wave has risen and is on its way, then before we suffer such a clash, let's put a bigger wave in front of it and break their wave."[5] It is a truism that classical Islamic thought gave a prominent place to the concept of tolerance before some leaders distorted it for opportunistic reasons. Even in the context of a critique of the Arab-Israeli conflict, Dr. Ismail Al-Faruqi left no room for any equivocation regarding the paramount importance of tolerance, not only in Islam, but also in Judaism and Christianity.

> Whether we like it or not, we, the adherents of the Abrahamic faiths, Jews, Christian, and Muslims are doomed to co-exist for long into the future. Moreover, we are doomed to do so as neighbors. Nay, as neighbors so inter-dependent that our livelihood, our prosperity, our happiness and security are extremely difficult, if not impossible, without cooperation . . . Understanding the other faith is a *conditio sine qua non* of recognition of that faith and cooperation . . . Islam's understanding of Judaism occurs on three

3. Knitter, *One Earth, Many Religions*, 15–16.
4. May, *Pluralism and the Religions*, 1.
5. Unal and Williams, *Advocate of Dialogue*, 189.

> distinctive levels: it sees members of that faith as humans, as heirs of the Semitic religious traditions, and, specifically, as Jews.[6]

In a more systematic study of the place of interfaith dialogue, Dr. Al-Faruqi wrote: "The ideal of universal community was equally taught by Jesus, son of Mary . . . The same teaching was promoted by his followers who took the new religion beyond the Jewish community and proselytized the world. The ideal remained active in the Roman Catholic Church for almost a millennium and a half."[7]

This absolute need for interreligious dialogue is all the more imperative as we learn from a PEW Research survey in April 2015 that predicts "a vibrant religious planet, not the withering away of religion predicted by some futurists," as reported by *The New York Times* of April 3, 2015. Other scholars have seen the necessity of interreligious dialogue in order to grasp the similarities and also the differences among the world religions. For such scholars,

> Judaism and Islam are compatible in that they concur that God cares deeply not only about attitudes but actions, not only about what one says to God, but how one conducts affairs at home and in the village . . . This is an age in which, in the US, in Europe, and in the Middle East, the monotheism of law in the service of the All Merciful (as both call God) intersects once more, as it did one thousand years ago.[8]

A Muslim scholar corroborates the same idea. "When a Muslim reads the Torah, he or she finds so many parallels that there can be no real question of our shared beliefs, and, indeed, their common heritage."[9] Using the traditional group discussion, the Shalom Hartman Institute held many seminars where representatives of the three monotheistic faiths used a cross-reading of the Holy Scriptures together.

6. Al-Faruqi quoted in Hechiche, *What Jews Should Know about Islam and Muslims*, xii.

7. Al-Faruqi, *Trialogue of Abrahamic Faiths*, 59.

8. Neusner et al. *Judaism and Islam in Practice*, vii.

9. Durkee, "Thoughts," 7.

Vatican II's Impact on Interfaith Dialogue

No interfaith study could be undertaken without giving credit to Vatican II's document *Nostra Aetate,* the 1965 "Declaration on the Church's Relationship toward Non-Christian Religions." Other respected scholars have also encouraged openness to other non-Christian religions and denominations.[10] For example, Betty Stafford considered Arnold Toynbee a "religious pluralist in the fullest sense. Even in a Utopian society, he would not envision or desire that there be only one religion. He believes that so long as human beings are genetically, not to mention culturally, diverse, religion must likewise be diverse," before adding: "His ecumenism, however, goes far beyond a mere plea for tolerance of those other faiths. For just as truly it can be said that his position calls for, not just one religion, but for a plurality of religions, it can be said that this same position recognizes that all religions are dimensions of each other."[11]

James Carse makes the point that "dialogue can occur only when each can criticize and challenge the other." Why so? He argued that "religions are so diverse that there is little common ground for agreement, or even for disagreement."[12] In tackling the question of interreligious dialogue, Mohammed Arkoun suggests that our thinking be conducted by "the philosophical perspective of the reciprocity of consciences." For him, one must recognize the existence of "a religious question which has to be dealt with in the all-embracing, universal question of meaning."[13] For Arkoun, the Judeo-Muslim dialogue has not started because the question

> remains as to when and at what price Islamic thought will welcome and encourage a critical theology comparable to that affirmed with such clarity, rigor, and promise in La Théologie en postmodernité. . . . As long as this approach is rejected in principle, its necessity denied, and its most instructive production ignored on the ground that Islam rejects 'Western' science and draws instead its conceptual resources and its processes of argumentation from the Quran and the teachings of the 'Pious Elders' alone, Muslims will go on seeking in the discourse of victimization alibis for the deficiencies of a thought paralyzed by its own scholasticism.[14]

10. Faggioli, "Vatican II," 38–49.
11. Stafford, *Radical Pluralism*, 823.
12. Carse, "Diversity in the World's Religions," 26–27.
13. Arkoun, "From Inter-Religious Dialogue," 124.
14. Ibid., 132.

Almost prophetically, seventeen years before the tragic Paris terror attacks of January 2015, the self-criticism of France and Great Britain regarding their failure in integrating religious minorities echoed Arkoun's warning that the "democratic" Europeans who ease their consciences by granting freedom of worship to the Muslims settled in their midst without ever bothering about the intellectual and cultural indigence in which they are kept, unwittingly foster Islam's drift toward political violence that is then stigmatized in inadequate terms, indeed in a contemptuous spirit.[15]

SACRED SPACE AND TIME IN JEWISH-MUSLIM TRADITIONS

Space and Time in Islamic Sociology

Joseph Chelhod proposed that Islam can be approached from without (through the "borrowings" the new religion made from older religions, in particular Judaism and Christianity) or from within (by studying the rich and complex personality of its founder) or even by mixing the two. In trying to comprehend "the phenomenon which is the sudden appearance of a new system of belief," Chelhod views it not "as a matter concerning a spontaneous creation, springing out of the mind of an illuminated person, but as an actual ideological revolution, the symptoms of which are detectable in the social life, in its economic problems, and in its malaises."[16] Chelhod's main contribution to the understanding of Islamic sociology and to the Islamic concept of sacred space and time is in his analysis of continuity and change in Arab-Islamic history. The appearance of Islam would be the fruit of a slow evolution which led the Arabs from the clan to the nation,[17] from the individual to the person, and, at the religious level, from animism to universalism. "The originality of the personality of the prophet of Islam would precisely come from his ability to impregnate himself with a sense of his milieu and with a sense of his time, understanding the aspirations of his people for a new ideology. Thus, he managed to offer them a religion better adapted to their customs and culture than any other alien system."[18]

15. Ibid.

16. Chelhod, *Les Structured de Sacré*, 7.

17. Today, it is tragic to see how Arab-Islamic tribalism has taken us back to pre-Islamic times. See Al-Ashmawy, "Terreur et Terrorisme," 66.

18. Chelhod, *Les Structures de Sacré*, 8–9.

As the title of his book indicates, Chelhod notes that the Arab factor in Islam concerns its language, traditions, and the interactions between humans and space and between humans and time. The Holy Quran contains a preponderance of Arab culture and lost tribes, which leads Chelhod to speak of "a stratification in Islam"; "the succession of various cultural periods marked by animism, national religion, Hanafism, and Judeo-Christian monotheism were an integral part of the evolution of the Arab religious thinking and attitude toward universalism."[19] As for the sacred space and time, the Quran refers to them abundantly.[20] How many times in recent history did we witness inter-Islamic warfare even during the holy month of Ramadan?

Religiously speaking, the debate over the similarities and linkages between Judaism and Islam has been a thorny issue. But some serious scholarly effort has been achieved in addressing this relationship in a Cartesian fashion. How so? Classical Islamic thought did have its precursors in modern rationalism, e.g., Descartes, who is often associated only with European thinkers in the seventeenth and eighteenth centuries. The scholar G. R. Hawting addressed the question of the Islamic sanctuary in its Judeo-Islamic historical context. His own question was "how the pre-Islamic sanctuary at Mecca became the Muslim sanctuary." He considered that "the one important concomitant of Mohammed's takeover of the Meccan sanctuary, the destruction of the idols," is seen as a harking back to Abraham's monotheism, "a purification of the sanctuary from the abuses which had been introduced in the Jahiliyya,"[21] or pre-Islamic time.

Islamic Time

For modern specialists of the "History of History," the historian should not judge the past, nor strive to instruct his/her contemporaries, but simply give an account of what really happened. Earlier historians were already concerned about this issue. "The modern world, as von Ranke saw it . . . was monarchical and Christian. The developments which led to the rise of

19. Ibid.

20. Mecca is declared sacred by God Himself (XXVIII, 57), (XXIV) The Kaaba is the sacred Abode (V, 97), and ancient (XXII, 3). Allah has also prescribed that out of the twelve months of the year, four should be sacred (IX, 36) during which no battle should be undertaken (V, 2). Pickthall, *The Glorious Koran*, 514, 455, and 245.

21. Hawting, *Pre-Islamic Arabia*, 23.

modern society were political and religious; the two could not be isolated."[22] Von Ranke added,

> Religious truth must have an outward and visible representation, in order that the State may be perpetually reminded of the origin and the end of our earthly existence; of the rights of our neighbors, and the kindred of all nations of the earth . . . Thus, then, independence of thought and political freedom are indispensable to the Church itself . . . She needs them to preserve her from the lifeless iteration of misunderstood doctrines and rites, which kill the soul.[23]

Here begins the dialectical issue between history and belief, eloquently described by Tarif Khaldi, who tried to distinguish between the apprehension of time in Judaism and Christianity on the one hand and in Islam on the other. In doing so, Khaldi wrote "The Quranic version of history rests upon a certain conception of time and space and a certain style to express that conception. Islam and history are coeval: 'It was God who called you Muslims from days of old' (Sura 22:78)."[24] Khaldi elaborates this view as follows:

> Thereafter, the Quran pans over a landscape where time is less a chronology than a continuum, where Abraham, Moses, Jesus, and Mohammed are all described in a grammatical tense which one is tempted to call the eternal present. The whole of history is at once to God. Within this design, events are arranged in clusters repetitive in form. This means that a Quranic *qissa* or tale is closer in function and meaning to a "case in point" or an "affair," or even a "parable" than it is to a story or narrative.[25]

When he refers to Ibn-Khaldun, Khaldi corrects a misperception of scholars who considered Ibn-Khaldun's *History* to be an "unworthy sequel of his celebrated *Muqaddima*."[26] But Khaldi asserts that, when Ibn-Khaldun looked at the relationship between *shari'a* and *syasa*, he

> highlighted a dominant concern of the age: the relationship between power and virtue [and] argued that power was necessary, that it was in itself neither good nor bad, but a special kind of skill

22. Iggers, "Introduction," xxxvi–xxxvii.

23. Von Ranke, *History of the Reformation in Germany*, 1–2.

24. "And strive for Allah with the endeavor which is His right. He hath chosen you and Hath not laid upon you any hardship," in Pickthall, *The Glorious Quran*, 347.

25. Khaldi, *Arabic Historical Thought*, 8.

26. Ibid.

> to be used badly or well in the maintenance of the state. Seen in their historical context, these views seem to emanate from reflections on government and justice . . . But Ibn-Khaldun startles his readers by both the consistency and the expansion of the vision . . . The universe of Ibn-Khaldun is a structured whole with its gradations of reality and meaning. History is the record of this structure and it too reflects the many permutations of *syasa*, the levels in which the levels interact and develop. The *Muqaddima* sets out the broad outlines of this scheme; the history demonstrates how that scheme operated in time.[27]

Khaldi offers us another perspective to better understand today's baffling debates about Islamic extremism and *jihad*ism within the Muslim world and beyond. It is Ibn-Khaldun's "ubiquitous correctives." According to Khaldi,

> In many instances, the boldness of the criticism is accentuated by the sensitive nature of the opinions expressed. Ibn-Khaldun was not only correcting historical reports but challenging the majority view of theologians, jurists, and historians on a large number of controversial issues. In re-writing history, he knew full well that ancient opinions needed to be questioned; prejudices cast away; fabrications exposed.[28]

Khaldi's meticulous analysis, supported by Ibn-Khaldun's exceptional authority, can be corroborated by a contemporary scholar with regard to the ongoing contradictions between established *hadiths* (the recorded statements of Muhammad) and the opportunistic use of *fatwas* (edicts) by Muslim leaders especially when Saudi Arabia juggled with the issues of sacred space, sacred time, and the need to have foreign non-Muslim troops stationed on its soil.[29]

ISLAM IN JUDAISM AND JUDAISM IN ISLAM

Arab-Jewish-Islamic Common Intellectual Heritage

In an important article, "An Approach to the Millennium," Timothy Jenkins asked: "How are we to think about the millennium?" He answers, first, that

27. Ibid.
28. Ibid., 225.
29. Redissi, *Le Pacte de Nadjid*, 287.

> it has a force of its own; it poses a demand and it cannot be ignored . . . Second, despite this force, it can take on many contents, from cheerful effervescence to apocalyptic doom, from frenetic partying to the end of time . . . This kind of existence is frequently discussed in terms of the distinction between *chronos* and *kairos:* The millennium is not simply a point in a chronological sequence, but an event.[30]

Rabbi David Hartman's book, *Israelis and the Jewish Tradition,* asks: How are we to reconcile modernity with Israel's three-thousand-year-old history, since the State of Israel gives a framework for Jewish membership/community apart from any particular religious content.[31] As Hartman notes, "Many Israelis are disturbed and angered by the dangerous polarization between a ghetto vision of Judaism that repudiates modernity and a radical secularism that ridicules the tradition."[32]

Directly or indirectly, Hartman's study led to the divisive debate at the Knesset in the 1990s over the question: "Who is a Jew?"[33] Hartman dealt with this ticklish question by a textual analysis of two great Jewish thinkers, viz., Yehuda Halevy and Moses Maimonides. These two eminent scholars shed a bright light on traditional Jewish values and modern democratic values. In a word, Hartman's comparative approach to these two thinkers is analogous to the complex relationship between the God of Abraham, that is, a faith perspective, and the God of the philosophers, that is, an approach based solely on reason.[34] Given the fact that Maimonides had an Aristotelian linkage with the Muslim, Al-Farabi, it seems natural to look for connections between Judaism and Islam, since as religions they have similar theological structures. For example, both are based on law, whether it be called *torah* or *shariah*. As Hartman notes, philosophers often tend to overlook historical, social, political, and economic concerns, focusing instead entirely on philosophical reflection.[35]

For several years, I shared Rabbi Hartman's views on Israeli-Palestinian peace and on the importance of interfaith dialogue. Inspired by his writings, and by his genuine fraternal leadership in actual intellectual and

30. Jenkins, "An Approach to the Millennium," 161.
31. Hartman, *Israelis*, 15.
32. Ibid., 165.
33. Ibid., 157–58.
34. Ibid., 29–31.
35. Ibid., 29–30.

spiritual studies of the three holy scriptures at the Shalom Hartman Institute in Jerusalem, I reached the point of looking at the tragic inter-Islamic and intra-Islamic conflicts of the time as belonging to a young *umma* (or Muslim community worldwide) debating its past. This tragedy seems to have been exacerbated since the Arab Spring that started in Tunisia in 2010–2011, before spreading to the Arab world, especially to Syria and Iraq. Very recently, a kind of reflux led to the March 18, 2015, terror attack against tourists visiting the Bardo Museum. The actual target was, indeed, the Tunisian dependence on tourism.[36]

Ethics in Islam: *Jihad* or *Salam*?

Like all other religions, faith and practice in Islam are intertwined. Corroborating the views of Cheikh Si Hamza Boubakeur, the former Head of the Grand Mosque of Paris, Mawlana Mohammed Ali sees "no dogma in Islam, nor mere beliefs forced upon a man for his alleged salvation," before adding, "Even in the earliest revelations to Prophet Mohammed as much stress was laid on prayers as on service to humanity, perhaps more on the latter." In fact, "Prayer to HIM was meaningless if not accompanied with service to humanity." This is explicitly prescribed by the Holy Quran: "Hast thou seen him who believes religion? That is the one who is rough with the orphan. And urges not the feeding of the needy."[37] As for the use and abuse of the word *jihad*,[38] Ali uses a quotation of D. B McDonalds in the *Encyclopedia of Islam* to refute the "great misconception that *jihad* is associated with war."[39] A philological analysis helps us better understand the true meaning of *jihad* and how it was so easily distorted from its original meaning by Muslims and by non-Muslims. *Jihad* derives from the root letters: *J/H/D* (*Jahd/Juhd*) meaning ability, exertion or power, strife leading to three kinds of struggle: Against the visible enemy, against the devil, and against the self (*jihad annafs).* It is the third *Jihad* that was identified by Prophet Mohamed as "*Jihad al-Akbar*" or the Greater *Jihad.*

For Asma Afsaruddin, the scholarly literature from the first three centuries of Islam reveals that there were various meanings attached to the

36. Kirkpatrick, "Militants, ISIS included."

37. Ali, *Religion of Islam*, 408.

38. For an extensive treatment of the use and abuse of *jihad*, Fregosi, *Jihad in the West*, 399–409.

39 Ali, *Religion of Islam*, 408–9.

term, *jihad*. Hence, there were competing views about how an individual should walk on the path willed by God.[40] We can already see that any search for the roots of the use of terror in Islam, especially in the case of its justification in the name of Allah, requires two historical considerations: early classical Islam and the modern resurgence of Islam in the eighteenth to nineteenth centuries. During the first phase, Islam was already divided between Mecca and Damascus, and both centers of power were threatened by Byzantium. The second phase was marked by the victorious march of Christian Europe into Muslim lands from Napoleon's expedition into Egypt, the colonization of the Maghreb, to the Anglo-French secret agreements during World War I. Mohammed Said Al-Ashmawy associates the use of terror to cultural traditions of pre-Islamic Arabs of Arabia.[41] But for Nadine Picaudou, the term *jihad*, formed from the same verbal root as *ijtihad*, was used for the interpretation of a text to translate or capture the general idea of an effort toward a determined goal, an effort against oneself, and at the same time, an effort on the path of God.

When seen in the context of the total fiasco of the June 1967 Arab-Israeli War, Nadine Picaudou offers us a very useful and authoritative historical and contextual definition of *jihad*. "Conceived as a permanent struggle between God's will and most of the forces which arise as obstacles to it, *jihad* traditionally follows a certain order by jurists in terms of four categories."

1. *Jihad* of the sword, or armed combat for God
2. *Jihad* of the heart, the inner *jihad* which is an effort for moral and spiritual development
3. *Jihad* of the tongue, associated with preaching
4. *Jihad* of the hand that encompasses most of the behavior compatible with God's will.[42]

However, Picaudou suggests that "sometimes, this hierarchy is simplified under the form of a dichotomy which would oppose the minor *jihad* or armed *jihad* to the major *jihad* or greater *jihad*, the inner struggle of the believer." Pursuing her analysis, Picaudou adds:

40. Afsaruddin, "*Views of Jihad*," 165–69.
41. Al-Ashmawy, "Terreur," 65–72.
42. Picaudou, *L'Islam entre Religion*, 212.

> The armed *jihad*, which is here the main object of our reflection, is submitted to precise criteria which determine its canonical character . . . Muslim societies think of war by defining the conditions of legitimate violence and the limits of its use. Two of these deserve to be mentioned: 1. Only the caliph, the legitimate leader of the community, is authorized to call *jihad*, and 2. The community, not the individual, has the obligation to undertake an offensive war, i.e., this action is the prerogative of the caliph's army.[43]

Picaudou is probably closer to the truth when she presents "offensive *jihad*" as a means to expand Islam territorially as a dream of a universal empire, more than a holy war for the faith, and also to think of classical *jihad* as referring to a legal war, rather than a holy war.[44]

FROM *JIHAD* TO *IJTIHAD*

The Evolution of Quranic Interpretation

If we place some *hadiths* (recorded statements of Prophet Muhammad) in their right contexts, we find that the word *jihad* is not used exclusively for fighting and killing. In part of Bukhari's collection of traditions, the Prophet refers to "a party of my community [that] shall not cease to be triumphant being the upholder of truths . . . and these are the men of learning (*Ahl al-Ilm*)."[45] Yet, surprisingly, and paradoxically, it was among the Muslim jurists (*Fuquaha*) that the word *jihad* lost its original wider significance and began to be used in its narrower sense of *quital* (fighting and killing). There are a plethora of views concerning the nature of *jihad* in early Islamic law. Moreover, it was not until the nineteenth century that Islamic law became codified authoritatively.[46]

How could the latter declare "*La Ikraha fiddeen*!" (No coercion in religion!) and concomitantly, how could the Qur'an countenance proselytizing by the sword? For the two above mentioned scholars, "Differences about the status of *jihad* are a marked feature of early Islamic law, and the details about the conduct of *jihad* continue to reflect historical circumstances throughout the history of Islamic law in the Middle East." What

43. Ibid.

44. Ibid., 215.

45. Bukhari, cited in Ali, *The Religion of Islam*, 213.

46. Mottahedeh, "The Idea of *Jihad*," 23.

is significant in this study is the negation of any "authoritatively codified Islamic law before the ninth century A.D."[47] In reviewing the available primary sources, these two aforementioned scholars tried to re-construct the earliest discussions about *jihad*. They found that

> the first half of the second Islamic century (which ends in 766 A.D.) saw the emergence of two genres of writing about *jihad* which either mixed history and legal thought or attempted to set down rulings of war that relied upon historical precedents. The first were the books dealing with the military expeditions organized by the Prophet in the Medinan period. Some of those books also included the military expeditions of early Caliphs.[48]

While books dealing specifically with *jihad* increased, they belonged to two categories: One consisted of specific sections of the collections of prophetic traditions, or separate books on "the virtues of *jihad*." Roy Mottahedeh and Ridwan Al-Sayyid consider that "The Kitab al-Jihad of Abdallah B. Al-Mubarak al-Marawazi (d.181/797) must surely have been one of the earliest examples of such individual books."[49]

The Militarization of the Ideology of *Jihad*

This interpretation is given even more authority with a reference to the eminent scholar, Dr. Jacqueline Chabbi, according to whom there was some divergence between the Hijazi and the Syrian scholars on the question of whether *jihad* refers to a defensive or offensive war. For her,

> It is possible to suppose that in the mid-second/eighth century, the Medinian editor . . . may have belonged to those who were skeptical about warfare on the frontier; particularly with regard to the purity of the intentions of the fighters . . . There is, furthermore, attributed to Malik the transmission of a *hadith*, according to which the most scrupulous piety (ablutions, attendance at the mosque, continuous observance and prayers) would be the true *ribat* (dwelling on the frontier) . . . That seems to represent a position which would effectively have been professed by Malik . . . It may be wondered whether these traditions support a conflict of opinion among traditionalists at the end of the second/eighth

47. Ibid.
48. Ibid.
49. Ibid., 25.

> century? These indications could permit the fixing of the time when *the ideology of jihad*, professed by circles yet to be identified, began to stress the meritorious aspects of military service on the frontier, while in other circles, there was manifest opposition to this new point of view . . . If such was the case, it could be said that this conflict would, as if symbolically, have divided those who, of quietist tendency, aspired to make *mujawara* (living close to the Kaaba) from those who aspired to make *ribat* (dwelling on the frontier). The latter would have professed a new type of activism.[50]

Although it is said that Ibn Abdelwahhab did not have a clear doctrine, he condemned disobedience to legitimate rulers, while also opposing self-proclaimed kings, shahs, and princes whose usurpation of God's power justified revolt. This critical issue became more problematical when the early Saud rulers had to face the traditional genealogical criterion: The religious prince had to belong to the Prophet's tribe, the Koreish.

This is a very serious and contentious principle that could re-emerge today, particularly when the so-called Islamic State/Caliphate established by Abu Baker Al-Baghdadi is challenging and threatening neighboring Arab-Muslim states, especially Saudi Arabia and the Hashemite Kingdom of Jordan, (the latter having more legitimacy to claim the right of succession). This was the reason for the *Sauds* to espouse Ibn-Taymiyya's interpretation of power and legitimacy, which did not require a Koreishi ascendancy for the *Ulemas* (religious and legal scholars to rule the *Umma* (the Muslim community). The Hanbali rule, espoused by Ibn Taymiyya, was that, as long as the ruler remained faithful to God's laws, he was to be obeyed even if he had taken power by force. This interpretation was supported by verses of the Holy Quran: "Remain united and firmly attached to God's Pact!" (3:103) and by a *hadith* "An unjust man is better than a prolonged discord." In trying to explain what sounded like servility (think of the causes of the 2011–2015 effects of the Arab Spring),[51] Hamadi Redissi found his answer

50. Ibid. In addition, one may think that Jacqueline Chabbi found the key to the controversial debate about *jihad* through her interpretation of *sura* XXIX, Al-Ankabut, (The Spider) 6.8, and the change of the centrality of the confrontation between the Prophet and his adversaries in Mekka before the challenge moved to Medina. See Chabbi, *Le Seigneur des Tribus*, 398.

51. La Boétie, *Discours de la Servitude Volontaire*,71. Beatrice Hibou expanded La Boétie's notion that humans have a tendency to remain passive under dictators. For a contemporary interpretation of the actual sources of the Arab Spring: See Hibou, *Economie Politique*, 121. Hechiche elaborated the same idea in *From the Arab Spring to the Islamic Spring?*

in the work of the late eminent Professor Henri Laoust.[52] "The duty of obedience to the Imam became one of the essential principles of the political sociology of Wahhabism." Thus, the Pact of Nadjd became the actual tradition.[53]

CONCLUSION

Year after year, world conferences and congresses have tried to convince world public opinion that acts of terror and intimidation in the name of Islam have no legitimacy and, on the contrary, that they are un-Islamic.[54] The *Fatwa* of Mardin, issued centuries ago by Ibn-Taymiyyah to justify resistance to and retaliation against the Mongols, seems to have totally transformed Islam as a religion into an ideology of combat, not taking into account the specific historical context. One must fully agree with Dr. Asghar Ali Engineer who recommended that

> our attention must now be shifted from *Jihad* to *Ijtihad*, which means to strive intellectually to comprehend the problems facing the Muslim world and find their solutions. In keeping with the basic principles and values enshrined in the Quran . . . "*Ijtihad* was very much a living process in early Islam; its gates were shut, many scholars maintain, around the sack of Baghdad by the Mongol hordes in 1258. Ironically, it was half a century later that Ibn Taymiyya, defining his own Hanbali school of thought, issued his *fatwa* on *jihad*. Thus the gates of *ijtihad* were closed, and those of *jihad* flung open."[55]

The late eminent scholar and orientalist Professor Jacques Berque used an authoritative *hadith* to demonstrate not only the possibility but also the

52. Professor Laoust was one of my Doctoral Defense Committee members at the Sorbonne.

53. Redissi, *Le Pacte de Nadjid*, 287.

54. Euro-Arab University Conference on Tolerance in Istanbul, Turkey; three world congresses Imams and Rabbis for Peace organized by Foundation Hommes de Parole; numerous UN Declarations, and the very recent White House Conference on Extremism of February 2015, all of which condemned the "high-jacking of Islam, the religion. *Imams and Rabbis for Peace*.

55. Engineer, Asghar Ali, "From Jihad to Ijtihad." The same author shared similar views at the Ibn-Khaldun Conference, held in the fall of 1995, near London, UK, where many Muslim women participated sharing one common point: the necessity to give a feminine interpretation of the Quran.

imperative duty for Muslims to strive in understanding some form or degree of renewal in the interpretation of the Quran. Berque went as far as to see an old theory of modernization in Islam that he compared to Kant's "practical reason."[56] Looking at the phenomenal development of *jihad* in memory and in history, and today at its phenomenal globalization world over, one must be skeptical regarding the "imagined truth of Salafism." Michel de Certeau reinforces this particular point. "Writing is the memory of a forgotten separation . . . It is the endless effect of loss and debt, but it neither preserves nor restores an initial content, as this is for ever lost (forgotten) and represented only by substitutes which are inverted and transformed according to the law set up for a founding exclusion. Scriptural practice is itself a work of memory."[57] This is but a natural phenomenon of the human condition. The danger is also due to the human condition.

> The willingness of ordinary people to let themselves be guided by slogans becomes obvious at certain periods in history and is easily accounted for. However, the endurance and effectiveness of slogans over long stretches of time or the entire lifetime of civilizations are difficult, if not impossible, to calculate and to explain. This applies with particular force to civilizations of the past where any documentation, however plentiful it may be, is fragmented in the extreme."[58]

Ed Hussain enlightens us with his narrative about his experience in his native country of Saudi Arabia.

> Salafi intolerance has led to the destruction of the Islamic heritage in Mecca and Medina. If ISIS is detonating shrines, it learned to do so from the precedent set in 1925 by the House of Saud with the Wahhabi-inspired demolition of 1,400-year-old tombs in the Jannat Al Baqui cemetery in Medina . . . What is religious extremism other than making *shariah* state law? This is exactly what ISIS is attempting to do with its caliphate. Unless we challenge this un-Islamic practice, that is, trying to govern by a rigid interpretation of *shariah*, no amount of work by a United Nations agency can unravel Islamist terrorism. Saudi Arabia created the monster that is Salafi terrorism . . . It must address the theological and ideological roots of extremism at home, starting in the cities of Mecca

56. Berque, *Efforts d'Innovation*, 74.

57. De Certeau, *The Writing of History*, 323.

58. Rosenthal, *Knowledge Triumphant*, 324.

> and Medina. Reforming the home of Islam would be a giant step toward winning against extremism in this global battle of ideas.[59]

Referring to the pact between the Saudis and the founder of Wahhabism, Hussain categorically states, "That 1744 desert treaty must now be nullified."[60] In actuality, the roots of extremism and puritanical Islam go back to thirteenth-fourteenth century Ibn-Taymiyya (d. 728/1328), the author of the *Mardin Fatwa.* Through that *fatwa*, Ibn-Taymiyya divided the world into two spaces: "Dar-al-Islam" (the Abode of Islam) and "Dar-al Harb" (the Abode of War or *Jihad*). Muslim scholars, facing the uses and abuses of Islam the religion to justify terrorism and fanaticism, decided to combat Ibn-Taymiyya on his ground. They met in Mardin in March 2010 to issue a *fatwa* condemning the Mardin Fatwa, at the conference held at Artikulu University. In essence, the results of the conference proclaimed that

> Ibn-Taymiyya's *fatwa* cannot, under any circumstances, be used as a justification and proof for excommunicating Muslims and taking up arms against their rulers, and shedding blood and taking their property, and terrorizing peaceful people, and betraying those living among Muslims and those whom Muslims live in their midst by virtue of citizenship and security. Whoever takes this *fatwa* as an excuse to fight Muslims and non-Muslims has erred in their interpretation and are wrong according to the scriptural texts.[61]

Is there a better explanation for the madness afflicting the Arab-Muslim and non-Arab Muslim worlds between March 2015 and January 2017 from Tunisia to Yemen and on to South Asia? Can a Muslim, in good faith, still convince her/his sisters and brothers of "*Ahl-Al-Kitab*"—*The People of The Book*—that Islam is a religion of peace and tolerance after the mass beheadings of Egyptian Copts in Libya, the Reina massacre in Istanbul, and the expulsion or forced conversion of Christians and other religious minorities in Mosul?[62] Do we need a Muslim Westphalia to stop the bloodshed? After all, "Verily, never will Allah change the condition of a people until they change it themselves."[63] On the other hand, how could any disciple of Dr. Martin Luther King Jr. surrender to despair in these very tragic days between April 2015 to April 2017 without remembering his words at the Nobel Prize cere-

59. Hussain, "Saudis Must Stop," 2014, A21.
60. Ibid.
61. Ibid.
62. CBS 60 Minutes Program of Sunday, March 22, 2015.
63. Michot, "Ibn Taymiyya's," 179–80.

mony of October 14, 1964: "After contemplation, I conclude that this award . . . is a profound recognition that nonviolence is the answer to the crucial political and moral question of our time—the need for man to overcome oppression and violence without resorting to violence and oppression. Civilization and violence are antithetical concepts"[64] Dr. King continued, "I believe that even amid today's mortar bursts and whining bullets, there is still hope for a brighter tomorrow. I believe that wounded justice, lying prostrate on the blood-flowing streets of our nations, can be lifted from this dust of shame to reign supreme among the children of men."

BIBLIOGRAPHY

Afsaruddin, Asma. "Views of *Jihad* throughout History." *Religious Compass* 1.1 (2007) 65–169.

Al-Ashmawy, Mohammed Said. "Terreur et Terrorisme au Moyen-Orient." In *Contre L'Intégrisme Islamiste une Expérience Égyptienne,* edited by Rifaat El-Said et al., 66–72. Paris: Maisonneuve et Larose, 1994.

Al Faruqi, Ismail Raji, ed. *Trialogue of Abrahamic Faiths: Papers Presented to the Islamic Studies Group of American Academy of Religion.* 4th ed. Beltsville, MD: Amana, 1995.

Ali, Mohammed Mawlana. *The Religion of Islam: A Comprehensive Discussion of the Sources, Principles, and Practices of Islam.* (Lahore) USA: The Ahmady'ya Anjuman Isha' At Islam, 1990.

Arkoun, Mohammed. "From Interreligious Dialogue to the Recognition of the Religious Phenomenon." *Diogenes* 46 (1998) 123–51.

Berque, Jacques. "Les Efforts d'Innovation dans L'Islam Moderne." In *L'Islam, La Philosophie et la Science: quatre conferences publiques organisées par l'Unesco,* edited by Muhammad Hamidullah et al., 67–93. Paris: Les Presses de l'Unesco, 1981.

Carse, James. "Diversity in the World Religions." *National Forum: Phi Kappa Phi Journal* 74 (1994) 26–27.

Certeau, Michel de. *The Writing of History.* Translated by Tom Conley. New York: Columbia University Press, 1988.

Chabbi, Jacqueline. *Le Signeur des Tribus: La Vie de Mahomet, Préface d'André Caqust.* Paris: Noesis, 1997.

Chelhod, Joseph. *Les Structures du Sacré chez les Arabes.* Paris: Maisonneuve et Larose, 1964.

Durkee, Abdulah Noorudeen. "Thoughts on Some Possibilities for Muslim-Jewish Dialogue." *Dialogue and Alliance* 14 (2000) 5–18.

El-Saïd, Rifaat, et al. *Contre l'Intégrisme Islamiste: Une Expérience Égyptienne.* Paris: Maisonneuve et Larose, 1994.

Encel, Stephan. *Histoire et Religion: L'Impossible Dialogue? Essais d'Analyse Comparative des Grilles de Lecture Historique et Monotheiste.* Paris: L'Harmattan, 2006.

64. King, *Nobel Prize Acceptance Speech,* 1964.

Engineer, Ashgar Ali. "From Jihad to Ijtihad." *The Afternoon Dispatch and Courier*, May 10, 2010. www.afternoondc.in/notes-from-new-delhi/from-jihad-to-ijtihad/article_1945.

Fregosi, Paul. *Jihad in the West: Muslim Conquests from the 7th to the 21st Centuries*. Amherst, NY: Prometheus, 1998.

Hartman, David. *Israelis and the Jewish Tradition: An Ancient People Debating Its Future*. New Haven: Yale University Press, 2000.

Hawting, Gerald R. *Pre-Islamic Arabia/the Jahiliyya*. New York: Oxford University Press, 2013.

Hechiche, Abdelwahab. "Da Primavera Arabe a Primavera Islamica." *Politica Externa* 21 (June, July, August, 2012). http://www.eei-unrsp.com.br/portal/wp-content/uploads/2012/03 /ENSAIO-DO-IEEI-12.pdf.

———. "The Roots of Jihad in Memory and History." *The Levantine Review* 4 (Winter 2015) 217–53.

———. *What Jews Should Know about Islam and Muslims: Remembering a Common Heritage*. Paris: Publisud, 2004.

Hibou, Beatrice. "La Tunisie en Révolution? Introduction au Thème, Tunisie, Economie Politique et Morale d'un Mouvement Social." *Politique Africaine* 121 (March 2011). www.politique-africaine.com/numeros/pdf/intro/121005.pdf

Hussain, Ed. "Saudis Must Stop Exporting Extremism." *The New York Times*, August 23, 2014, A21.

Iggers, Georg G., and Konrad von Moltke, eds. *The Theory and Practice of History*. New translation by Wilma A. Iggers and Konrad von Moltke. New York: Bobbs-Merrill, 1973.

Imams and Rabbis for Peace: A Historical Meeting. Translated by John Kinsella. Geneva: Hommes de Parole, 2005.

Jenkins, Timothy. "An Approach to the Millennium." *Theology* 807 (1999) 161–69.

Khaldi, Tarif. *Arabic Historical Thought in the Classical Period*. Cambridge Studies in Islamic Civilization. Cambridge: Cambridge University Press, 1994.

King, Martin Luther, Jr. "Nobel Prize Acceptance Speech." In *A Testament of Hope: The Essential Writings of Martin Luther King, Jr.* by Martin Luther King Jr. and J. M. Washington, 217–20. New York: Harper & Row, 1986.

Kirkpatrick, David D. "Militants, ISIS Included, Claim Tunisia Museum Attack." *The New York Times*, March 19, 2015. https://www.nytimes.com/2015/03/20/world/africa/militants-isis-included-claim-tunisia-museum-attack.html.

Knitter, Paul F. *One Earth, Many Religions: Multifaith Dialogue and Global Responsibility*. Maryknoll, NY: Orbis, 1995.

La Boétie, Etienne de. *Discours de la Servitude Volontaire*. Paris: Gallimard, 2009.

May, John D'Arcy, ed. *Pluralism and the Religions: The Theological and Political Dimensions*. London: Casssell, 1998.

Mensching, Gustav. *Tolerance and Truth in Religion*. Translated by Hans-Joachim Klimkeit. Tuscaloosa: University of Alabama Press, 1971.

Michot, Yahya. "Ibn Taymiyya's 'New Mardin Fatwa': Is Genetically Modified Islam (GMI) Carcinogenic?" *The Muslim World* 101 (2011) 130–81.

Mottahedeh, Parviz Roy, and Ridwan Al-Sayyid. "The Idea of Jihad in Islam before the Crusades." In *The Crusades from the Perspective of Byzantium and the Muslim World*, edited by Angeliki E. Laiou and Roy Mottahedeh, 23–29. Washington, DC: Dumbarton Oaks and Research Library, 2001.

Neuhaus, Richard, John. "The Approaching Century of Religion." *First Things* 10 (1997) 75–79. https://www.firstthings.com/article/1997/10/the-approaching-century-of-religion.

Picaudou, Nadine. *L'islam entre Religion et Ideologie: Essais sur la Modernité Musulmane*. Paris: Gallimard, 2010.

Pickthall, Mohammed Marmaduke. *The Meaning of the Glorious Koran*. An explanatory translation by Mohammed Marmaduke Pickthall. London: Allen & Unwin, 1969.

Ranke, Leopold von. *History of the Reformation in Germany*. London: Routledge, 1905. https//archive.org/details/cu31924029240020.

Redissi, Hamadi. *Le Pacte de Nadjid: Comment L'islam Sectaire est devenu l'Islam*. Paris: Seuil, 2007.

Rosenthal, Frank. *Knowledge Triumphant: The Concept of Knowledge in Medieval Islam*. Leiden: Brill, 1970.

Stafford, Betty. "The Radical Pluralism of Arnold Toynbee—Its Implications for Religion." *Journal of Ecumenical Studies* 9 (1972) 819–40.

Unal, Ali, and Alphonse Williams, eds. *Advocate of Dialogue: Fethullah Gülen*. Fairfax, VA: The Fountain, 2000.

5

"Whirling Diversions" in Turkey

John A. Tures[1]

ABSTRACT

The paper employs the diversionary theory of conflict to Turkey, to determine if the country's recent leaders are employing such tactics in their policies toward internal and external rivals. Unlike traditional uses of diversionary theory of conflict, where a leader seeks internal unity with a

1. This paper's research was made possible by a grant from LaGrange College, which included a component for undergraduate research. As a result, two collegiate classes got to participate in the literature review and gathering of evidence. The research assistants who participated include Lydia A. Arflin, Sydney Q. Aronson, Travis W. Beaird, Lavurn P. Billups, Daniel R. Blankenship, Abigail C. Bowen, Elijah M. Brague, Kadeshia L. Brown, Jalen J. Butler, Audrey K, Chancellor, Stephen J. Coelho, Davis P. Conley, Wesley L. Dismuke, Brian S. Fincher, Jeffrey T. Garner, Daniel S. Garrett, Nina M. Gorrell-Wyman, Sean M. Greer, Kristen A. Grover, Shekinah G. Hall, Hamilton V. Harp, Richard C. Howell, Janice L. Job, Chandler E. Joyner, Faisal A. Khan, Zachary J. Kudwa, Tyler V. Langston, Veronique J. Mattox, Michael S. McCauley, Leah S. McGibbon, Corey B. Morgan, Ryan P. Najim, Jessica K. Nelson, Giovanna Ortiz, Duncan M. Parker, Jeremiah A. Parks, Matthew C. Pogue, Benjamin J. Puckett, Nicholas J. Rawls, Jason D. Ray, LaNisha C. Rivers, Michael T. Shaw, Bre'Lan A. Simpson, Dustin L. Tardy, Esteban Vidal, Mark R. Wagner and Karly B. Williams.

war abroad, such rulers engage in verbal threats, demonstrations of force, and even limited uses of it (as opposed to a full-scale conflict), attempting to link enemies abroad to opponents at home. The paper concludes with a connection of the results to the importance of peacebuilding

LINKING ENEMIES ABROAD TO ENEMIES AT HOME

On December 17, 2013, elements of the Turkish government conducted a sting operation on family and friends with business ties to Turkish President Recep Tayyip Erdoğan. His response in 2014 was to link domestic opponents with unpopular foreign countries like Israel, Germany, and even the United States.[2] Meanwhile, these local political rivals attempted to connect Erdoğan to al-Qaeda, ISIS, and even Hitler. The diversionary theory of conflict seems to be employed in full swing, though the targets may be internal, not external.

Erdoğan served as Prime Minister of Turkey from 2003 to 2014, and then proceeded to be elected president, a head of state role that is normally ceremonial, but will get more powers if he succeeds.[3] His party, the AKP, was aligned with Hizmet (which means "Service"), a Muslim group calling for interfaith dialogue and a focus on science and culture.[4] (It is led by Fethullah Gülen, an Islamic cleric living in self-imposed exile in the United States.)[5] But that relationship soured in 2009 over concerns by Gülen's followers about Erdoğan's alleged corruption, nepotism, and an increasing desire to hold on to power in Turkey's democratic regime.[6] Furthermore, numerous members of Gülen's movement were key figures in exposing the alleged corruption in the Erdoğan regime with widespread wiretaps.[7] The combined problems of the Gezi crackdown, the corruption probes, and problems with neighbors all took a toll on Erdoğan's standing in Turkey. Erdoğan's popularity before his election as President had dropped from 74% to 51% in Turkey.[8]

2. *Cihan News Agency,* "Presidential Hopefuls."
3. Ibid.
4. Alpay, "True Anatolian Marvel."
5. *Cihan News Agency,* "Intel Agency's Warnings."
6. Cengiz, "Why the Case Is Suspicious."
7. Turam, "Gulen, Erdogan and Democracy."
8. Poushter, "Support for Turkey's Erdogan."

Erdoğan, for his part, accused Gülen's followers, and allies in the government, of running a "parallel state" intent on usurping Turkish democracy and thwarting the will of the majority, as Erdoğan and his party have won all elections.[9] Things came to a boil on December 17, 2014, when Erdoğan ordered the arrest of media opposition, as well as law enforcement officials responsible for the corruption probe, earning international condemnation for such actions.[10]

DISTRACTING DOMESTIC CITIZENS

But what makes this dispute different from your traditional political spat is the possible presence of a behavior known as the diversionary theory of conflict. Scholars contend that leaders employing this tactic seek to distract their citizens from domestic problems with an international war. Such a conflict would divert the people's attention and promote a "rally 'round the flag" behavior, a nationalist spurt that would boost the leader's popularity."[11]

The origins of this theory come from Lewis Coser, who claimed that social conflict "serves to establish and maintain the identity and boundary lines of society and groups."[12] "Additionally, conflict . . . may help to establish unity or reestablish unity and cohesion where it has been threatened by hostile and antagonistic feelings among the members."[13] Therefore, scholars concluded that when facing a dangerous external threat, it might promote unity within a group. A war could bring a divided country together. "When faced with a threat from an external force, individual members of a group tend to become more cohesive and supportive of their leader,"[14] something which Morgan and Anderson examine in their own research.[15]

Political scientists seemed to lose interest in the theory when they found only modest support for this argument. That was because it was typically tested on Western leaders, like British Prime Ministers and United

9. *Cihan News Agency*, "TUSIAD Chairman."

10. *Cihan News Agency*, "Gov't Tries To Frame Hizmet."

11. Tures, "Moammar Gadhafi Lashes Out."

12. Coser, *Functions of Social Conflict*, 33.

13. Ibid., 153.

14. Mitchell and Prins, "Rivalry and Diversionary Uses," 939.

15. Morgan and Anderson, "Domestic Support and Diversionary Conflict," 800–801.

States Presidents.[16] Recent research has refocused these efforts on Middle East rulers. And the targets are not random, as a crisis is fomented with a country with which there have been past differences, like an enduring rivalry, so the public is not confused by who the enemy is. "We believe that states involved in enduring rivalries can more easily justify the use of force when domestic turmoil is high."[17]

Moreover, scholars only focused on the internal unity from external conflict link in Coser's argument. They ignored Coser's writings about how internal and external conflict might be linked. "Yet not every type of conflict is likely to benefit group structure," he writes. "Whether social conflict is beneficial to internal adaptation or not depends on the type of issues over which it is fought as well as on the type of social structure within which it occurs."[18] Nor are all enemies foreign by nature. "The chosen antagonist can be substituted for by any other 'suitable' target."[19] In fact, an internal conflict where there is a domestic target, might be more intense and dangerous. "The closer the group, the more intense the conflict . . . It is likely to threaten the very roots of the relationship."[20]

Chiozza and Goemans examine the relationship between leaders who are at a higher risk of losing office and the decision to initiate a crisis or not. One such tactic in the arsenal of such an embattled leader is the "scapegoat mechanism," where someone is targeted to blame for a country's problems. By linking the local scapegoat to a foreign country, a leader can also mobilize people to "put aside their differences with leaders and support them in times of international crisis."[21] Tir finds a similar link between a leader's popularity, or lack thereof, and diverting the public's discontent with a foreign policy crisis. Here such leaders manufacture the crisis for selfish reasons, not for the national interest.[22] An economic downturn[23] or even a corruption scandal could make a leader fairly unpopular, precipitating the crisis (domestic, international, or both). And leaders above all desire

16. Tures and Beaver, "Selective Saber Rattling," 4–26.

17. Mitchell and Prins, "Rivalry and Diversionary Uses," 938.

18. Coser, *Functions of Social Conflict,* 153.

19. Ibid., 156.

20. Ibid., 155.

21. Chiozza and Goemans, "Peace through Insecurity," 443–5.

22. Tir, "Territorial Diversion," 422.

23. Mitchell and Prins, "Rivalry and Diversionary Uses," 937.

power, something which internal problems clearly threaten, increasing the probability of conflict.[24]

But Tir and Jasinski find that domestic targets are even more tempting. "With a state, certain segments of society may feel a greater affinity to their own group or even to another state than to the state of which they are nominally citizens. This means that the embattled leader's constituency often does not include the entire population of the state." Therefore, "Leaders can 'exploit the society's fragmentation' in his or her favor."[25]

Findings show that while internal chaos does not always lead to external war,[26] leaders in Western Asia have a penchant for linking domestic opponents to enemies abroad in a bid for better domestic coalitional power.[27] And those same opponents have shown that people out of power can also play the game.

ERDOĞAN'S ACTIONS

Connect Gülen to Israel and the West

Take the case of Erdoğan's actions after the corruption probe and protests that swept the country. The Turkish leader blamed the foreign media for the Gezi Park Protests of 2013. "Numerous attacks were made [against Turkey] here and abroad, in the national and international media, several finance circles, foreign countries and intelligence organizations," Erdoğan said while describing how his government survived last year's Gezi Park protests and corruption investigations," according to the *Cihan News Agency*,[28] though Istanbul-based news agency points out that Erdoğan has given interviews to these very same media, even penning a piece in *The Wall Street Journal* that he lambasted over the Gezi Park incident.[29]

But other times, Erdoğan has a specific domestic opponent linked to a specific foreign opponent. In order to deal with angry demonstrators and charges of corruption, Erdoğan has since attempted to link Gülen and his followers to Israel, which had conducted a commando raid on a ship full of

24. Sobek, "Rallying Around the Podesta," 29.
25. Tir and Jasinski, "Domestic-Level Diversionary Theory," 644.
26. Ibid.
27. Tures and Beaver, "Selective Saber Rattling," 4.
28. *Cihan News Agency*, "Erdogan Returns."
29. *Cihan News Agency*, "Erdogan Drifts."

Turkish activists trying to run the Gaza blockade and help the Palestinians. Nearly ten Turks died in that conflict, with hundreds injured.[30]

According to the *Cihan News Agency* on December 15, 2014, "the pro-government [paper] *Aksam* also focused on the fact that Israel's *Haaretz* daily newspaper was the first to publish coverage of the raid on the 'parallel organization,' which *Aksam* interpreted as a sign of support. Erdoğan has criticized Gülen on countless occasions by claiming his Hizmet movement has alleged ties with Israel."[31]

Additionally, according to *Cumhuriyet*, another newspaper, Hizmet leader Gülen "noted that when Israeli babies who were killed and injured as a result [*sic*] Iraq's rocket attacks on the Israeli cities made him more upset and that he cried for them"[32] during the 1991 Gulf War. That piece, written by Ahmet Sik of the AKP, took place the same day as the raid on Gülen's followers.

It is not just Gülen whom Erdoğan links to Israel. According to Emre Uslu, law enforcement officials investigating his government and family for corruption share the same fate "Erdoğan's long-standing claim against the police officers was that they had committed treason. He also claimed that they are foreign spies dedicated to toppling his government on behalf of foreign powers, implying that the officers work for Israel and the US."[33] And reporters have plenty to fear from the Erdoğan regime. "In the summer of 2013, he cracked down on peaceful demonstrators in Gezi Park and arrested scores of journalists who are still languishing in jail. According to the Committee to Protect Journalists, there are more journalists in prison in Turkey than in China or Iran."[34] A prime example of this was when President Erdoğan authorized the investigation and arrest of journalist Mehmet Baransu on "espionage' charges," for leaking "classified documents to the media."[35]

How do we know this is a diversionary theory game, instead of a genuine hatred of two groups, and simply putting two and two together? Emre Uslu wrote about Erdoğan's public anger against Israel, coupled with private dealings behind the scenes with Israel.

30. BBC, "Turkey Election"; Koplow, "Israel and Turkey."
31. *Cihan News Agency*, "Zaman Hits Turkish Headlines."
32. Sik, "Turkish Paper Views Gulen."
33. Uslu, "Arresting Police."
34. Ben-Meir, "What Happened?"
35. "Ergodan v. Gulen."

> A few years ago when Erdoğan said 'one minute' to Israel's leader and challenged Israel's bullying attitude in Palestine and the region, he was welcomed by the majority of the people in Turkey, the Muslim world and his tone of criticism even found sympathizers in the West. However, as years passed, it turned out that while he was protesting Israel's unjust blockade of Gaza, his son's ships were trading with Israel.[36]

Opposition Nationalist Movement Party (MHP) leader Devlet Bahçeli

> stated that Erdoğan just tries to manipulate the Israeli offensive by showing perfunctory reactions for influencing voters in the upcoming presidential race. Accusing Erdoğan of being insincere in the Palestinian crisis, Bahçeli stated that while Erdoğan has been repeatedly showing harsh reactions against Israel in his rally or meeting speeches, his government has sold 124 tons of jet fuel to Israel to be used in aircrafts that are currently bombing Palestinians in Gaza.[37]

And Uslu adds,

> Let me share a striking example from Turkey. It has been argued that Prime Minister Erdoğan's son Burak Erdoğan has not hesitated to continue trading with Israel when Turkey-Israeli relations soured. Yet, Erdoğan's daughter showed up in front of the Israeli embassy to protest Israel's offensive against Gaza. So far, neither Erdoğan nor his son have denied the allegations that they have conducted business with Israel.
>
> Turkish media reported that Turkey is selling cheap Kurdish oil to Gaza, perhaps used as fuel for Israeli fighter jets to bomb Gaza, but the same government is also supporting the protests against Israel. Turkish Energy Minister Taner Yıldız said that, as a government, Turkey has not sold cheap Kurdish oil to Israel. Well, the Turkish government has not sold any oil to any party in the world because there is no such thing as a government selling oil. It is private companies that sell oil.
>
> Moreover, Erdoğan's government and its supporters, political Islamists, use Israel's attack on Gaza as a pretext to criticize the opposition. Political Islamists use language against domestic opposition that they cannot use against Israel. Political Islamists criticize domestic opposition groups for not showing enough "courage" to stand against Israel, as if they were the ones who attacked Gaza.

36. Uslu, "Erdogan."
37. *Cihan News Agency*, "Erdogan Drifts."

> For instance, Justice and Development Party (AKP) officials as well as pro-AKP figures and media outlets criticize the Nationalist Movement Party (MHP), the Peoples' Republican Party (CHP) and the Gülen movement for being silent in the face of Israel's aggression toward Gaza. They hammer the domestic opposition, using cruel language that they cannot use against Israel.
>
> This is the main problem for the people of Gaza. Since it has been an instrument to be used against domestic opposition and not against Israel, the crisis in Gaza will never end. It is obvious that any peace deal between Israeli and Palestinian people would harm the interests of political Islamists around the world. If there were peace in Palestine, political Islamists would find it very difficult to generate political discourse for their domestic political agendas.[38]

Erdoğan also has a long history of playing both the peace card and the conflict card with Israel, when it suits his needs to do either one. He has criticized Israel for building a wall with Palestine and its policies vis-à-vis the Palestinians.[39]

> A clear illustration of this took place in early 2009, when Recep Tayyip Erdoğan stormed out of the discussion when he was asked by Shimon Peres how he would react if Turkey were attacked every night. A report from *The Guardian* (2009) describes the event. "It all started when, facing criticism from Erdoğan during a panel discussion, Peres asked the Turkish prime minister: 'What would you do if you were to have in Istanbul every night a hundred rockets?'"[40] Erdoğan did not make light of this question and was visibly upset with Peres. According to Tait, "Erdoğan responded by admonishing his interlocutor for raising his voice, and added: 'The reason for you raising your voice is the psychology of guilt. I will not raise my voice that much, you should know that. When it comes to killing you know very well how to kill. I know well you hit and kill children on the beaches.'"[41]

But behind the scenes, it is a different story. Shortly after assuming office, Erdoğan was on the phone with Israeli Prime Minister Ariel Sharon and Sharon's Palestinian counterpart Mahmoud Abbas, an attempt to bring

38. Uslu, "Gaza's Biggest Problem."

39. *Anatolia News Agency*, "Premier Condemns Use of Force"; *Washington Times*, "Turkish peacekeepers."

40. Tait, "International: Diplomacy."

41. Ibid.

both sides together.[42] He offered the same mediation for the Israeli-Syrian disputes as well.[43]

This goes beyond offers to negotiate. Turkey arrested numerous suspects after Israeli synagogues were bombed in Turkey.[44] The Turkish government also criticized attacks on Israelis,[45] and the two countries signed a series of bilateral economic agreements[46] and proposed enhancing these.[47] Those commercial deals, given his family's economic connections to Israel and potential corruption, are especially enlightening.

Connect Gülen to the West

While most of the diversionary tactics have been to tie Gülen to Israel, it is by no means the only case. Though a NATO ally, the United States has not always found itself the most popular country in the region. And given that Gülen lives in Pennsylvania, Erdoğan has taken every opportunity to link the 79-year-old cleric to America. The former prime minister, now President of Turkey, even demanded the extradition of Gülen from the United States to Turkey. "'Deport him or give him to us,' the pro-government Yeni Şafak daily and other newspapers quoted Erdoğan as saying of Gülen. 'Let him come and live in his own country if he says he hasn't committed a crime.'" Additonally, "Gülen is in self-imposed exile in the US, though there is no legal hurdle preventing him from returning to Turkey. Shortly after he went to the US in 2000, he was charged with establishing an illegal organization in Turkey, but he was eventually acquitted in 2008," writes the *Cihan News Agency*.[48]

Despite this, Erdoğan has revoked or suspended Gülen's passport. "The move could bring Ankara a step closer to issuing a formal extradition request for Gülen. Washington is expected to reject such a demand, further fraying bilateral ties already strained over regional policy and enhancing US concerns over what some see as Erdoğan's increasing authoritarianism."[49]

42. *BBC*, "Turkey Election."
43. *Anatolia News Agency*, "Turkish premier says ready."
44. *Anatolia News Agency*, "Turkey Marks Anniversary."
45. *Anatolia News Agency*, "Turkey Condemns Suicide Bombing."
46. *Anatolia News Agency*, "Turkey, Israel Sign Memorandum."
47. *Anatolia News Agency*, "Turkish Business, Israeli Envoy Discuss."
48. *Cihan News Agency*, "Media: Erdogan To Seek Extradition."
49. Hogg, "Turkey Revokes Passport."

Hogg also claims that "the case against Gülen was politically motivated."[50] And the government attempted "to abolish private institutions [because they are] the strongholds of Gülenists to educate their reserve armies of cadres."[51]

Abdullah Karakus adds this quote from the current Turkish President: "Erdoğan, reproaching Obama with regard to Fethullah Gülen, conveyed the message of: 'Either extradite him to us or else expel him. When you ask us for terrorists, we give them to you. We expect the same approach from you.'"[52] Gülen is therefore likened to a terrorist.

How do we know that this attempt to claim Gülen is a terrorist and to stoke the flames of anti-Americanism aims to distract from the growing corruption scandal? Behind the scenes, Erdoğan has worked to cultivate close ties with President Obama and work together on issues, especially Syria.[53] It appears to be another case where the people are being told one thing, while Erdoğan does something else privately. But his "tough talk" against Washington is proving itself to be counterproductive. "In June 2012 when Syria shot down a Turkish fighter near the Syrian coast, Ankara called on NATO to meet and take action against Syria, but NATO only denounced the Syrian act and declared that it was not ready to get militarily involved in Syria."[54] Erdoğan has complained about the lack of Western support on the issue[55] (but has only himself to blame for the icy relations between Turkey and NATO).

When it was revealed that Germany and other Western countries had been spying on Turkey, Erdoğan's Foreign Minister Ahmet Davutoglu tried to link it to the Hizmet movement. Davutoglu claimed the record of critical meeting on Syria was leaked on the Internet before March elections. "In an interview, he talked about three possibilities, supporters of Syrian President Bashar al-Assad, elements of the parallel structure, and pro-Iranian figures. Now, Germany has also been added to this list."[56]

Erdoğan's critics have now made a point of pointing out when the Turkish leader links domestic and foreign opponents. "Erdoğan's harsh

50. Ibid.

51. Toprak, "What's behind the Fight."

52. Karakus, "Messages of Reproach and Warning."

53. Stuster, "Turkish Protest."

54. Wakim, "End of El-Assad?" 195.

55. Fradkin and Libby, "Erdogan's Grand Vision."

56. Bilci, "Who Wiretapped Turkey?"

discourse indicates that he will cause more polarization in Turkish society, trying to pit different groups against one another in order to survive politically and to distract people from talking about corruption and other wrongdoings in the government," reports the *Cihan News Agency*. Moreover, "Erdoğan, the chief political Islamist, turned foreign policy into a domestic political battleground in order to score points in the election, and thereby antagonized allies and partners," said Ekmeleddin İhsanoğlu, the former secretary-general of the Organization of Islamic Cooperation (OIC) according to the *Cihan News Agency*.[57]

THE RESULT FOR TURKEY

And such diversionary tactics are stoking conflict at home for Turkey and problems abroad. According to Cook, Turkey "has become an insular, prickly, nationalist one-man show that is alienating Turkey from its traditional allies in the United States and Europe and making the country increasingly irrelevant to the Middle East."[58] And Lowen concludes "Recep Tayyip Erdoğan is building what he calls a 'New Turkey.' Others call it a polarized, unhappy Turkey—and one where friends at home and abroad are fading fast."[59] This is despite Erdoğan's claims to have a policy with zero problems for neighbors. Yet, according to Ben-Meir, "Turkey today has problems with every neighbor."[60] As a result, "Turkey has become a very lonely country because of its seclusion from other countries."[61]

ERDOĞAN'S OPPONENTS FIGHT FIRE WITH FIRE

But the Turkish opposition, the media, and Gülen's Hizmet followers have also demonstrated an ability to lump Erdoğan with other unpopular actors abroad, like ISIS and al-Qaeda.

White contends, "It now appears that Turkey has provided military and medical assistance to ISIS . . . The Turkish IHH organization even played a

57. *Cihan News Agency*, "Erdogan Returns."
58. Cook, "Emperor Erdogan."
59. Lowen, "Erdogan's 'New Turkey.'"
60. Ben-Meir, "What Happened?"
61. Genc, "Erdogan Usess Gaza."

prominent role in this." She goes on to show that the IHH, a pro-Hamas aid agency is a 'cat's paw' that "the government can disavow formally."[62]

Abdullah Bozkurt concurs. He claims "Erdoğan, Davutoglu and other members of the Cabinet have all avoided criticizing ISIL directly." That is contrasted with Gülen, "who has come out with the most unambiguous statement against ISIL, saying he deplores 'the brutal atrocities' being committed by what he called a terrorist group hiding behind a false religious rhetoric."[63] Additional evidence is provided of earlier anti-al-Qaeda raids and how those who conducted them were fired from their jobs. Most disturbing was the report from the independent newspaper Taraf, which ISIL fought using Turkish ammunition, and some of its fighters sought medical aid in Turkey.[64]

But ISIS is hardly the only group to which Erdoğan's opponents tried to connect him. In another publication, Bozkurt links the Turkish President to a leader of Hamas (Khalid Mashaal), the Muslim Brotherhood, and Iran.[65]

In one case, a Turkish newspaper even tried to tie Erdoğan to Hitler. "'Hitler, too, started like this,' headlined the critical Taraf daily, comparing the crackdown by President Recep Tayyip Erdoğan on Zaman and Samanyolu, two Hizmet movement-affiliated media groups, to the origins of Hitler's rise to power with the Nazi Party," reported the *Cihan News Agency*.[66] Not only was this a reference to a historically odious character, but also linked Erdoğan to the unpopular Germans who had recently spied on Germany.

Even the controversial raid on Gülen's Hizmet organization, the media, and law enforcement, was not without an international element, according to Erdoğan's rivals. "The recent government crackdown on media outlets seen as sympathetic to Gülen's views was initiated by the government after a letter of complaint from a member of the radical group Tahsiyeciler, which is openly supportive of al-Qaeda ideology."[67] Additional details link Tahsiyeciler and their leader, Mehmet Dogan, to Osama bin-Laden, the war in

62. White, "Salafi Switcheroo."

63. Bozkurt, "Regime Sends Wrong Signals."

64. Ibid.

65. Bozkurt, "Turkey, Caliph and Erdogan."

66. *Cihan News Agency*, "Zihan Hits Headlines."

67. *Cihan News Agency*, "Gov't Tries to Frame Hizmet."

Afghanistan, and attacks on Americans.[68] But Erdoğan couldn't resist copying the opposition strategy, insinuating that Gülen was the one backing al-Qaeda. "Describing the Hizmet movement, inspired by Turkish Islamic scholar Fethullah Gülen, as a criminal organization, Küçük said in his column on Tuesday: 'In the same way al-Qaeda cannot [be allowed to] have TV channels and dailies, this parallel crime organization cannot possess television channels and dailies.'"[69]

CONCLUDING THOUGHTS ABOUT THE DIVERSIONARY THEORY AND PEACEBUILDING

The 2015 Elections and Conflict Spillover from Turkey to Syria

Many scholars and nonacademics are familiar with the diversionary theory of conflict or the "wag the dog" hypothesis, from the 1990s American film by that name, where a US President's advisers manufacture a war abroad to improve his domestic standing at home and distract the public from an embarrassing scandal.[70] What they do not always realize is that these leaders with incentives to divert the public attention actually connect domestic opponents to rival factions abroad.

For Turkey, this became perfectly clear in the two elections held in 2015. By labeling Gülen and his followers "terrorists,"[71] the current regime could tie the group that exposed Erdoğan's scandals to enemies abroad, those responsible for bomb blasts that struck Turkey during the election, even if no Gülen follower ever engages in a terror attack or is directly accused of doing so. This has the effect of distracting the public from corruption and authoritarianism at home, which is the goal of the strategy.

Gülenists are hardly the only targets. Kurds have earned the ire of the Erdoğan regime. The plucky pro-Kurd party HDP, which appeals to many Turks (especially the youth) won enough votes to be seated in parliament, depriving Erdoğan of the power to remake the country's constitution and install himself as a strong president (instead of a ceremonial one). In fact, Erdoğan's party (AKP) didn't even win a majority in June, forcing a need for

68. Bozkurt, "Jailed Journalist"; Uslu, "Does Erdogan Support Preacher?"

69. *Cihan News Agency*, "Judicial Package Authorizes Seizure."

70. Tures, "How Gadhafi Lashes Out."

71. Mezzofiore, "Tukey Puts Gulen on List."

either a coalition government (with opposition parties like the CHP, MHP or HDP) or a new election.[72]

Rather, Erdoğan turned to his old diversionary tactic. The ceasefire with Kurdish fighters was removed, and armed forces attacked the Kurds, leading to reprisals. Erdoğan repeatedly attempted to link HDP party members to the PKK insurgents, despite repeated denials. The conflict spread to Syria, and in the months and days before the fall elections, Erdoğan ordered attacks on Kurds across the border, while claiming he was fighting ISIS. Bombs exploded at HDP events and those for the country's Communist Party.[73] Though ISIS was blamed, Turkish armed forces were ordered to bomb ISIS's enemy, the Syrian Kurds.[74]

In the new elections, the AKP won back their majority, though not enough votes to make Erdoğan a powerful president via a constitutional legislative action. The HDP even held on to their spot in parliament, despite the necessity of a double-digit election threshold (for most countries that have one, the threshold is 5 percent or less). But in the process the AKP usurped the nationalist MHP, which normally takes a tough line on the Kurds, in order to win the most votes (49.4 percent). The "extra votes" taken from parties not making the threshold put the AKP over the top and gave them the right to have at least a plebiscite on presidential powers.[75] As of the writing of this article, Erdoğan's prime minister has accused Syrian Kurds of an attack on the military and is escalating the bombing attacks across the border.[76]

This most recent series of events show why diversionary tactics employed by leaders should not be ignored as political "cheap talk," or "harmless" pre-election bantering. These strong words and accusations have the power not only to produce domestic conflict with targeting, but to widen conflicts into regional wars. What can be done about this problem?

The Potential for Peacebuilding in Solving the Crisis

Just as the problem from this case emerged in the Middle East, a solution may come from there as well. In 1992, United Nations Secretary-General

72. Arango and Yeginsu, "Party Loses Majority."
73. Coskun and Toksabay, "Turkey Sees State Hand."
74. *Al-Jazeera,* "Turkey Attacks Kurdish Fighters."
75. BBC. "Turkey Election."
76. Hjelmgaard, "Turkey Bombs Kurds."

Boutros Boutros-Ghali adopted the phrase "peacebuilding" in his report "An Agenda for Peace." He called for the United Nations to solidify peaceful institutions as an antidote to conflict. This was augmented by a subsequent report eight years later (the Brahimi Report), which identified peace as something to be built, rather than something to serve merely as an antithesis of war. A 2009 report flushed out more details about the peacebuilding strategy.

> At an aggregate level, one could distinguish four broad theories of change.
>
> 1) Address drivers and root causes (e.g. horizontal inequalities).
>
> 2) Build institutions and capacities of individuals, communities and authorities to manage conflict and deliver services
>
> 3) Enhance social cohesion and build trust among social groups
>
> 4) Build trust in and legitimacy of governments."[77]

The reason why Westerners and others outside the conflict fail to grasp the situation is due to a lack of understanding of the problem. The drivers and root causes are passed off as religious (secular vs. Islamist) or ethnic (Turk vs. Kurd). In reality, the struggle is about power and control, whether it will be in the hands of many or few. A lack of cohesion exists because of the diversionary policies, where a leader pits one group against another.

As for institutions, they do not need to be built so much as saved. In order to hold power, Erdoğan has either co-opted institutions or attacked them if he can't control them. This involves rooting out those not loyal to him or shutting down business enterprises that oppose him.

But social cohesion can be built. Already, we have seen how Turks have stood with Kurds, rejecting calls to pit one against the other.[78] They have shown that diversionary tactics are starting to lose their appeal. In the face of withering assaults by the regime, Gülenists still loyally stand by their principles and posts where they can, rather than cave in.[79] And as the Gezi Park demonstrators showed, Turks will try to stand up to the regime.[80]

As for building trust and legitimacy in government, people in Turkey have done that. If anything, the polls showed a dramatic interest in, and

77. United Nations, "What Is Peacebuilding?"

78. Gursel, "Erdogan's War Backfires."

79. Alliance for Shared Values. "Turkey Current Events."

80. *Cihan News Agency*, "Erdogan Drifts."

excitement about, the democratic process, as people swarmed the ballot boxes to express their political rights, on all sides. Turnout in the June election approached 90 percent.[81]

There are two ways in which peacebuilding can work in Turkey. One is internal and one is external. Internally, Erdoğan's AKP still clings to their beloved strongman, displaying a belief that he supports their ideals and will take care of their basic needs. At a recent meeting this year at the Alliance for Shared Values,[82] Gülenists presented to a Western audience what was happening in Turkey. They pointed out that they (Gülen's followers) overlooked abuses committed by the Erdoğan regime, because they were wielded against secularists or those who supported the old coups against Islamists.[83] Moreover, Gülenists and the AKP were allies. "We should have recognized the signs that this could happen to us," the conference organizers told the audience.[84] The AKP is in the same position as the Gülenists. They are tolerating the campaign against followers of Fethullah Gülen, reasoning that "it's not me who is under attack," unable to realize that one day, this idealistic party will either outlive its usefulness for Erdoğan or become a threat to his rule. Then the AKP will take their place as the persecuted party.

That's why peacebuilding is so important in Turkey. That's why social cohesion needs to occur between the AKP and their old Gülenists allies, or the Kurds, who once enjoyed a ceasefire with the AKP-led government and nearly a decade of relative peace.[85]

But this is not a lesson just for Turks. Westerners observing what's going on in Turkey seem to accept whatever the Turkish government is telling them. Journalists pass on reports and quotes from President Erdoğan and Prime Minister Ahmet Davutoglu without engaging in any critical analysis; (Why is "ISIS" primarily bombing Erdoğan's election opponents at rallies?). Fearful of losing the war on terrorism, Western leaders work with Erdoğan and rarely rebuke him when those air attacks kill Kurds instead of ISIS, even though the former is a Western ally and the latter is a Western enemy. Anyone who is less of a strongman is seen as too weak to combat terrorism. Anyone who is Muslim is not to be trusted, even if we're talking about

81. Arango and Yeginsu, "Party Loses Majority."
82. Alliance for Shared Values, "Turkey Current Events."
83. Mezzofiore, "Turkey Puts Gulen on List."
84. Alliance for Shared Values, "Turkey Current Events."
85. Tol, "Clash of Former Allies."

those who condemn terrorism (like Gülen) or oppose it with force (like the Kurds).

Moreover, other scholars have found that other countries are not immune from employing the diversionary theory of conflict, often in a more dangerous context. For example, in their article on the diversionary theory of conflict, Clark, Fordham, and Nordstrom found that

> during the United States-Iraq crisis of 2002 to 2003, North Korea withdrew from the Nuclear Nonproliferation Treaty, restarted nuclear facilities and directly threatened the United States with nuclear attack. US preoccupation with its imminent invasion of Iraq, to some extent, provided North Korea with an opportunity to press the United States aggressively for direct talks on security and aid, perhaps in an effort to gain bargaining leverage in the face of US distraction."[86]

Though the case involves the traditional diversionary theory of conflict (North Korean leaders seeking legitimacy by demonizing a foreign country), there are some similarities between their theory and the modified version employed in this paper, especially with regards to limited uses of force. "It is important to notice here that efforts to exploit do not necessarily or even primarily mean that a foreign state physically attacks," Clark, Fordham, and Nordstrom write.[87] What is important is that this shows that not only can such tactics be found outside of the Middle East, but, if left unchecked, can eventually involve more serious actions, including threats to use nuclear weapons.

The "peacebuilding" that Boutros-Ghali and Brahimi[88] wrote about need not be a prescription for a third world country with internal problems. Addressing underlying causes, building institutions and individual capacities, enhancing social cohesion, and building trust and legitimacy is also a recipe for international relations, where Westerners and Turks can put aside past suspicions and fears and seek greater cooperation. Had the European Union not stymied Turkey, it would have had more leverage. Had the Americans not panicked about solving the Syrian crisis and stopping ISIS, they wouldn't have given Erdoğan the green light to widen the conflict by making it a Turkey-Kurdish War.

86. Clark et al., "Preying on Misfortune," 254.

87. Ibid.

88. United Nations, "What Is Peacebuilding?"

At the conclusion of their February 2016 talk, the Alliance for Shared Values team requested these very peacebuilding initiatives among those who had already taken steps to connect with Turkey. Reach out, understand what's going on, build connections, we were advised. It was a small-scale call for what Westerners and Turks must do on a wider scale, if peace is to return to the region.

BIBLIOGRAPHY

Al-Jazeera. "Turkey Attacks Kurdish Fighters Inside Syria." *Al-Jazeera,* October 27, 2015. http://www.aljazeera.com/news/2015/10/turkey-attacks-kurdish-fighters-syria-151027082432729.html.

Alliance for Shared Values. "Turkey Current Events." Presentation at the Atlantic Institute, Atlanta, GA, February 12, 2016.

Alpay, Sahin. "A True Anatolian Marvel." *Cihan News Agency*, November 10, 2014.

Anatolia News Agency. "Turkey Condemns Suicide Bombing in Israel." August 31, 2004.

———. "Turkey, Israel Sign Memorandum at End of Economic Committee Meeting." Relisted by *BBC*. July 16, 2004.

———. "Turkey Marks Anniversary of Istanbul Synagogue Bombings." November 15, 2004.

———. "Turkish Business Body Head, Israeli Envoy Discuss Enhancing Economic Ties." October 14, 2004.

———. "Turkish Premier Condemns Israel's Use of Force in Palestinian Territories." September 16, 2004.

———. "Turkish Premier Says Ready To Mediate in Syria-Israel Talks." October 28, 2009. http://infoweb.newsbank.com/resources/doc/nb/news /12BA639B749A52E8?p=AWNB.

Arango, Tim, and Ceylan Yeginsu. "Erdogan's Governing Party in Turkey Loses Parliamentary Majority." *The New York Times*, June 7, 2015. http://www.nytimes.com /2015/06/08/world/europe/turkey-election-recep-tayyip-erdogan-kurds-hdp.html?_r=0.

Ben-Meir, Alon. "What Happened to Recep Tayyip Erdogan?" *History News Network*, November 30, 2014. http://historynewsnetwork.org/article/ 157660.

Bilici, Abdulhamit. "Who Wiretapped Turkey?" *Cihan News Agency*, August 23, 2014.

Bozkurt, Abdullah. "The Case of Jailed Journalist Hidayat Karaca." *Cihan News Agency*, December 23, 2014.

———. "Erdogan Regime Sends Wrong Signals About ISIL." *Cihan News Agency*, September 13, 2014.

———. "Turkey, Caliphate and Erdogan." *Cihan News Agency*, December 30, 2014.

British Broadcasting Corporation. "Gaza Flotilla Raid: No Israel Charges Over Mavi Marmara." November 6, 2014. http://www.bbc.com/news/world-middle-east-29934002.

———. "Turkey Election: Ruling AKP Regains Majority." British Broadcasting Company, November 2, 2015. http://www.bbc.com/news/world-europe-34694420.

———. "Turkish Premier Discusses Ties, Mideast with Palestinian, Israeli." BBC Monitoring Middle East—Political, January 10, 2003.

Cengiz, Orhan Kemal. "Why The Case Against These Journalists Is So Suspicious." *Cihan News Agency*, December 19, 2014.

Chiozza, Giacomo, and Hein E. Goemans. "Peace through Insecurity: Tenure and International Conflict." *Journal of Conflict Resolution* 47.4 (2003) 443–67. http://www.jstor.org/stable/3176204.

Cihan News Agency. "Erdogan Drifts between War and Peace in Relations with Foreign Markets." July 24, 2014.

———. "Erdogan Returns to Hate Speech, Drops Pledge to 'Embrace All.'" August 14, 2014.

———. "Gov't Tries To Frame Hizmet with Secret Statements from Shady Sources." December 26, 2014.

———. "Intel Agency's Warnings Set Off Probe into Turkish Al-Qaeda-Affiliated Group." December 17, 2014.

———. "Media: Turkey's Erdogan to Seek Gulen Extradition in Obama's Talks." September 5, 2014.

———. "Presidential Hopefuls Make Last-Minute Pitch as They Wrap Up Their Campaign." August 8, 2014.

———. "TUSIAD Chairman Says Does Not See 'Parallel Structure' within State." December 29, 2014.

———. "Zaman Hits Turkish Headlines, Newspapers Show Measures of Influence." December 15, 2014.

Clark, David H., et al. "Preying on the Misfortune of Others: When Do States Exploit Their Opponents' Domestic Troubles?" *Journal of Politics* 73.1 (2011) 248–64.

Cook, Steven. "Emperor Erdogan." *Politico*, February 2015. http://www.politico.com/magazine /story/2015/02/turkey-emperor-erdogan-114835.

Coser, Lewis. *The Functions of Social Conflict*. New York: Glencoe, 1956.

Coskun, Orhan, and Ece Toksabay. "Turkey Sees Islamic State Hand in Bombing, Vows Election Will Go On." *Reuters*. October 12, 2015. http://www.reuters.com/article/us-turkey-explosion-idUSKCN0S407020151012.

"Erdogan v. Gulen: Who Will Prevail?" *The Economist*, December 13, 2013. http://www.economist.com/news/europe/21591645-who-will-prevail-erdogan-v-gulen.

Fradkin, Hillel, and Lewis Libby. "Erdogan's Grand Vision: Rise and Decline." *World Affairs Journal*, March/April, 2013. http://www .worldaffairsjournal.org/article/erdogan%E2%80%99s-grand-vision-rise-and-decline.

Genc, Savas. "Erdogan Uses Gaza as Domestic Policy Instrument." *Today's Zaman*, August 4, 2014. http://www.todayszaman.com/monday-talk_erdogan-uses-gaza-as-domestic-policy-instrument_354488.html.

Gursel, Kadri. "Erdogan's War Backfires." *Al-Monitor*. August 15. http://www.al-monitor.com/pulse/originals/2015/08/turkey-kurds-pkk-elections-erdogan-war-backfiring.html#.

Hjelmgaard, Kim. "Turkey Bombs Syrian Kurds after Ankara Attack." *USA Today*. February 18, 2016. http://www.usatoday.com/story/news/world/2016/02/18/turkey-says-syrian-kurds-behind-ankara-attack/80543852/.

Hogg, Johnny. "Turkey Revokes Passport of Bitter Erdogan rival Gulen." *Reuters*, February 3, 2015. http://www.reuters.com/article/2015/02/03/us-turkey-gulen-idUSKBN0L71NW20150203.

Karakus, Abdullah. "Messages of Reproach and Warning from Erdogan." *Milliyet*, September 6, 2014.

Koplow, Michael J. "Why Israel and Turkey Got Back Together." *Foreign Affairs*, March 23, 2013. http://www.foreignaffairs.com/articles/139076 /michael-j-koplow/why-israel-and-turkey-got-back-together?page=show.

Lowen, Mark. "Erdogan's 'New Turkey' Drifts towards Isolation." *BBC News Europe*, November 19, 2014. http://www.bbc.com/news/world-europe-30111043.

Mezzofiore, Gianluca. "Turkey Puts Fethullah Gulen on Most-Wanted Terrorist List." *International Business Times*, October 29, 2015. http://www.ibtimes.co.uk/turkey-puts-fethullah-gulen-most-wanted-terrorist-list-1526305.

Mitchell, Sara McLaughlin, and Brandon C. Prins. "Rivalry and Diversionary Uses of Force." *Journal of Conflict Resolution* 48.6 (2004) 937–61. https://www/jstor.org/stable/4149801.

Morgan, T. Clifton, and Christopher J. Anderson. "Domestic Support and Diversionary External Conflict in Great Britain, 1950–1992." *Journal of Politics* 61.3 (1999) 799–814.

Poushter, Jacob. "Support for Turkey's Erdogan Drops Sharply in Middle East." *Pew Research*, July 30, 2014. http://www.pewresearch.org/fact-tank/2014/07/30/ support-for-turkeys-erdogan-drops-sharply-in-middle-east/.

Sik, Ahmet. "Turkish Paper Views History of Gulen Community, Ties with Ruling Party." *Cumhuriyet*, December 17, 2014.

Sobek, David. "Rallying around the Podesta: Testing Diversionary Theory across Time." *Journal of Peace Research* 44 (2007) 29–45.

Stuster, Dana. "Turkish Protest Obama's Close Friendship with Erdogan." *Foreign Policy*, June 2013. http://foreignpolicy.com/2013/06/04/turkish-protests-test-obamas-close-friendship-with-erdogan/.

Tait, Robert. "International: Diplomacy: Turkey Gives Erdogan a Hero's Welcome after Clash with Israeli President over Gaza Attack: Angry Leader Walked out of Debate at Davos Forum: Peres Seeks to Defuse Row in Phone Call to Ankara." *The Guardian*, January 31, 2009. http://www.theguardian.com/world/2009/jan/30/turkish-prime-minister-gaza-davos.

Tir, Jaroslav, and Michael Jasinski. "Domestic-Level Diversionary Theory of War: Targeting Ethnic Minorities." *Journal of Conflict Resolution* 52.5 (2008) 641–64. https://www.jstor.org/stable/27638632.

———. "Territorial Diversion: Diversionary Theory of War and Territorial Conflict." *Journal of Politics* 72.2 (2010) 413–25. https://www .jstor .org /stable/10.1017/s0022381609990879.

Tol, Gonul. "The Clash of Former Allies: The AKP Versus the Gulen Movement." *Middle East Institute*, March 7, 2014. http://www.mei.edu/content /clash-former-allies-akp-versus-gulen-movement.

Toprak, Levent. "What's behind the Fight between Erdogan and Gulen Movement?" *Marksist Tatum*, January 2014. http://en.marksist.net/levent-toprak /whats-behind-fight-between-erdogan-and-gulen-movement.htm.

Turam, Berna. "Gulen, Erdogan and Democracy in Turkey." *Al Jazeera*, March 13, 2014. http://www.aljazeera.com/indepth/ opinion/ 2014/03/ gulen-vs-erdogan-struggle-thre-201431114482929946.html.

Tures, John A. "How Moammar Gadhafi Lashes Out at Western Governments to Distract Libyans at Home." *Pacific Standard*, March 28, 2011.

Tures, John A., and Kim S. Beaver. "Selective Saber Rattling by Iraqi Politicians." *Digest of Middle East Studies* 20.1 (2011) 4–26.

United Nations. "What Is Peacebuilding? Definitions and Policy Development." The United Nations. 2009. http://www.unpbf.org/application-guidelines/what-is-peacebuilding/.

Uslu, Emre. "Arresting Police To Make Erdogan Happy." *Cihan News Agency*, July 31, 2014.

———. "Does Erdogan Really Support An Al-Qaeda Preacher?" *Cihan News Agency*, December 20, 2014.

———. "Erdogan: From World Leader to World Comedian." *Cihan News Agency*, December 1, 2014.

———. "Gaza's Biggest Problem: Political Islamists." *Cihan News Agency*, July 19, 2014.

Wakim, Jamal. "End of Al-Assad, Or of Erdogan?" *Arab Studies Quarterly*, (Summer 2014) 186–200. http://proxygsu-lag1.galileo.usg.edu/ login?url=http://search.ebscohost.com/login.aspx?direct=true&db=lfh&AN=98612332&site=eds-live&scope=site.

Washington Times. "Turkish Peacekeepers in Lebanon?—Ankara Wants U.S. Action against PKK." August 9, 2006. http://www/washingtontimes.com /news/2006/aug/8/20060808-095630-3701lr/.

White, Jenny. "Salafi Switcheroo." *Kamil Pasha*, August 14, 2014. http:/kamilpasha.com /?p=7770.

6

Peacebuilding according to Daisaku Ikeda and Sōka Gakkai International

Richard Penaskovic

> Our world continues to be threatened by more than 20,000 nuclear warheads—the capacity to kill or grievously injure all people living on Earth, and to destroy the global ecosystem many times over. We are impelled to ask what it is, exactly, that is being protected by this unimaginable destructive capacity.
>
> Daisaku Ikeda

> Be the change you wish to see in the world.
>
> Mahatma Gandhi

INTRODUCTION

On March7, 2017, Ja Song Nam, the North Korean Ambassador to the United Nations, in a letter to the UN Security Council stated that the United States-South Korean military exercises are driving the Korean Peninsula toward "nuclear disaster." He also stated that "It may go over to an actual war."[1] What drove Ja Song Nam to make this statement? The United States is setting up the Terminal High-Altitude Area Defense system (THAAD) in South Korea in order to knock out short- and medium-range ballistic missiles during the last part of their flights.[2] North Korea, along with Russia and China see the THAAD system as a huge threat to their own security. For their part, the United States and South Korea are cognizant that North Korea possesses the mobile KN-08, KN 14, and, most importantly, Nadong NRBM intercontinental ballistic missiles that can reach the shores of the United States, and that they are, most likely, nuclear armed.[3] Hence the United States and South Korea feel that they must set up the THAAD system for their own security and these countries are convinced that THAAD is a purely defensive system. In this connection, the thought of Daisaku Ikeda, particularly in regard to nuclear weapons, is *au courant*, as we shall see in this chapter.

This chapter deals with the Sōka Gakkai movement and the thought of Daisaku Ikeda, a Buddhist and an Honorary President of Sōka Gakkai. Part 1 of this essay deals with the history of the Sōka Gakkai movement in Japan, including the influence of the Nichiren Shoshu school of Buddhism, while the second section looks at the life and controversy surrounding Sōka Gakkai and Daisaku Ikeda. The third section discusses the writings of Daisaku Ikeda, while the final section offers some reflections on Daisaku Ikeda and the Sōka Gakkai movement, particularly regarding the building of nuclear weapons.

SŌKA GAKKAI OR THE VALUE CREATING SOCIETY: A NEW RELIGIOUS MOVEMENT?

Scholars in religious studies argue that the Sōka Gakkai movement that began in Japan after World War II bears a striking similarity to other new

1. "North Korea Warns," 7a.
2. "US Moves Controversial Missiles," 10A.
3. Woolsey and Pry, "Don't Underestimate North Korea."

religious movements that began in Japan around the same time, e.g., the "Dancing Religion" called Tensho Kōtai Jingūkyō,[4] plus two other sects with an affinity to Nichiren Buddhism, viz., Reiyūkai (Spiritual Friends Association) founded in 1925 and Risshō Kōseikai (Society Establishing Righteousness & Harmony) established in 1938.[5] Sōka Gakkai shares some features that the new religious movements in Japan have such as (1) these new religious movements give their adherents a sense of belonging and (2) they have a charismatic leader who embodies the faith. For the Sōka Gakkai movement, Jōsei Toda, the second President after Makiguchi gave the sect a charismatic leader.[6] Although scholars see an affinity between Sōka Gakkai and these new Japanese religious movements, adherents of the Sōka Gakkai do not agree with these academics. According to their own self-understanding, members believe that the Sōka Gakkai movement began over seven hundred years ago with the medieval thinker, Nichiren (1222–82), who interpreted the *Lotus Sutra* as the final message of Shakyamuni or the Buddha. Nichiren claimed to be Jō gyō, (mentioned in the *Lotus Sutra*), a saint or the bodhisattva, viz., a person who, on the verge of nirvana, works to teach others how to find enlightenment.[7]

Nichiren, a charismatic individual, attracted many followers and taught them the *Daimoku* or the sacred phrase, *Nam-myoho-rengo-kyo* or "Homage to the *Lotus Sutra*." One should note that the Sanskrit word *nam* means "devotion or dedication," while *myoho* may best be translated as "mystic law." *Renge* refers to the lotus flower that in seeding and blooming serves as a symbol for cause and effect, while *kyo* stands for the teachings of the Buddha.[8] Members of Sōka Gakkai regard the *Daimoku* as "the agency of enlightenment itself."[9] Tradition states that Nichiren wrote this invocation on the sacred mandala scroll at the famous Taisekjji shrine near Mt. Fuji in Japan. Devotees regard this sacred scroll as the key to unlocking nirvana, hence they recite or chant some portion of the *Lotus Sutra* on a daily basis.

The Sōka Gakkai movement began with Makiguchi Tsunesaburo (1871–1944) who infused new blood into the Nichiren Shōshū movement

4. Brannen, *Sōka Gakkai*, 26.
5. Ellwood, "New Religions," 6573.
6. Brannen, *Sōka Gakkai*, 29.
7. Ellwood, "New Religions," 6574.
8. Goulah and Urbain, "Daisaku Ikeda's Philosophy," 318.
9. Wilson, "Sōka Gakkai," 406.

with his book, *Kachiron* (Philosophy of Value) which was greatly influenced by the thought of Nichiren. Makiguchi, primarily an educator, established the Value Creating Educational Society, and sixty students of Makiguchi established the Sōka Gakkai or Value Creation society in 1937.[10] The movement had three thousand members in 1941. However, Japan's military government imprisoned Makiguchi and other leaders for not placing the movement under state-controlled Shintoism.

Makiguchi spoke about three basic virtues that his followers should put into practice: truth that brings about happiness; beauty; and goodness. The members of Sōka Gakkai are to put these three virtues into practice by (1) chanting the *Daimoku* and other verses of the *Lotus Sutra,* (2) meditating deeply on the writings of Nichiren, and (3) proselytizing others so they might also enjoy the good life. Daily chanting of the *Daimoku* by members of the Sōka Gakkai International contributes to good health, inner peace, prosperity here on earth, wisdom, and eventual salvation. Members of Sōka Gakkai emphasize doing good deeds on earth, rather than waiting for a reward in the hereafter.[11] Values are created by making Buddhism part of one's daily life on earth. If this is accomplished, world peace will eventually come about.[12]

After Makiguchi died, his famous student, Toda Jōsei (1900–1958) gave Sōka Gakkai new life with the popular slogan, *shakubuku* or "break and subdue." The Japanese press found this formula disturbing because it sanctioned an aggressive style of winning new converts, but for Jōsei and his followers, *shakubuku* annihilates falsity while at the same time giving new converts the benefits associated with Nichiren Buddhism.[13] The organization grew under Jōsei but even more so under its third president, Daisaku Ikeda, who established the Sōka Gakkai International in 1975. Yet despite its lofty and noble goals, the Sōka Gakkai movement has had more than its share of controversy, almost from its inception.

10. Dawson, "Cultural Significance," 343.

11. Wilson, "Sōka Gakkai," 407.

12. Ibid., 406.

13. Ibid.

WHY CONTROVERSY HAS SURROUNDED THE MOVEMENT

Although it may be difficult to argue with the stated ideals of the movement, such as its stand on human rights, the emphasis put on dialogue with others, the strong focus on world peace, and the concern for the environment, nevertheless, there are several reasons why the Sōka Gakkai movement has been controversial. At the inception of the movement Sōka Gakkai members utilized "pep" songs, "many of which were popular tunes among soldiers during the Second World War."[14] Members carried with them in a black zipper case the *Manual on Forced Conversions*, or *Shakubuku Kyōten*. This business of proselytizing in the 1950s and 1960s called *shakubuku* (break and subdue) served a dual function, viz., propping up one's own faith in the movement and giving members a sense that they were fulfilling an important function as missionaries or ambassadors of the movement. On the downside, however, some adherents of the movement had a hand in smashing the icons of other religious sects and attacked their "false beliefs." This also played a role in putting the movement under the cloud of suspicion.

This method called *shakubuku*, inaugurated under the second President, Jōsei Toda, set the movement back and was replaced by the method called *shoju,* that is, leading others to the truth through persuasion, in other words, without attacking their cherished beliefs as false.[15] As sociologists point out, new religious movements (NRMs) recruit best by using "pre-existing networks of social relations and developing interpersonal bonds between members and non-members."[16]

A more important source of controversy surrounding the Sōka Gakkai movement concerns its involvement in Japanese politics. In this connection, what upset many Japanese happened in 1964 when Sōka Gakkai established a political party called *Komeito*. Some observers argued that this move on the part of Sōka Gakkai was unconstitutional since it violated the separation of religion and politics according to the Japanese Constitution.[17] However, Sōka Gakkai International and *Komeito* went their separate ways back in 1970. At that time *Komeito* shed its religious language and had an

14. Brannen, *Sōka Gakkai,* 47.

15. Dawson, "Cultural Significance," 346.

16. Ibid., 348.

17. Aoki, "Komeito's 50 years."

important role to play in Japanese politics. However, *Komeito* changed its stance starting about fifteen years ago, when it formed an alliance with the reigning Liberal Democratic Party and began calling itself the New *Komeito*. When P.M. Shinzo Abe's cabinet reinterpreted Japan's Constitution to allow for Japan to fight back if attacked by another nation, the New *Komeito* party went along with the change, thus compromising its pacifist stance, in order to remain in the coalition with the Liberal Democratic Party. As a result of this merger the *Komeito* Party reinvented itself as a political party without any vestiges of religion.[18]

DAISAKU IKEDA AND THE SŌKA GAKKAI INTERNATIONAL

Daisaku Ikeda (b. 1928) has been active throughout his life as a philosopher, the prolific author of two hundred books, and the founder of numerous educational institutes, such as Sōka University, that opened its newest campus in Aliso Viejo in California, as well as the Sōka School system in Japan, Hong Kong, Singapore, and Malaysia. Ikeda founded the Fuji Art museum, the Oriental Institute of Academic Research, and the Seikyo Press. Best known perhaps as a peace activist, he received the United Nations Peace Award in 1983. Ikeda has been an ambassador for world peace that involves social justice, sustainable development, and a nuclear free world. In 1964 he established the Min-On Concert Association to further global peace via international exchanges of the performing arts.[19]

In 1960 Ikeda became President of the Sōka Gakkai or Value Creating Society International that has about ten to twelve million members in over 150 countries. These numbers are approximations since we have no exact statistics on the number of members worldwide. The Value Creating Society International has always been connected with Nichiren Shoshu or the True School of Nichiren, a Buddhist priestly order in Japan. Nichiren (1222–82) had a special place in his heart and mind for a famous Buddhist text, *The Lotus Sutra*. Nichiren interpreted this sacred text as the Buddha or Shakyamuni's final revelation. Tradition has it that he told his followers that he himself was Jogyo or the *bodhisattva* (saint) spoken of in *The Lotus Sutra*.[20] Nichiren taught his disciples the *Daimoku* or invocation, "Homage to

18. Ibid.

19. Ikeda, *For The Sake of Peace*, 223.

20. Dawson, "Cultural Significance," 345.

the Lotus Sutra," writing this invocation on the sacred mandala scroll (the *Gohonzon*) at the Taiseikji shrine near Mt. Fuji in Japan. Devotees regard this scroll as the key to finding happiness or *nirvana*. Nikko, a student of Nichiren, established *Nichiren Shoshu*, one of the 31 Nichiren denominations. Later on, Nikkan (1665–1726) systematized the doctrines of Nichiren Shoshu, arguing that Nichiren was indeed the eternal Buddha, whereas the Buddha himself simply paved the way for Nichiren.[21]

There are a host of benefits associated with chanting the verses of the *Daimoku*, namely, wisdom, health, prosperity, inner peace, global peace, and salvation for all of humanity.[22] Hence members of the Value Creating Society "strongly encourage others to chant" while emphasizing the importance of actions on earth, rather than in the afterlife.[23] For members of Sōka Gakkai, incorporating Buddhist values like compassion into one's daily life brings about the creation of moral values. Today members of the Value Creating Society take part in discussion groups or circles that serve as a venue for making converts. Members also make a pilgrimage to Taisekji near Mt. Fuji. At one time, the Value Creating Society had a political arm called *Komeit*o or Clean Government Party. However, the Value Creating Society broke off its affiliation with the Clean Government Society in 1970 but still remains its chief supporter. The break occurred because of tension between the priests of Nichiren Shoshu and the lay-run Value Creating Society.[24]

In his book, *For the Sake of Peace*, Daisaku delineates several ways or paths to global peace and harmony from a Buddhist perspective. Daisaku calls the first path that of self-mastery and discipline, noting that religious practices build lasting peace because they teach discipline and self-restraint. Religions also instill in their followers the spiritual base that helps them become citizens of the world since norms generated internally are most effective. For example, Leonardo Da Vinci learned self-discipline so well that he then had the courage to face any challenge life thrust in his path. When individuals nourish their inner, spiritual selves, they become capable of overcoming any obstacle. As Shakyamuni admonishes, "We are to be lamps unto ourselves."[25]

21. Wilson, "Sōka Gakkai," 406.

22. Ibid.

23. Ibid., 407.

24. Stone, "Sōka Gakkai," 781.

25. Ikeda, *For The Sake of Peace*, 35.

Human beings contain both good and evil; that is, no one is totally good and, conversely, no one is totally evil. For this reason the *Lotus Sutra* states that we should not despise anyone. Why so? Every person possesses the Buddha nature, i.e., the eternal, immutable nature of all beings, and can attain *nirvana*. Ikeda notes that there exists in every person a "greater self" and a "lesser self." The greater self gives us the ability to reach out to others and to seek their happiness and well-being. The lesser self, on the other hand, make us egotistical and self-centered.[26]

Ikeda also speaks of the path of community and that of nations. Those on this path are concerned with maintaining ethical values, practicing altruism, and fighting for social justice around the globe. He sees relationships between nations as analogous to interpersonal relationships. The community of nations cannot get along well, i.e., peacefully, if one nation holds stubbornly to its own point of view with complete disregard to the views of other nations. Instead of competition on the political, economic, or military levels, nations must compete with other nations in doing good, that is, by competing on the humanitarian level. In this connection Ikeda stresses the value of "soft power," that is, winning others over on the basis of moral persuasion, as opposed to hard power, be it military superiority or economic clout.[27]

Ikeda enunciates the adage that "in helping others we, simultaneously, help ourselves." Shariputra, one of the Buddha's disciples, notes that when two bundles of reeds lean against each other, they are able to stand upright. However, when one bundle tries to stand alone, it falls down.[28] This goes along with the theory known as "dependent origination."[29] This simply means that ours is a thoroughly interdependent world, where whatever happens in one part of the world has an effect on the entire world, just as when one throws a pebble in the pond, the ensuing waves reach the shore. Not everyone believes that our world is interdependent. There are the rugged individualists like my former logic teacher, Gervase Beyer, who claimed that contrary to John Donne's axiom "No person is an island," he believed that "Every person is an island with at most a leaky rowboat."

26. Ibid.
27. Ibid., 72.
28. Ibid., 75.
29. Ibid., 67, 122.

Ikeda raises this urgent question: How do we promote world citizens committed to the shared welfare of humanity?[30] There exists no simple answer to this important question; however, Ikeda does offer some pointers that help us come up with an answer. First, humanity has a strong need to find its ethnic, racial, and national identity. For example, the Kurds in Syria, Iraq, and Turkey long for a separate Kurdish nation. This will be exceedingly difficult to achieve but it will give them their own identity as a separate nation and this may also be in the best interest of surrounding nations like Turkey whose President Erdoğan wants to eliminate them from Turkey. This will only come about by the shedding of blood on both sides, the Turks and the Kurds.

Second, nations can no longer rely on military might alone to buttress their security concerns. We saw this on 9/11 when al Qaeda destroyed the Twin Towers and part of the Pentagon building in Washington, DC. Security can only be attained when nations highlight the importance of human rights, social development, and democracy. We cannot, for example, expect the Gulf States and other nations on the Arabian Peninsula to become democratic overnight. This will take at least a decade or more, just as it took the United States time to develop into a democracy.

Third, Ikeda argues that we must implement the Five Principles of Peace drawn up in 1954 by the first Afro-American Conference in Bandung, Indonesia. The first principle states that countries must respect the territorial rights of other countries. In this connection it appears that the United States violated this principle by invading Iraq to topple the regime of Saddam Hussein. Also, Russia seems to be doing the same thing under Vladimir Putin when it attempts to annex the Crimean region of the Ukraine, a sovereign country. The second principle of peace concerns the notion of mutual nonaggression. ISIS continually flaunts this principle today in Iraq, Syria, and Boka Haram does the same thing in Nigeria.[31]

The third principle of peace states that there ought to be no intervention in the domestic politics of another sovereign nation.[32] According to this principle, for example, the bombing of Yemen by Saudi Arabian fighter jets is morally wrong. The fourth principle of peace deals with the notions of equality and reciprocity. The United States does nothing diplomatically to stop Israel from building settlements on Palestinian land, thus making it

30. Ibid., 160.

31. Ibid., 15.

32. Ibid., 152.

impossible to have a Palestinian state, yet it allows the Israeli Defense Force to occupy the West Bank and Gaza Strip, thus keeping the Palestinians in what amounts to an open-air prison.

Ikeda also writes about the path of dialogue and toleration.[33] He believes that dialogue creates an open space whereby individuals and nations can become whole. Extremists use violence and terror as their modus operandi, whereas gradualists like former President Obama believe in negotiating a treaty with Iran so that they do not develop a nuclear weapon. Obama's policy of negotiation and dialogue with Iran is entirely in line with the Buddhist perspective of Ikeda and the Value Creating Society. As Ikeda notes, discussion and dialogue or "soft power" help nations solve their differences peacefully.[34]

Ikeda remarks that stereotyping causes us to consider those who disagree with us as the primary enemy to be conquered. Dialogue, on the other hand, presupposes the existence in us of self-discipline and compassion for others. In this matter Ikeda speaks of "the greater self." Those who have in themselves the "greater self" are united with others "in a web of relationships that transcend space and time."[35] These individuals are altruistic in that they are concerned with the happiness of others and at the same time earnestly desire to end their pain and suffering. In regard to politics, Ikeda argues that we must look beyond superficial solutions and figure out the underlying causes of ethnic and racial strife, be it in Ferguson, Missouri, or in Staten Island, New York. Failure to do so will be tantamount to putting out the fire in one location, while watching it flame up elsewhere. In order to get beyond our parochial thinking, we must become transnationalists, that is, thinking on a global scale rather than looking at the world only from the perspective of how such an action will best serve the economic and financial interests of our own country. In this connection Ikeda would have us become "world citizens."[36]

Ikeda strongly believes in the elimination of nuclear weapons and speaks about the path of disarmament. He notes that most of the citizens of the world believe that nuclear weapons should be totally abolished. There exists no justification for the stockpiling of nuclear weapons because they are from a moral perspective unshootable. If morally unshootable, there

33. Ibid., 12.
34. Ibid., 57–62.
35. Ibid., 62, 35–37.
36. Ibid., 79.

exists no good reason to stockpile nuclear weapons the way the United State* and Russia continue to do. Does it make sense for there to be over 15,000 nuclear warheads in the world, particularly when such weapons can easily fall into the hands of unscrupulous terrorists and hold an entire nation at bay?[37]

In his dialogue with M. S. Swaminathan in 2005, D. Ikeda noted that in the 1950s the two world super powers at that time, the Soviet Union and the United States, began stockpiling nuclear weapons, including the hydrogen bomb.[38] M. S. Swaminathan took the position that rather than focusing on military aspects, we ought to concentrate on overcoming violence in our mind by looking at the security of the entire human race. We must always remember that in a nuclear war everyone loses. Ikeda argues that every life is sacred and has a right to exist. Ikeda has in mind the Buddhist teaching that there exist two poles: the basic nature of nirvana that works for good and its opposite the basic nature of darkness that attempts to snuff out life.[39]

At first, five nations (the United States, the Soviet Union, China, France, and the United Kingdom) possessed nuclear weapons. Then Israel, Pakistan, and India had them. Recently, North Korea has acquired a nuclear arsenal. With enriched uranium 235 available, terrorists are able to make a nuclear bomb and hold the world hostage. Ikeda worries that instead of regarding nuclear weapons "as a last resort," nations or even terrorist groups will "think of them in terms of actual combat use."[40] It seems that the gap between conventional warfare and nuclear warfare is closing. This is a scary thought. In his first term, former President Obama argued that he desired a world free of nuclear weapons. However, in his second term, Obama has made an about-face with his program of "nuclear modernization."[41] The United States is upgrading its nuclear program at a projected cost of upwards of $1 trillion. How so? The Pentagon is developing "air-launched cruise missiles" and long-range bombers with nuclear warheads, plus "steerable" dial-a-yield" nuclear bombs. Yet nuclear weapons cannot be used to solve today's military challenges. The logic behind this development of updating the US nuclear program is this: new, nuclear weapons would frighten enemies so that they would not use or develop

37. Ibid., 194.

38. Swaminathan and Ikeda, *Revolution in Green,* 112.

39. Ibid., 115.

40. Ibid., 119.

41. Bacevich, "New Nukes," 8.

nuclear weapons. That argument is seriously flawed since (1) North Korea is already intent on developing nuclear weapons under its president, Kim Jong-un, (2) even our allies may fear us as we modernize our nuclear capability since we are the only nation in the world that has actually used an atomic bomb on another country, viz., Japan, and (3) the United States tends to attack those it dislikes or fears, e.g., think of our invasion of Iraq under the pretext of eliminating "weapons of mass destruction."[42]

Ikeda argues that the United States and other countries like Russia and Saudi Arabia ought to cut their military budgets and spend the money on eliminating poverty around the globe. This may sound utopian to some, but Costa Rica under President Oscar Arias Sanchez eliminated that country's armed forces in 1949 and has not incurred any untoward consequences. Ikeda also wants a ceiling put on a country's military expenditures, including conventional arms. He writes, "Other research confirms that areas experiencing regional conflict continue to be the major export market for the arms trade."[43] An example may clarify this matter for us today. In the fall of 2015 Saudi Arabia used sophisticated bomber jets bought from the United States to destroy parts of Yemen in order to restore the past government to power. The Saudis might have better used the money to break the cycle of poverty in Yemen where the per capita income is less than $2.00 a day. As Ikeda notes, poverty destabilizes a society and gives rise to conflict that further increases the poverty and creates millions of homeless people as we see today in the failed states of Iraq, Syria, and Afghanistan.[44]

Ikeda makes the point that deterrence simply does not work. He questions whether the Big Five nations should have nuclear weapons while not allowing other countries to have them. Positively, he thinks that the Big Five, along with Israel, Pakistan, and India, should reduce their nuclear arsenals in accordance with the Nuclear Nonproliferation Treaty ((NPT) and the unratified Comprehensive Test Ban Treaty (CTBT). Ikeda sees dialogue and trust as the keys to nuclear disarmament. To freeze nuclear arsenals as they exist now won't work either. There must be a reduction of nuclear and conventional weapons.[45] The notion of deterrence does not work, particularly in today's world where terrorist groups like Boka Haram hold nothing sacred, neither human life nor test ban treaties. Nothing prevents a terrorist

42. Ibid.

43. Swaminathan and Ikeda, *Revolution in Green*, 200.

44. Ibid., 207.

45. Ikeda, *For the Sake of Peace*, 201.

group from holding a country hostage using an atomic bomb as its trump card.[46]

What can be done, if anything? Both Ikeda and Swaminathan agree that in order to cut violence and terrorism in today's world we must look at its deepest causes, viz., dire poverty, overpopulation, world hunger, discrimination, and social injustice. Ikeda notes that "terrorism is often a last attempt to be heard—its language requires no translation."[47] Ikeda sees a huge imbalance between North and South, i.e., between industrialized countries and developing ones. The developing nations in the South decry the consumerist mentality of the North, in tandem with the structure of the international economy that has brought about the total degradation of the environment.[48] Ikeda cites the Human Development Report of the United Nations in 1996 that states, "If present trends continue, economic disparities between industrialized and developing nations will move from inequitable to inhuman."[49] Unfortunately, "present trends" have continued so that this is precisely our situation today in terms of the economic gap between the industrialized nations, (such as Germany, the Scandinavian countries, Japan, Canada, and the United States) as opposed to Third World countries (like Haiti, Bangladesh, Yemen, and others).

Similarly, Terrence E. Paupp in his book, *Redefining Human Rights in the Struggle for Peace and Development*, argues that one of the biggest problems in international law concerns the neglect by the countries of the Global North to respect the valid claims of the countries of the Global South. He writes that the Global North fails to adhere to the "legal mandates contained in the human rights to peace and development."[50] By accepting the global order as it currently exists, scholars in the West think in terms of a "capitalist domination by a transnational capitalist class." By doing so, Western "legal discourse" buys into Eurocentric values, thus dismissing the "substantive claims" found in the human rights to peace and development.[51]

46. Ibid., 119.

47. Ibid., 122.

48. Ibid., 163.

49. Ibid. See Terrence E. Paupp in *Redefining Human Rights*, 1, who argues that one of the biggest problems in international law concerns the neglect by countries of the Global North to respect the values of the countries of the Global South.

50. Paupp, *Redefining Human Rights*, 1.

51. Ibid.

What can be done about dire poverty, overpopulation, and the gap between the rich and the poor? For starters, both Ikeda and Swaminathan believe in the "Ever-green Revolution" and the importance of living in a sustainable way. Ikeda notes that "We all want to help children develop their immense potential and we want the Earth we bequeath to them to be both beautiful and peaceful."[52] To meet these twin goals of saving the planet and living in a simple way so that future generations can meet their needs, Ikeda and Swaminathan see education as the way to go. Ikeda and Sōka Gakkai International were instrumental in getting the United Nations to call for the "Decade of Education for Sustainable Development" starting in 2005.[53] Swaminathan established the Swaminathan Research Foundation that has 240 staff members living in villages throughout India to save the environment, to do research on "coastal mangrove ecologies," to study microorganisms in order to make the soil more fertile, and to preserve the "genes of endangered species."[54]

In his dialogue with Swaminathan about these biovillages, Ikeda notes the importance of training personnel and staff since they can function as role models for the poor. Rather than give the villagers handouts, staff members attempt to improve the lives of the poor villagers. For example, in one village the staff created a "touch-and-smell garden" for the blind children in the village.[55]

In this connection Swaminathan speaks of ecotechnology that has five key elements: employment, energy (renewable), equity, economics, and ecology. Eco-technology, then, involves using "community knowledge and ecological prudence" combined with cutting edge "science and technology like renewable energy."[56] A key facet of eco-technology involves a flexible approach toward solving local problems rather than a one size fits all model.[57] Ikeda speaks of this as "respect for diversity."[58] Ikeda observes that just as each tree, peach, plum, apricot, or cherry has its own particular quality, so do human beings. Swaminathan notes that in the poor region of Orissa, tribal women set up a gene bank in order to preserve and conserve various

52. Swaminathan and Ikeda, *Revolution in Green*, 71.

53. Ibid.

54. Ibid., 59.

55. Ibid., 61.

56. Ibid., 62.

57. Ibid., 63.

58. Ibid., 64.

crops. Moreover, they organized a "seed bank, a water bank and a food bank" in order to produce food and ward off starvation.[59] Ikeda and Sōka Gakkai International, on the other hand, founded the Amazon Ecological Research Centre (AERC), members of which planted over twenty thousand seedlings of sixty kinds of tree species using a method termed *enriquecimento* or "increasing the property." The aim is to establish a seed bank in the Amazon forest to "preserve the seeds of more than sixty tree species."[60]

SOME REFLECTIONS

First, it comes as no surprise that the Sōka Gakkai International has millions of followers in Japan and throughout the world. They have many cutting edge notions, for example, the need for people around the world to live in a sustainable way and to lessen their carbon footprint, thus leaving the Earth in better shape than they found it. Members of the movement have been working for decades to bring about a "green revolution" before it became popular to do so. Moreover, Ikeda's numerous writings have shown the absolute folly of stockpiling conventional and nuclear weapons when the latter are, from a moral point of view, unshootable. In sum, there can be no justification to employ nuclear weapons, no matter the provocation. Of course, Ikeda's Buddhist views on peacebuilding would not sit well with the military-industrial complex in the United States, where we often arm both sides of a conflict, just to make money. They would also be at variance with Vladimir Putin, who treats weaker nations, e.g., the Ukraine, as his fiefdom.

Second, there are a multitude of problems connected with bringing about peace on earth, some of which are caused by nations that are jingoistic, epitomized in the slogan, "My nation, right or wrong." This was apparent in the United States when George W. Bush invaded Iraq under the pretext that Saddam Hussein possessed "weapons of mass destruction," when, in fact, we, apparently, were interested in Iraq's oil deposits. There is also the problem that the United Nations has little power when it comes to reining in the world's superpowers. In fact, it appears to be the case that Pope Francis has more moral and spiritual power than the United Nations, for example, he helped engineer a rapprochement between the United States and Cuba.

59. Ibid., 66.

60. Ibid., 67.

Third, most of the Republican Presidential hopefuls, including Donald Trump, believed that the United States should take the lead with our NATO allies and fight ISIS with ground troops. That, I would argue, would be an egregious and costly mistake for several reasons: (1) the conflict in Syria, for example, is extremely complex and involves multiple parties: President Assad and the Alawite party backed by Vladimir Putin versus the Kurds who are fighting against ISIS with Syrian rebels backed by NATO and the United States. NATO and the United States cannot win this civil war, says David Schanzer.[61] There must be a political settlement among the various warring parties. Also, what would it mean to win this war since the United States and NATO would then have to see to it that there's a new governing power in place in an area rife with deep sectarian divisions?[62]

Durukan Kuzu, a research associate at Coventry University in England, notes that "a third of the Europeans fighting with IS [*sic*] in Syria are known to be coming from France."[63] Why is that the case? It seems that discrimination and hate speech against Muslims have been on the increase in France for the past decade. For instance, think of the controversy in France about Muslims wearing religious garb in public. Also, the riots in 2005 by Muslim youths in a section of Paris were caused by racial segregation and socioeconomic injustice that had nothing to do with the formation of a global caliphate ruled by *sharia*. France must treat and respect all of its citizens, particularly its Muslim minorities. Tougher border controls will not eliminate the terrorist attacks, nor will a more stringent immigration policy. Such measures might exacerbate rather than solve the problem.

Fourth, we have nine countries that possess nuclear weapons: Russia, (c. 7,500 weapons), the United States, (7,200), France, (fewer than 300), China, (250), the United Kingdom, (215), Pakistan, (110–20), India, (90–110), Israel, (c. 80) and North Korea, (c. 12 nuclear weapons).[64] In addition, fifty other nations have nuclear materials and can theoretically make their own nuclear weapons. The main reason countries have nuclear weapons is for deterrence, that is, to fend off a nuclear attack from another country. However, many years ago scientists who made the first nuclear weapons established a group called Global Zero: The International Movement for the Elimination of Nuclear Weapons. This group believes strongly that the

61. Schanzer, "More and More."

62. Ibid.

63. Kuzu, "Paris Attacks."

64. *Global Zero Commission*, 161.

consequences of nuking another country are so devastating that nuclear weapons are, morally speaking, unshootable. Global Zero feels that no nation should have a nuclear weapon. Global Zero also points out that there have been twenty-five cases in which nuclear explosive materials have been stolen or lost. It seems that Global Zero has been making the same case as that made by Daisaku Ikeda and Sōka Gakkai over the past three decades or more.

Fifth, the writings of Daisaku Ikeda demonstrate that to ensure world peace we must utilize "soft power" along with military might. Soft power enabled Secretary of State John Kerry to work out a historic deal with the Iranian government that prevents Iran from acquiring a nuclear weapon. Moreover, the Iranian Atomic Energy Agency on January 6, 2016, verified that Iran completed the necessary steps under the Iran deal to ensure that "Iran's nuclear program is and remains exclusively peaceful."[65] If this deal had not been completed, the possibility existed that Israel, fearing for its own security, might have initiated a first strike against Iranian nuclear facilities, since Prime Minister Netanyahu has for at least a decade feared Iranian intentions vis-à-vis Israel.

Soft power also brought about the "Kyoto Protocol" that commits its Parties to reduce greenhouse gas emissions since human made CO2 emissions have caused global warming. The Kyoto Protocol is linked to the U.N. Framework Convention on Climate Change and commits its Parties by setting binding emission targets internationally. Adopted on December 11, 1997, in Kyoto, Japan, this Protocol entered into force on February 16, 2005, and rules for its implementation were adopted in Marrakesh, Morocco in 2001. Then, the Protocol was amended in Doha, Qatar on December 8, 2012.[66]

BIBLIOGRAPHY

Aoki, Mizuho. "Komeito's 50 Years of Losing Religion." *Japan Times*, November 21, 2014. http://www.lexisnexis.com.spot.lib.auburn.edu/Inacui2api/delivery/Pri.

Bacevich, Andrew J. "Election 2016: New Nukes? Turning away from Disarmament." *Commonweal* 143 (2016) 8–10.

Brannen, Noah. *Sōka Gakkai: Japan's Militant Buddhists*. Richmond, VA: John Knox, 1968.

Dawson, Lorne. L. "The Cultural Significance of New Religious Movements: The Case of Sōka Gakkai." *Sociology of Religion* 62.3 (2001) 337–64.

65. "The Historic Deal."

66. "Kyoto Protocol."

Dumoulin, Henri. "Buddhism in Modern Japan." In *Buddhism in the Modern World*, edited by Henri Dumoulin and John Maraldo, 215–76. New York: Macmillan, 1976.

Ellwood, Robert S., and Shimazono Susumu. "New Religious Movements in Japan." In *Encyclopedia of Religion*, edited by Lindsay Jones, 6572–75. New York: Macmillan, 2005.

Global Zero Commission on Nuclear Risk Reduction Report De-alerting and Stabilizing the World's Nuclear Force Postures, April, 2015. www.globalzero.org.

Goulah, Jason, and Olivier Urbain. "Daisaku Ikeda's Philosophy of peace, education proposals, and Sōka education: convergences and divergences in Peace Education." *Journal of Peace Education* 10 (2013) 303–32.

"The Historic Deal that Will Prevent Iran from Acquiring a Nuclear Weapon." *The Iran Deal*, July 14, 2015. https://obamawhitehouse.archives.gov/issues/foreign-policy/iran-deal.

Huyghe, René, and D. Ikeda. *Dawn after Dark*. Translated by Richard L. Gage. New York: Weatherhill, 1991.

Ikeda, Daisaku. *For the Sake of Peace: Seven Paths to Global Harmony*. Santa Monica, CA: Middleway, 2001.

———. *Life: An Enigma, A Precious Jewel*. Translated by Charles S. Terry. New York: Kodansha America, 1982.

Ikeda, Daisaku, and Yasushi Minogue. *Letters of Four Seasons*. Translated by Richard L. Gage. New York: Kodansha America, 1980.

Koonin, Steven E. "Can We Trust Our Aging Nukes." *The Wall Street Journal*, October 15–16, 2017, C3.

Kuzu, Durukan. "Paris Attacks Closing Migration Routes into France Won't Stop Terrorism—Resisting Xenophobia Might." *Informed Comment: Thoughts on the Middle East, History and Religion*. https://www.juancole.com/2015/11/migration-resisting-xenophobia html.

"Kyoto Protocol." *United Nations Framework Convention on Climate Change Warns of Potential 'Nuclear Disaster.'"* unfcc.int/Kyoto__protocol/items/2830.php.

Mecklin, John, ed. "It Is Two and a Half Minutes to Midnight: 2017 Doomsday Clock Statements." *Bulletin of the American Scientists*, Jan. 27, 2017. thebulletin.org/sites/default/files/ Final2017 Clock Statement.pdf.

"North Korea Warns of Potential Nuclear Disaster." *Opelika-Auburn News*, March 7, 2017, 7A.

Paupp, Terence E. *Redefining Human Rights in the Struggle for Peace and Development*. New York: Cambridge University Press, 2014.

Schanzer, David. "More and More U.S. Military Power not Answer to Isis Threat." *IslamiCommentary*, Nov. 16, 2015. https://www.islamicommentary.org/../more-and-more-us-military-power-not-answer-to-isis-threat/.

Stone, Jacqueline I. "Sōka Gakkai," In *Encyclopedia of Buddhism*, edited by Robert E. Boswell Jr., 781. New York: Gale, 2004.

Susumu, Shimazono. "Sōka Gakkai." In *Encyclopedia of Religion*, edited by Lindsay Jones, 8508–10. New York: Macmillan Reference USA, 2005.

Swaminathan, Monkombu Sambasivan. *Revolutions: To Green the Environment, to Grow the Human Heart. A Dialogue between M.S. Swaminathan, Leader of the Ever-green Revolution and Daisaku Ikeda, Proponent of the Human Revolution*. Chennai, India: East West Books, Madras, 2005.

Toynbee, Arnold J., and Daisaku Ikeda. *The Toynbee-Ikeda Dialogue: Man Himself Must Choose.* New York: Kodansha International, 1976.

"US Moves Controversial Missile Defense to South Korea." *Opelika-Auburn News*, March 8, 2015, 10A.

Wauran, Markus, "Donald Trump and US Nuclear Policy In East Asia—OpEd." *Geopolitical Monitor.* February 6, 2017. https://geopoliticalmonitor.com/donald-trump-and-us-nuclear-policy-in-east-asia/.

Wilson, Bryan N. "Sōka Gakkai." In *Encyclopedia of Religion*, edited by Mircea Eliade, 405–7. New York: Macmillan, 1987.

Woolsey, R. James, and Peter Vincent Pry, "Don't Underestimate North Korea's Nuclear Arsenal." *Wall Street Journal*, February 27, 2017. https.//www.dont-underestimate-north-korea's-nuclear-arsenal-1488239693.

7

The Israeli-Palestinian Peace Process, the United Nations, and Nongovernmental Organizations

Jason R. Tatlock

In the early days of its existence, the United Nations became deeply entrenched in the Israeli-Palestinian peace process, and the international body has continued to be of importance in efforts to establish security, to foster peaceful cohabitation, and to meet the needs of the inhabitants of the region. Nongovernmental organizations or NGOs have sought to improve the lives of people in Israel/Palestine; some of this work is done in coordination with the international community. Utilizing the United Nations as its primary focal point, this chapter examines the relationship between the United Nations and the peace process, while bearing in mind the roles played by nongovernmental actors in building peace. Utilizing as a case study the Israeli–Palestinian crisis that transpired in the Gaza Strip during the summer of 2006, the chapter concludes that NGOs have an integral role to play in the peace process, fulfilling the partnership relationship outlined by the UN Secretary-General Boutros-Ghali in 1994.

The following comments are organized into five sections: (1) The United Nations: Origins and Structure; (2) The United Nations and Nongovernmental Organizations; (3) The United Nations and Israel–Palestine;

(4) Nongovernmental Organizations, the United Nations, and Israel–Palestine: A Case Study; and (5) Conclusions.

THE UNITED NATIONS: ORIGINS AND STRUCTURE[1]

Founded in an era of global war and a period characterized by terrible atrocities, the United Nations has become a focal point of peace since its inception in 1945. While flawed, as are all institutions, the United Nations seeks to foster significant and lasting change around the world. It has been a place for governments, as well as the stateless and nongovernmental actors, to meet in solidarity or acrimony under the banner of the United Nations Charter, which speaks to the lofty principles upon which the organization was built, like ending war, promoting human rights, maintaining international law, and furthering societal progress.[2] There are six divisions of the United Nations that have been tasked with meeting such ideals: the Secretariat, Security Council, General Assembly, Economic and Social Council, International Court of Justice, and Trusteeship Council. Each may be summarized as follows:

The Secretariat is the key administrative body of the United Nations, led by the Secretary-General. Currently, the position is held by Ban Ki-moon, who is the eighth individual to hold the office. All UN organs, excluding the International Court of Justice, serve under his administrative authority. Management of the UN's Peacekeeping Forces falls under his purview as well. The earliest force of this kind was the United Nations Truce Supervision Organization, whose headquarters is situated in Jerusalem and whose mandate to monitor the peace between Israel and its neighbors has continued until today.[3]

The Security Council has five member states with permanent positions and veto authority, namely, China, France, Russian Federation, United Kingdom, and United States of America. This core group is supplemented by ten delegations with nonpermanent status that serve two year rotations.

1. This section incorporates some concepts from Tatlock, "United Nations," which was prepared in consultation with Baehr and Gordenker, *The United Nations*; and Fasulo, *An Insider's Guide*.

2. United Nations, "Charter of the United Nations."

3. UN Peacekeeping, "Helping to Bring," and United Nations document S/RES/50. United Nations documents are available at http://www.un.org/en/documents/index.html.

According to Article 24 of the UN Charter, the Security Council has been given the "primary responsibility for the maintenance of international peace and security."[4] To accomplish this task, the council can approve military action, as it did with the Korean War[5] and more recently with the First Gulf War;[6] however, it mainly chooses to sanction errant states.

The General Assembly is the primary body for member states to address relevant concerns, but despite its ability to pass resolutions, the General Assembly must typically work with the Security Council in order to take practical measures for conflict resolution. This is the general principle, but the General Assembly can authorize military action if the Security Council proves unable to establish a unanimous course of action.[7]

The Economic and Social Council has fifty-four members who are elected for three year terms. The purposes of the council are varied, but the organ is particularly concerned with examining "international economic, social, cultural, educational, health, and related matters"; and it has been given the authority to "make recommendations for the purpose of promoting respect for, and observance of, human rights and fundamental freedoms for all."[8] According to Article 71 of the UN Charter, the council has been given the ability to establish consultative arrangements with international and national nongovernmental agencies.[9]

The fifteen elected justices of the International Court of Justice mainly adjudicate conflicts between states, as in the disagreement between Qatar and Bahrain over territory,[10] or in the contentious matter of the creation of an Israeli defensive barrier throughout the West Bank. The court deemed the construction unlawful.[11]

An additional organ, the Trusteeship Council has completed its function of helping designated territories in the work of self-governance and is, therefore, not an active division of the United Nations. Of interest to Middle

4. United Nations, "Charter of the United Nations."

5. United Nations documents S/RES/83 and S/RES/84.

6. United Nations document S/RES/678.

7. United Nations document A/RES/377 (V).

8. United Nations, "Charter of the United Nations," Article 62.

9. United Nations, "Charter of the United Nations," Article 71.

10. United Nations document A/55/4; International Court of Justice Press Release 2001/9. International Court of Justice Press Releases are available at http://www.icj-cij.org/presscom/index.php?p1=6&p2=1.

11. United Nations document A/ES-10/273.

Eastern affairs is the fact that this council did not have Middle Eastern territories under its purview, although its forerunner, the League of Nations, oversaw mandates in the region, such as the British Mandate for Palestine, which did not expire until after the United Nations was already established.

THE UNITED NATIONS AND NONGOVERNMENTAL ORGANIZATIONS

Of the United Nations organs, NGOs have their most significant role in UN affairs through the Economic and Social Council. Indeed, according to the UN Non-governmental Liaison Service (UN-NGLS), it is only through this branch, as outlined in the charter of the UN, that such organizations have recognized rights for observance and participation; it is through the council that NGOs obtain consultative status and the attached privileges, such as entrance into the council's meetings.[12] UN Charter Article 71, which addresses NGOs, was not originally part of the charter, but through negotiations, NGOs were able to influence its inclusion as an amendment to the charter. This occurred in 1945; in Willetts's estimation, it was one of two victories obtained by NGOs at that time. The other was fostering the inclusion of language into the charter that identified human rights promotion as a fundamental purpose of the world body. Willetts also noted that NGOs were unable to secure a seat at two important tables in terms of gaining rights with the Security Council and General Assembly.[13] While lacking formal recognition by the General Assembly, NGOs may participate in the sessions of the assembly when invited, which is a commonly occurring aspect of NGO-UN relations. Their lobbying activities consist of such things as presenting issue papers or meeting with delegates. Advocating for their causes with the Security Council occurs even more informally than with the General Assembly. In addition to engaging government representatives informally, NGOs have of late been included in less formalized Security Council meetings and briefings. In this way, NGO have been able to provide testimony on particular concerns, such as country specific humanitarian matters and the effects of warfare on civilian populations.[14]

12. UN Non-Governmental Liaison Service (NGLS), *Intergovernmental Negotiations*, 12.

13. Willetts, "Consultative Status," 31.

14. UN Non-Governmental Liaison Service (NGLS), *Intergovernmental Negotiations*, 7, 14–15.

Utilizing their knowledge of local populations and politics, NGOs have also been active within a subordinate body of the General Assembly, namely, the Human Rights Council. In the case study chosen for this chapter, for instance, World Vision International was able to present, at least by letter, information to the Human Rights Council derived from its work in the Gaza Strip. Therein, the organization notes that it has conducted humanitarian work for decades in the Strip and that it is "the largest of the UN implementing partners."[15] According to the document, the circulation of the statement was done under the provisions established by the Economic and Social Council Resolution 1996/31.[16] That resolution recognizes that the nature of the NGO sector had changed with the increase in the number of regional and national NGOs.[17]

Tony Hill, coordinator with the UN-NGLS, has identified three phases of NGO involvement at the UN.[18] The first phase corresponds to the days of the creation of the UN through the Cold War period, in which international NGOs were particularly associated with the UN. Yet, in Hill's estimation, these NGOs made little impact, being mainly excluded from the UN political process. In the second phase, starting in the 1990s, national and regional NGOs become more involved, actively seeking to shape intergovernmental decisions. It was also at this time that members of the private economic world became more engaged. The third phase, which was in its infancy at the time of Hill's publication, constitutes coalitions between NGOs and governments, as well as "various forms of multi-stakeholder, public-private, public policy networks and partnerships."[19] Just before the adoption of Resolution 1996/31, Richard Stanley, at a Stanley Foundation Conference on "The UN System and NGOs: New Relationships for a New Era," remarked:

> Non-governmental organizations are not new. What is new is that the revolution in information and communications has created an environment in which NGOs are flourishing, have become transnational in character, and can help to build civil society on a global scale. While the nation-state and international institutions will continue, their influence and control over humankind is now

15. United Nations document A/HRC/S–1/NGO/2.

16. See United Nations document E/1996/96.

17. Ibid.

18. Hill, "Three Generations," 135–41.

19. Ibid., 140.

> shared with market-driven economic activity on one hand and private voluntary organizations, associations, and networks on the other. Societal decision-making becomes a shared interactive process rather than an autocratic, hierarchical one.[20]

What Stanley identified is in line with the reality of UN relations, as explained by Hill above. Hill specified that "at the political level, the UN has shifted from an organization in which only governments spoke only to governments, to one that now brings together the political power of governments, the economic power of the corporate sector, and the "public opinion" power of civil society (and the global communication and information media) as participants in the global policy dialogue."[21] During his time as Secretary-General, Boutros-Ghali similarly explained that with the end of the Cold War, the UN moved from an institution with a reputation of being the purview of nation-states to one that more greatly recognized the inclusion of NGOs in the political process.[22] Focusing on the role of NGOs in promoting peace, Boutros-Ghali outlined three areas for NGO participation in peace building: "assistance, mobilization and democratization activities."[23] In the area of assistance, he considered NGOs as instrumental in peacekeeping by being involved in preventive diplomacy through acting as early warning sentries to growing crises in the regions they work. In terms of mobilization, Boutros-Ghali tasked NGOs with the mission of helping sway public opinion in order to get states to act for peace in conjunction with the United Nations. For democratization, he identified that NGOs can help democracy through spreading democratic ideals and notions of peace, by supporting democratic growth within nations, and by monitoring democratic processes around the globe.[24] It is the role of NGOs in peace building that will be demonstrated in the case study examined shortly, but first I will set the context by briefly discussing the role of the United Nations in Israel–Palestine.

20. Stanley, "Opening Remarks," 7.
21. Hill, "Three Generations," 140.
22. Boutros-Ghali, "Statement," 311.
23. Ibid., 313.
24. Ibid., 313–16.

THE UNITED NATIONS AND ISRAEL–PALESTINE

Regarding the initial work of the United Nations, it is important to note that the organization entered into discussions with representatives of the Arab and Jewish camps shortly after the body was inaugurated in 1945. The result of these meetings, as reflected in the *Report to the General Assembly* of 1947, was that the United Nations Special Committee on Palestine considered both sides to have legitimate claims of ownership.[25] Importantly, the committee recommended the partitioning of the area into three separate areas: a state controlled by Arabs, a state administered by Jews, and an area governed by the international community.[26] The partition plan was never implemented, although the post-Mandate era war of 1948 to 1949 resulted in areas controlled by Jews and Arabs; an autonomous Palestinian state was not realized, however. Subsequent warfare, specifically the Six Day War of 1967, and settlement activities have increased the space filled by Israeli occupation, while the number of Palestinian refugees has grown significantly and the status of Jerusalem continues to be a matter of contention. United Nations resolution after resolution has been approved,[27] but little has changed to establish the two-state solution envisioned by the committee. Indeed, the borders of that two-state solution are not truly under consideration any longer; instead, the pre-1967 borders are the sought-after demarcations for a potential Palestinian state.[28] In the contemporary context, Palestinian statehood has been a prominent matter during the current tenure of Secretary-General Ban Ki-moon. The last days of 2014 saw, for instance, a defeated attempt to gain Security Council support for an Israeli withdrawal from territory and the recognition of full UN member status for Palestine.[29]

25. United Nations documents A/364 and A/364/Add.2.

26. United Nations document A/RES/181.

27. In a draft resolution submitted to the Security Council for consideration at a July 2006 meeting, the key Security Council resolutions on Israel–Palestine were identified as resolutions 242, 338, 1397, and 1515. United Nations document S/2006/508.

28. United Nations document S/RES/242.

29. UN News Centre, December 30, 2014.

NONGOVERNMENTAL ORGANIZATIONS, THE UNITED NATIONS, AND ISRAEL–PALESTINE: A CASE STUDY

Nongovernmental organizations operate outside the confines of state governance, but they are certainly engaged in political matters and are committed to fostering governance that promotes their agendas. As we have seen, they are incorporated into the United Nations bureaucracy, albeit they only have a consultative status. NGOs function as lobbyists when necessary, which, no doubt, is a common requirement and constitutes their primary role at the United Nations. Prior to the aforementioned vote at the Security Council, the CEO and president of Americans for Peace Now, Debra DeLee, asked the Obama administration to allow the resolution to pass, suggesting that it was in line with US policy and interests.[30] The group and its sister organization, the Israeli Shalom Achshav or Peace Now movement, seek to establish a peaceful resolution to the Israeli–Palestinian conflict. Peace Now, as well as other nongovernmental organizations, represents mobilization for change by nonstate actors at the grassroots level. In this instance, the lobbying efforts of the Peace Now movement failed to sway the government of the United States, which voted against the aforementioned draft resolution on Palestine because it was deemed one-sided, divisive, antithetical to negotiations, potentially volatile, and staged.[31] The concept of a Palestinian state with a democratically elected government is a particularly complicated matter since the election of a Hamas-led government at the start of 2006, for it created a rift in Palestinian unity, pitting the Fatah movement against a group that is regarded as a terrorist organization. The situation was exacerbated when in May 2006, Fatah and Hamas-affiliated security personnel entered into armed clashes in Gaza.[32] Shortly thereafter, our case study begins with a crisis that drew NGOs into peace building efforts in conjunction with UN responses to the violent affairs starting at the end of June 2006.

The most salient points related to the sequence of events that transpired before the UN Security Council took up the matter on the afternoon of June 30 are: (1) Palestinian militants exited the Gaza Strip, attacked an Israeli Defense Forces (IDF) position, and kidnapped a soldier named Gilad Shalit on June 25, 2006; (2) three groups, including Hamas's military

30. Nir, "Press Release."

31. United Nations document S/PV.7354.

32. Butler, "Gaza Chronology," 117–18.

organization (Izz el-Din al-Qassam Brigades) claimed responsibility and demanded the release of Palestinian prisoners in exchange for Gilad Shalit; (3) the Palestinian Authority under President Abbas requested Shalit's release and the Israeli government declined to negotiate a prisoner exchange; (4) Israel started a military campaign using aircraft and ground forces to secure Shalit from Gaza on June 28; (5) on June 29, the IDF explained that the operations were also aimed at responding to rockets fired from the Gaza Strip into Israel by Palestinians; (6) during the night of June 29, Israel arrested more than sixty Palestinian Authority government officials and nearly two dozen individuals suspected of being militants in Jerusalem and the West Bank, and the IDF continued air strikes in the Strip; and (7) it was reported that two Palestinian militants were killed in the West Bank on June 30. In addition to the military operations, the inhabitants of the Gaza Strip faced shortages in power and water, and limited food and fuel supplies.[33] This was the start of what the Israeli government called "Operation Summer Rains," which primarily transpired in June and July of 2006, but has been regarded as lasting for months.[34]

Beginning in 2007, I began to examine the Israeli–Palestinian conflict on the issue of accusations of genocide as concentrated in United Nations' discourse. This study, which resulted in a 2009 article, followed on the hills of Hamas's recent usurpation of the Gaza Strip and it was also contemporary with the early days of Iran's nuclear ambitions, which is still a matter of concern today. I discovered that both Hamas and the then Iranian president, Ahmadinejad, were being accused of violating the UN Genocide Convention (1948), and that NGOs were behind some of these accusations; for instance, the World Union for Progressive Judaism and the International Association of Jewish Lawyers and Jurists (two Jewish NGOs that have enjoyed consultative status at the United Nations for several years, particularly the World Union for Progressive Judaism, which earned its status in 1972).[35] These groups leveled accusations against the Hamas government for engendering genocidal views, utilizing the Hamas Charter as the basis for these allegations and noting parallels between it and the work of Adolf Hitler. As one of the NGOs explained: the charter "calls for politicide of Israel and the genocide of its population in unmistakably explicit terms

33. United Nations document S/PV.5481.
34. Esposito, "Israeli Military," 134–35.
35. United Nations document E/2014/INF/5.

rivalling those of Hitler's *Mein Kampf*."[36] These accusations and concerns were presented in the material prepared for the First Special Session of the UN Human Rights Council, which met in July of 2006.[37]

Other NGOs presented statements for consideration at the Human Rights Council, too, although it should be noted that the debate ended before NGOs were given the chance to speak at the special session.[38] Hence, the formal submission of statements prior to the meeting by NGOs entered into the session's document list, but were not read by the authors. A joint statement by several groups, such as the International Youth and Student Movement for the United Nations, welcomed the call for a special session and denounced what was considered the excessive use of force by Israel, even calling it "barbarous warfare." In promoting the Palestinian cause, the NGOs explained that Israel is in violation of the Geneva Conventions, is culpable of crimes against humanity and war crimes (but not explicitly genocide), and should be held accountable.[39] They believed that the Human Rights Council was being given the chance to participate in "a defining moment for the future credibility of the United Nations human rights system."[40] Amnesty International, whose statement called upon the council to send a group of experts to investigate violations by both sides of the conflict,[41] shared with the authors of the joint statement the view that through the council, the United Nations was poised to reshape the international body's response to the Israeli–Palestinian conflict. More specifically, Amnesty International called upon the Human Rights Council to correct the errors of its predecessor, the UN Commission on Human Rights, which often considered the conflict, but did little about it.[42] Another NGO, the International Commission of Jurists, considered the crisis to be a significant test of the council's credibility, but the group was not content with simply requesting an investigation. For the jurists, the criminality of the actions, mainly on the part of Israel, was evident. They believed that words were

36. United Nations document A/HRC/S–1/NGO/5.

37. United Nations documents A/HRC/S–1/NGO/5 and A/HRC/S–1/NGO/4. The World Union for Progressive Judaism statement was co-authored by the Association for World Education.

38. United Nations document A/HRC/S–1/3.

39. United Nations document A/HRC/S–1/NGO/6.

40. Ibid.

41. Human Rights Watch similarly requested an investigation into the violence. United Nations document A/HRC/S–1/NGO/7.

42. United Nations document A/HRC/S–1/NGO/1.

insufficient and fact-finding investigations would delay a resolution to the conflict. The jurists, therefore, called upon the Human Rights Council to urge the Security Council to do its job in responding with action, and failing movement by the Security Council, to summon the General Assembly to exercise its authority to act when the Security Council is at an impasse.[43]

It is significant that the initial special session of the Human Rights Council was focused on the Israeli–Palestinian conflict. The council had just been created by the General Assembly in March of 2006 to take the place of the Commission on Human Rights.[44] In the resolution, the assembly acknowledged "that nongovernmental organizations play an important role at the national, regional and international levels, in the promotion and protection of human rights."[45] Thus, NGOs were seen as an integral part of the human rights process. The primary purpose of the session, the background, and the results were as follows:

To begin with, the special session was requested by the Tunisian delegation at the United Nations on June 30, 2006, in order to examine the intensification of the situation in the Israeli occupied territories.[46] The delegation did so at the behest of the Group of Arab States,[47] which are members of the League of Arab States.[48] One NGO, namely, UN Watch, which considers the "UN, Israel & Anti-Semitism" as one of its three primary areas of focus (UN Watch), indicated that while the meeting was supposedly connected to Israeli actions in the Gaza Strip, the "special session, if we consider the larger picture, is actually not that special at all. It is merely the latest instance of something that for over three decades has pervaded the United Nations: the demonization of Israel."[49] The NGO explained that the call for the special session occurred soon after the Human Rights Council condemned Israel during its initial conference, which devoted time to consider the Israel–Palestine conflict in the midst of its varied deliberations. UN Watch expressed its concern that the Group of Arab States was behind a month's long campaign to denigrate the Jewish state through the

43. United Nations document A/HRC/S–1/NGO/8.

44. United Nations document A/RES/60/251.

45. Ibid.

46. United Nations document A/HRC/S–1/1.

47. Ibid.

48. United Nations document NPT/CONF.2010/PC.III/WP.23.

49. United Nations document A/HRC/S–1/NGO/3.

new council.[50] In truth, during its first regular session, the Human Rights Council did pass a resolution that singled out Israelis as violators of human rights in occupied areas without emphasizing potential violations by any Palestinian actors (Resolution 2006/106). The draft resolution was presented by Pakistan and sponsored by the Organisation of the Islamic Conference,[51] an intergovernmental organization composed of fifty-seven member states with substantial Muslim populations.[52] Palestine has been an issue of concern from the group's beginnings.[53] The representative of Pakistan justified the necessity of the resolution because of indiscriminate targeting of noncombatants, Israel's oppressive economic policies, and the worsening situation in Gaza.[54] Representing the Group of Arab States, the Tunisian delegate expressed support for Pakistan and concern over the state of Palestinian affairs.[55] The Israeli delegate followed, explaining that the resolution was one-sided—sentiments shared by the Canadian delegation[56]—and that "the Council must not let itself become a mere instrument for Israel-bashing and be politicized and subverted by propaganda."[57] He also noted that the Secretary-General previously expressed concerns over the Commission on Human Rights's unbalanced focus on Israel. The Israeli representative, therefore, encouraged the new Council to move in a new

50. Ibid.

51. United Nations documents A/HRC/1/SR.24 and A/HRC/1/L.10/Add.1.

52. UN Non–Governmental Liaison Service (NGLS), *Intergovernmental Negotiations*, 32.

53. It is intriguing to note that the United Nations considers the organization to be the sole group of its kind in terms of its affirmation that politics and religion are intertwined, UN Non–Governmental Liaison Service (NGLS), *Intergovernmental Negotiations*, 32. Indeed, the group explains its origins as developing "when the First meeting of the leaders of the Islamic world was held in the wake of the criminal Zionist attempt to burn down the Blessed Al-Aqsa Mosque on 21 August 1969 in the occupied city of Al-Quds," Organisation of the Islamic Conference, "About OIC."

54. United Nations document A/HRC/1/SR.24.

55. Ibid.

56. The representative of the United Kingdom expressed his government's dissatisfaction with the resolution on Israel–Palestine during the first regular session on the basis that it was lopsided and because it was too soon for the burgeoning council to commit to the frequency by which it would examine specific areas of concern, United Nations document A/HRC/1/SR.24. This is ostensibly a diplomatic way of saying that the British government did not approve of the resolution's intent to make Israel a consistent focus of future meetings of the Human Rights Council.

57. United Nations document A/HRC/1/SR.24.

direction by disapproving the draft resolution.[58] As noted, the resolution was passed.

Certain of the views of the Israeli delegation were similarly espoused by an NGO prior to the June 30, 2006, passing of the resolution. B'nai B'rith International, a Jewish group, expressed its concern that the Human Rights Council would be repeating the failings of the Commission on Human Rights by making the Israeli–Palestinian conflict a matter of such focus, particularly with its agenda item 8. The organization cautioned that if the new council fails to improve upon the old, then there will be ripple effects throughout the United Nations, undermining the process of reform ushered in by the Secretary-General. B'nai B'rith International expressed the desire that the council should not continue the commission's repeated use of agenda item 8.[59] In fact, when the General Assembly established the Human Rights Council, the representative of Syria expressed the opposite: he hoped that the council would continue the agenda, particularly as it relates to an annual focus on Israeli actions in areas under its occupation.[60]

According to Neuer, agenda items for the commission related to human rights violations were unbalanced. Two items were addressed explicitly to human rights violations: one devoted exclusively to Israel and one focused more generally on any other place in the world.[61] In 2007 the Human Rights Council since followed in the footsteps of the commission to have a consistent agenda item on Israel's human rights record.[62] One can see that the new council was already moving in this direction during its first regular session, inasmuch as the resolution on Israel–Palestine that was adopted at that time reads:

> *Decides* to undertake substantive consideration of the human rights violations and implications of the Israeli occupation of Palestine and other occupied Arab territories at its next session and to incorporate this issue in following sessions.[63]

On the day it was adopted, the first special session was called by the Tunisian delegate. During that session, the Israeli representative opined that "it

58. Ibid.

59. United Nations document A/HRC/1/NGO/45.

60. United Nations document A/60/PV.72.

61. Neuer, "The Struggle."

62. Anti-Defamation League, "Israel at the UN."

63. United Nations document A/HRC/1/L.10/Add.1; emphasis original.

had taken Arab and Islamic countries only two weeks to reintroduce the flaws of the Commission and render the notion of a transparent, equitable and non-selective Human Rights Council a dead letter."[64] The resolution that was adopted during the first special session was much more extensive than that of the first general session, specifically addressing the situation in the Gaza Strip with an emphasis upon the actions of the Israeli government. A limited amount of text was reserved for any Palestinian actors who were contributing to the crisis and the strongest language was focused on demanding that Israel cease its military activities in Palestinian territory, adhere to humanitarian and human rights law, and exercise restraint so as not to punish civilians collectively. In the part of the resolution leveled at both sides, it urged all actors to abide by the principles of humanitarian law, to show restraint for the protection of civilians, and to deal with detainees according to the standards of the Geneva Conventions.

Despite the recommendation of the International Commission of Jurists, the resolution did not contain any statements urging the Security Council or General Assembly to respond with force. Instead, the Human Rights Council chose to send a fact-finding mission, which is exactly what the jurists discouraged. The resolution was passed on July 6, 2006.[65] This does not mean that those present at the Human Rights Council were not interested in bringing the Security Council into the matter. In fact, the Group of Arab States through the Algerian delegation had already requested that the Security Council take up the issue.[66] The request was submitted on June 29, 2006, even before the first special session of the Human Rights Council was called. The Security Council held a meeting on June 30, but voted on a draft resolution during its July 13 meeting, which was after the Human Rights Council already passed its resolution during the special session. At the Security Council, the United States exercised its veto power to defeat a resolution proposed by Qatar, condemning acts of aggression on both sides.[67]

64. United Nations document A/HRC/S–1/SR.1.

65. United Nations document A/HRC/S–1/3.

66. United Nations document S/2006/458. Qatar also requested such a session on June 29, 2006, United Nations document S/2006/462.

67. United Nations documents S/2006/508 and S/PV.5488.

CONCLUSIONS

Given the failures of states and the international community to bring about long-lasting peace in Israel–Palestine, I initially wondered if more had been accomplished outside of governmental intervention to foster peace, security, and well-being than within the confines of UN diplomacy. I have changed this line of inquiry, recognizing now that nongovernmental actors have become an integral part of UN efforts to foster peace, particularly in the post-Cold War era. The failures and successes of the United Nations are closely linked to the nongovernmental groups that partner with the body as part of the civil society surrounding the organization. In the case study chosen for this chapter, one can see the involvement of NGOs in their capacity as policy advocates related to their varied areas of expertise and work. The Human Rights Council was a fitting focal point for the study in light of the fact that NGOs were behind the incorporation into the UN Charter of a stronger human rights agenda.

Peace building is a key part of securing fundamental human rights and Boutros-Ghali identified three areas in which NGOs should actively participate in the peace building process, i.e., by working in the fields of mobilization, democratization, and assistance. NGOs have been involved in all three areas as related to the Israel–Palestinian conflict, but it is assistance and democratization that shone forth most brightly in the documents examined for the case study. Regarding assistance, Boutros-Ghali mentioned that NGOs can practice preventive diplomacy because of their work with people around the world. World Vision International utilized its extensive experience in the Gaza Strip to call attention to matters of grave concern to the Human Rights Council.

Concerning democratization efforts, Boutros-Ghali apparently envisioned NGO support for democracy within nation-states, but the case study demonstrates that NGOs have been working not only to enhance democratic processes within states, but also within the UN itself. Thus, there were efforts, such as those by B'nai B'rith International, to encourage the Human Rights Council to be fairer in its deliberations on Israel–Palestine than its predecessor, the Commission on Human Rights. Such sentiments were similarly shared by nation-states familiar with the commission.

Despite NGO advocacy efforts, member states of the United Nations, particularly the five permanent members of the Security Council, possess the power to further human rights and to build peace. They hold the greatest responsibility for the successes and failures of the international community. We should remember that actors in any given conflict, not the United Nations, are ultimately accountable for the maintenance of peace. The United Nations may even go so far as to pass resolutions or impose sanctions intent on stability and peace, but if they are not backed by the cooperation of individual states, they lack efficacy. The United Nations has passed numerous resolutions but the situation in Israel–Palestine has not improved in terms of establishing the type of peaceful cohabitation envisioned by the creators of early UN policy.

BIBLIOGRAPHY

Anti–Defamation League. "Israel at the UN: A History of Bias and Progress." http://www.adl.org/israel–international/un–international–organizations/c/Israel–at–the–UN.pdf.

Baehr, Peter R., and Leon Gordenker. *The United Nations: Reality and Ideal*. 4th ed. New York: Palgrave Macmillan, 2005.

Boutros-Ghali, Boutros. "Statement by the UN Secretary–General, Boutros Boutros-Ghali at the UN Department of Public Information Forty-Seventh Annual Conference of Non–governmental Organisations, 'We the Peoples: Building Peace.'" In *'The Conscience of the World': The Influence of Non–governmental Organisations in the UN System*, edited by Peter Willetts, 311–17. Washington, DC: The Brookings Institution, 1996.

Butler, Linda, compiler. "A Gaza Chronology, 1948–2008." *Journal of Palestine Studies* 38.3 (2009) 98–121. http://www.jstor.org/stable/10.1525/jps.2009.xxxviii.3.98.

Esposito, Michele, compiler. "Israeli Military Operations against Gaza, 2000–2008." *Journal of Palestine Studies* 38.3 (2009) 122–38. http://www.jstor.org/stable/10.1525/jps .2009.xxxviii.3.122.

Fasulo, Linda. *An Insider's Guide to the UN*. New Haven: Yale University Press, 2004.

Hill, Tony. "Three Generations of UN-Civil Society Relations: A Quick Sketch." In *Intergovernmental Negotiations and Decision Making at the United Nations: A Guide* by UN Non-Governmental Liaison Service (NGLS) with Gretchen Sidhu, 135–43. 2nd ed. New York: United Nations, 2007.

Neuer, Hillel. "The Struggle against Anti-Israel Bias at the UN Commission on Human Rights." *Jerusalem Center for Public Affairs*. January 1, 2006. http://www.jcpa.org/phas/phas-040-neuer.htm.

Nir, Ori. "Press Release: APN to Obama: Don't Block UNSC Resolution on Israeli-Palestinian Peace." *Americans for Peace Now*. December 30, 2014. http://peacenow.org/entry .php?id=9983#.VRRnE_nF9XE.

Organisation of the Islamic Conference. "About OIC." http://www.oic–un.org/about_oic.asp.

Stanley, Richard. "Opening Remarks." In *The UN System and NGOs: New Relationships for a New Era? Report of the Twenty-Fifth United Nations Issues Conference* by The Stanley Foundation, 6–12. Muscatine, IA: The Stanley Foundation, 1994.

Tatlock, Jason. "Genocidal Rhetoric and Remembrance Concentrated on the Israeli–Palestinian Conflict as Contextualized in the United Nations." *Journal of Third World Studies* 26.1 (2009) 77–97.

———. "United Nations." In *Encyclopedia of Middle East Wars: A Social, Political, and Military History*, edited by Spencer C. Tucker. Santa Barbara, CA: ABC–CLIO, 2010.

———. "The United Nations and the Bible." *Journal for Peace & Justice Studies* 22.2 (2012) 49–72.

UN Charter. "Charter of the United Nations." *United Nations*. http://www.un.org/en/sections/un-charter/preamble/index.html; http://www.un.org/en/documents/charter/chapter5.shtml; and http://www.un.org/en/documents/charter/chapter10.shtml.

UN News Centre. "UN Security Council Action on Palestinian Statehood Blocked." *United Nations*. December 30, 2014. http://www.un.org/apps/news/story.asp?NewsID=49709# .VRRpHvnF9XE.

UN Non-Governmental Liaison Service (NGLS) with Sidhu, Gretchen. *Intergovernmental Negotiations and Decision Making at the United Nations: A Guide*. 2nd ed. New York: United Nations, 2007.

UN Peacekeeping. "Helping to Bring Stability in the Middle East; UNTSO Mandate." *United Nations Truce Supervision Organization*. http://www.un.org/en/peacekeeping/missions /untso/ and http://www.un.org/en/peacekeeping/missions/untso/mandate.shtml.

UN Watch. "Issues In Focus." http://www.unwatch.org/site/c.bdKKISNqEmG/ b.1313899/k.948D/Issues_in_Focus.htm.

Willetts, Peter. "Consultative Status for NGOs at the United Nations." In '*The Conscience of the World:' The Influence of Non-governmental Organisations in the UN System*, edited by Peter Willetts, 31–62. Washington, DC: The Brookings Institution, 1996.

8

The Symbolic Power for Peace in the Encounter between Saint Francis and Sultan Al-Kamil

Wm. Loyd Allen

INTRODUCTION

In Assisi, Italy, in October 1986, religious leaders from various world religions gathered for the first World Day of Prayer for Peace at the invitation of Pope John Paul II. Assisi hosted an interreligious prayer meeting again in 1993 to pray for peace in the Balkans, and yet another months after 9/11 and in September 2016. Why the little town of Assisi? Because St. Francis, who met with Sultan Malik al-Kamil of Egypt during the siege of Damietta in 1219, was born there. This little-known encounter between a Christian saint and a Muslim sultan is a popular symbol among peacebuilders and those involved in interfaith dialogue. Cardinal Ratzinger, who became Pope Benedict XVI, made this connection explicit at the 2002 Assisi meeting, saying, "This man Francis . . . continues today to glow with the splendor of the same peace that convinced the sultan, the peace that truly demolishes any wall."[1] (Just what Francis convinced the sultan of, the cardinal does not say.)

These Assisi meetings are examples of the many authors, artists, and peacebuilding groups in the last century or so who have taken up the encounter of this sultan and this saint as a model for interreligious dialogue and peacemaking. John V. Tolan analyzes over a dozen of these in "Francis, Apostle of Peace," the fourteenth chapter of his book *Saint Francis and the Sultan*. He cites G. K. Chesterton, Nikos Kazantzakis, Idries Shah, Julien Green, and Carlos Carreto, as well as the two popes mentioned above. The flow of works in this genre continues unabated. Recent publications include Paul Moses's *The Saint and the Sultan*; Kathleen Warren's video, *In the Footprints of Francis and the Sultan*; and Joan Acocella's article in the 2013 edition of *The New Yorker*, among others.[2]

This recent output of works on Francis and al-Kamil's meeting as a model for peacebuilding through people-to-people relationships rather than political processes led me to write this article. Is the connection of the saint and the sultan to peacebuilding justified? In answer, first I will survey the historical context of Francis's meeting with the sultan, then relate ways the West employed it through the centuries, and end with an analysis of its value as a model for peacebuilding in the twenty-first century.

THE ENCOUNTER: ITS CONTEXT AND CENTRAL CHARACTERS

Ayyubid sultan, Malik al-Kamil, was a worldly leader personally acquainted with and adept at intercontinental diplomacy, brutal war, and the harsh realities of power politics. He was seven when his uncle Saladin recaptured Jerusalem from the Crusaders in 1187. At age eleven, as part of a truce negotiated by his father, al-Adil, he was knighted by England's King Richard the Lionhearted, who had recently ordered 2,700 Muslim prisoners decapitated in full view of Saladin's defeated army at Acre.[3] Al-Adil, who succeeded his brother Saladin as sultan, appointed al-Kamil ruler and protector of Egypt at age twenty.

1. Ratzinger, "30DAYS," para. 9.

2. See Moses, *The Saint and the Sultan*; Warren, *In the Footsteps of Francis and the Sultan*; and Acocella, "Rich Man, Poor Man."

3. Dardess, *In the Spirit of St. Francis and the Sultan*, loc. 1561 Kindle Edition.

An orthodox Sunni Muslim, Sultan al-Kamil is remembered among Christians as a tolerant ruler. Like his father and his uncle Saladin, he was typically quick to negotiate settlements and lenient on prisoners of war. Crusader and chronicler Oliver of Paderborn, a prisoner taken at the end of the Fifth Crusade, praised the sultan upon his release, saying he was more of a benefactor than a jailer.[4] Christian subjects of the sultan found him just and forgiving. Paul Moses in *The Saint and the Sultan* gives several examples. One is the story told of a Coptic Christian monk who converted to Islam but later appealed to al-Kamil to let him return to Christianity. Muslim law forbade conversion to Christianity, sometimes imposing death as the penalty, but al-Kamil allowed his petitioner to return to his monastery. Al-Kamil's father refused to sanction the decision and overturned it with death threats against the petitioner.[5]

Al-Kamil was open to interreligious discussions. He presided over a religious debate between Muslim scholars and the Coptic patriarch of Alexandria.[6] History portrays Sultan Al-Kamil as a just, tolerant, and pious leader with an openness to engage other faith perspectives. In all this, he reflected the best of his faith's social justice tradition. For a more lengthy discussion of the Muslim religious and social roots of al-Kamil's leadership, see George Dardess's chapter four, "The Fundamentals of Islamic Social Justice."[7]

In 1217, Western powers launched the Fifth Crusade to take Jerusalem back from Muslim control. Their strategy was to capture Egypt, the center of Ayyubid strength, then move on to undefended Jerusalem. In 1218, the Crusaders lay siege to the Egyptian port of Damietta, gateway to Cairo on the Nile. Malik al-Kamil's forces tried to lift the siege. They failed. After a long and bloody struggle, the Crusaders took the city in November 1219. Sultan al-Kamil's forces later defeated the Crusaders as they marched toward Cairo, ending the invaders' crusade in utter failure. Later al-Kamil negotiated with Emperor Frederick II the 1229 Treaty of Jaffa, which delivered Jerusalem to the Crusaders for ten years.[8]

4. Tolan, *Saint Francis and the Sultan*, 5.

5. Moses, *The Saint and the Sultan*, 70–73.

6. Kedar, *Crusade and Mission*, 123.

7. *Dardess, The Spirit of St. Francis and the Sultan.*

8. See Abu-Munshar, "Sultan Al-Kamil, Emperor Frederick II and the Submission of Jerusalem."

August 1219, though, found Christian and Muslim armies locked in battle in the sands around Damietta. In an abortive attack on the Sultan's position that month, the Crusaders suffered thousands of casualties. Al-Kamil proposed a truce by renewing a previous offer to exchange Jerusalem for Damietta. The Crusaders, under the command of papal appointee Cardinal Pelagius, eventually refused the truce, as they had all previous peace offers. Pelagius hoped to conquer Egypt as well as Jerusalem. As al-Kamil awaited the Crusaders' response, two dirty, barefoot monks left the Crusader camp, crossed into enemy territory, and succeeded in having an audience with the sultan.

One of these monks was Francis of Assisi, arguably Catholicism's best known and most beloved saint. He received canonization only two years after his death in 1226. Francis Bernadone was about the same age as al-Kamil. The carefree son of a wealthy Italian merchant, Francis went to war against neighboring Perugia at about age twenty. Captured and imprisoned for a year, he returned to Assisi a troubled veteran. A conversion process followed that would last a lifetime. Friend and first biographer of Francis, Thomas Celano, wrote a 1229 *Life of Saint Francis*[9] in which he expresses this conversion as a way of "'seeing' the visible mystery of Jesus Christ in the poor and in all of creation," in everything, everyone, everywhere, according to Michael Blastic.[10] In Francis's *Testament*, written just before his death, he names the turning point of this conversion as an encounter with a leper, in whom Francis saw the connection between God's love and personal contact with the suffering other. He wrote: "Afterward I delayed a little and left the world."[11]

Francis permanently abandoned every vestige of his former life of wealth and privilege to embrace a life of total poverty and humility in imitation of the "poor and crucified Christ." Francis called his followers to "follow the teaching and footprints of our Lord Jesus Christ, Who says: If you wish to be perfect, go, sell everything you have and give it to the poor, and you will have treasure in heaven (Matt 19:21); and come, follow me (Matt 19:21)."[12] Just as al-Kamil was entering the ranks of the privileged and powerful, Francis abandoned them. For many in his time, and afterward through the centuries, Francis became a visible image of the gospel

9. Thomas of Celano, "The Life of Saint Francis [Thomas of Celano]."

10. Blastic, "Franciscan Spirituality," 409.

11. Francis of Assisi, "The Testament," par. 1.

12. Francis of Assisi, "The Earlier Rule," chapter 1, v. 2.

to which he conformed. Francis modeled a radical expression of Christian living which he understood as living the "apostolic life" in the "form of the Holy Gospel"[13] found in the life of Christ and his disciples in the Bible. The way of Francis was fresh and attractive in its simplicity, joy, and sense of community with all of creation.

Other Catholic Christians of his day joined Francis in ever increasing numbers. They called themselves the friars minor (little brothers), and Francis they called *il poverello* (the little poor one). By 1221, there were an estimated three to five thousand brothers in various European nations.[14] Two decades after Francis's death, they numbered between thirty and thirty-five thousand from Scandinavia to Mongolia.[15] This movement became formalized in the Roman Catholic Church as the Order of Friars Minor or Franciscans. In 1219, however, it was still a novel and spontaneous movement, though swiftly expanding.

Francis's 1219 trip to Egypt was probably his third attempt to preach to the Muslims. Shipwreck foiled a try in 1212 and illness another in 1214. At any rate, he eventually reached the Fifth Crusade army's camp at Damietta, probably in July or August 1219, where he achieved his audience with Sultan al-Kamil.

Considering the great number of words published describing the encounter between St. Francis and Sultan Malik al-Kamil, history provides remarkably little evidence about the actual event. (This fact has not kept people from filling the historical vacuum with myriad presuppositions supporting their own purposes, as we shall see.) Two persons who saw Francis in Damietta during the siege wrote surviving descriptions of the encounter. One was Jacques de Vitry, Bishop of Acre, who left two versions of the meeting of the saint and sultan. The other was the anonymous author of the *Chronicle of Ernoul*. He was apparently a non-cleric nobleman closely associated with the Crusader King of Jerusalem, Jean de Brienne. Tolan publishes in English translation the pertinent passages of these sources, along with extensive context, in *Saint Francis and the Sultan*, chapters 1 and 2. Not surprisingly, a pair of impoverished monks who had no official business with the sultan merited no mention in Muslim sources from the era. The two Christian sources that first related the event considered it a

13. Francis of Assisi, "The Testament," par. 3.

14. "St. Francis of Assisi," *New Advent Catholic Encyclopedia*.

15. Tolan, *Saint Francis and the Sultan*, 117.

curiosity of no real importance. Only with the rise of Francis's reputation did it take on significance for Christians.

Based on the witness of de Vitry and the anonymous *Chronicle*, historians agree about the following essentials of the Damietta meeting. Francis of Assisi and a companion monk gained permission from the Crusade's leadership to cross enemy lines in order to seek an audience with Sultan al-Kamil. They arrived safely in the sultan's tent and returned unharmed to the Crusader camp some days later. All else must be inferred from circumstantial evidence. No description by Francis or al-Kamil or others actually present exists. From these bare outlines of the meeting, Christians have found fertile ground for employing this Christian-Muslim encounter for various purposes, including as a model for peacemaking.

(MIS)APPROPRIATING THE ENCOUNTER

Many writers and artists have used the encounter between St. Francis and Sultan al-Kamil to support various purposes. Whether the historical facts lend themselves to any particular cause requires careful discernment. Enough is unknown about Francis's motives, the meeting itself, and its aftermath to leave space for persons with specific agendas plenty of room to fill in the blanks with their own presuppositions, and they have. The process of legendary elaboration began immediately.

John Tolan's book is a scholarly tour de force exposé of the ways Christians (and a few Muslims) through the centuries have projected the preoccupations of their own time and place on the Damietta event, making it mirror their own concerns. Chapter by chapter, Tolan demonstrates the flexible, not to say ephemeral, use made of the facts of this Muslim/Christian encounter throughout history. The following paragraphs summarize Tolan's research in order to illustrate the diversity of interpretations of the encounter over the centuries.

In de Vitry's presentation, Francis is a winsome preacher with an eager Muslim sultan who is almost persuaded, providing hope for the East to be conquered for Christ by preaching even as the promise of military conquest began to fade. In the *Chronicle* by the anonymous lay noble, Francis has a failed witness to a wise, tolerant sultan who cannot hear the words of the gospel in the midst of war. The *Chronicle* implies resolution could only come through the political negotiations of competent statespersons, not through church ideologues like Cardinal Pelagius, whom the chronicler clearly despises.

Hagiographer Thomas of Celano wrote his 1229 *Life of Christ* for Francis's canonization as a means to bolster Francis's reputation as a brave soul eager for martyrdom. In this telling, the Muslim soldiers beat and torture poor Francis and his companion, but God miraculously intervenes to prevent martyrdom, so that Francis may continue his work. Instead of martyrdom, Francis is destined to receive the miracle of the stigmata, the wounds of Christ in his flesh. Martyred saints are commonplace, stigmata are special.[16]

Henry of Avranches, perhaps the most prestigious poet of his era, wrote his major work in 1229/30, *The Legend of Saint Francis*, for Pope Gregory IX, who paid him handsomely.[17] The Francis who shows up in this poem is less mystic monk and more imminent university professor, who seizes the opportunity to teach the sultan the fine points of theology. "'Of that first principle is a simple substance . . . simpler than a mathematical point . . . its essence is wondrously present . . . outside of place and time,'" preaches Francis.[18]

By 1266, Franciscan and future saint Bonaventure had completed his life of Francis, the *Legenda maior*, which the Church declared the only officially accepted life of Francis from henceforth. In it, Francis preaches unsuccessfully and then rejects as useless the sultan's suggestion of a reasoned debate with Muslim scholars. (In Bonaventure's day, the Franciscans were arguing about whether scholarly teaching at the University of Paris fit their vocation.) Instead the saint calls for a fire into which he and the sultan's Muslim religious leaders will step in order to see whom God protects. The sultan refuses.

This unlit fire continues to burn for centuries as further legend lights it and soon has Francis step into it unharmed. Bonaventure's test by fire illustration engulfs much of the future retelling of the story, especially the artistic representations of it. Tolan devotes chapters six, seven, and ten to its influence. As the power struggle between East and West gave one or the other the upper hand, so did the figures of Francis and al-Kamil dominate or recede in the images produced. The scene of Francis in al-Kamil's tent with fire blazing, Muslim's shrinking back, and Francis moving fearlessly

16. See Tolan, *Saint Francis and the Sultan*, chapter 3, for this interpretation.

17. Ibid., chapter 4.

18. Quoted in ibid., 74.

toward danger swiftly became by far the most oft recreated image of the encounter in paint and sculpture from the thirteenth to the twentieth century, according to Mahmood Ibrahim.[19]

During the Reformation and the Enlightenment, Protestants and *philosophes* employed the story of the saint and the sultan to show the ridiculousness of the Catholic faith and the fanaticism of Franciscan monks in particular. Who could believe such superstitious nonsense as seeking martyrdom by stepping into a live flame, or thinking a sultan would or should give up influence to become a pauper and a celibate? Francis was lucky the sultan was an enlightened statesman. In response, Counter-Reformation Catholic representations focused on the courage of Francis and the help of God against heretics like Protestants and unbelieving sceptics, as he had shut the mouth of the heretic sultan.[20]

In 1333, the Franciscans gained by negotiation with the Mamluks the privilege to have a presence in Jerusalem's and Bethlehem's Christian holy places, such as the Church of the Holy Sepulcher and the Church of the Nativity. They retained these rights for over five hundred years, during which a fourteenth-century legend that Francis was granted permission by Sultan al-Kamil to visit these sites was used as evidence of Franciscan claims over all other Christians in the Holy Land.[21]

Thus, the obscure incident at Damietta has been used to present the founder of the Franciscans variously as a worthy university academic, a fire-walking miracle worker, and a superstitious religious fanatic. It also has been employed to depict the sultan as a just statesman, an obstinate warmonger, a cringing barbarian, and a reasonable Enlightenment statesman. Given this instability of meaning, can the authentic historical event legitimately model peacebuilding in the twenty-first century?

John Tolan answers no. The most thorough interpreter of the history of the texts and images of the encounter ends his final chapter, "Francis, Apostle of Peace," with the following verdict on recent efforts to base peacemaking on the encounter of saint and sultan: "The authors of the twentieth and twenty-first centuries do nothing more or less than their predecessors: create a saint that fits their ideological needs."[22] I find this assessment too negative, but admit those who undertake to create a model for peacebuilding drawn from

19. Ibrahim, "Francis Preaching to the Sultan," 48.

20. Tolan, *Saint Francis and the Sultan*, chapter 11.

21. Ibid., 287.

22. Ibid., 322.

the Francis and al-Kamil encounter must proceed with considerable humility and careful discernment, if they desire to be taken seriously.

PEACEMAKING MOTIVES THAT OUTRUN THE EVIDENCE

The encounter of St. Francis of Assisi and Sultan al-Kamil of Egypt during wartime in 1219 makes real contributions to peacebuilding, if not overburdened by anachronistic motives the historical evidence cannot bear. Contemporary peacebuilders do well to know their history and realize its limitations. Questionable assertions only undermine the value of the encounter as an emblem of peacemaking. The simplest explanation of the saint and the sultan yields the most support for peacebuilding. Allegations that Francis planted interfaith dialogue in Jerusalem or confronted (invited?) a trial by fire at the sultan's tent, or that al-Kamil heard the gospel from the monk for the first time, or that Francis was a pacifist come to Damietta to protest the Crusades are best left aside.

The Jerusalem connection is political fabrication. The evocation of a dramatic trial by fire either to show the monk's courage and/or the Muslim's fear, as Lawrence Cunningham does,[23] is a legendary accretion that introduces an element of competitive confrontation unsupported in any of the rest of Francis's personal witness. Al-Kamil was already familiar with Christianity, if not with its Franciscan expression.

Fourth, and most difficult for many peacemakers to surrender, is the portrayal of Francis as a pacifist antiwar figure going eastward to talk the Crusaders out of continuing the Crusade. No doubt Francis opposed violence, but it does not follow that he actively opposed the Crusades, much less went to Egypt to end them. Many soldiers oppose war and preach peace. Francis preached to the Muslims as a part of the apostolic imitation of Christ, but in the thirteenth century that was an orthodox practice that existed alongside support for crusades.[24] Francis declares himself an obedient servant of "Almighty God and the Lord Pope."[25] Pope Innocent III had first declared the Fifth Crusade, and Pope Honorius III continued it. To say, as the authors of *St. Francis and the Foolishness of God* do, that

23. Cunningham, *Francis of Assisi*, 62.

24. See Kedar, *Crusade and Mission*, as cited in Tolan, *Saint Francis and the Sultan*, 306.

25. Francis of Assisi, "The Earlier Rule," chapter 24, v 4.

Francis "pleaded with the Christian commander Cardinal Pelagius, to end the fighting," or that Francis was, "diametrically opposed to the mindset of both society and the church," and "implored political leaders to stop waging war," goes beyond the facts.[26] (To their credit, the authors of *St. Francis and the Foolishness of God* radically modify this perspective in their 2015 revision of the book.) The slender reed from the early sources upon which this argument often rests is Thomas of Celano's note that Francis prophesied defeat for the Damietta Crusaders in a certain battle and advised them to wait for another day. This is far from preaching against the Crusades, much less war in general.[27]

PEACEMAKING AND THE HISTORICAL CONTEXT: A MODEST ASSESSMENT

What then, can we infer to support the model of peacebuilding from what we know about the saint and the sultan meeting in 1219? For one thing, we may assume certain values and practices of Francis's religious life that brought the ill-clad, barefoot monk to the door of the sultan's tent in Egypt. In historical context, it makes the most sense to understand Francis's main motivation was his pursuit of the apostolic or gospel life, which provided his sense of mission. This mission included going two by two into all the world to preach the gospel, as Jesus had sent out the original apostles in the same manner (Mark 6:7–8). Closely allied with this calling for Francis was ready acceptance of the danger of martyrdom. Most of Jesus' disciples had died at the hands of unbelievers. The possibility of martyrdom was a given in the Franciscan apostolic life. On January 16, 1220, while Francis was probably still in the East, a reluctant Muslim ruler in Marrakech martyred five Franciscans who persistently insulted the Prophet Mohammed,[28] something Francis never encouraged or showed any inclination to do.

Francis would have submitted to the sultan's authority while simultaneously hoping to convert him. After returning from Egypt, Francis presented his own views on Franciscan mission among Muslims in Chapter XVI of his *Earlier Rule* of 1221 titled, "Those Going Among the Saracens and Other Believers." There he gives two ways to proceed among the Saracens (Muslims): first, to live as obedient subjects of "every human creature," without

26. Dennis et al, *St. Francis and the Foolishness of God*, 84 and 93.

27. Tolan, *Saint Francis and the Sultan*, 305.

28. Ibid., 6.

argument or debate, while acknowledging Christ; second, to "announce the Word of God" that nonbelievers might believe and be baptized.[29] It is likely that he followed the latter in al-Kamil's presence, since he had gone through so much trouble and danger to get the opportunity to speak to him. I believe it safe to assume Francis in Damietta sought primarily to convert the sultan to Christianity. If his later writings reflect his 1219 encounter, Francis likely obediently surrendered to Sultan al-Kamil's authority while acknowledging he hoped the Muslim ruler would convert to Christ.

Given that assumption and his customary deportment, some further inferences about the manner of Francis's presentation may be safely made. He would have approached the sultan as a friend. Very likely Francis began by blessing the abode of Sultan al-Kamil. Chapter IV of the *Earlier Rule,* which is titled, "How the Brothers Should Go Through the World," commands them to say upon entering any home, "Peace to this house."[30] In Chapter XXII, Francis admonishes all Franciscans to "'Love your enemies and do good to them that hate you'" (Mt 5:44). He continues in verses 3 and 4: "Our friends, therefore, are all those who unjustly inflict upon us distress and anguish, shame and injury, sorrow and punishment, martyrdom and death. We must love them greatly for we shall possess eternal life because of what they bring us."[31] Francis would have reversed the usual stereotyped Christian dismissal of the sultan's value and met him as a friend worthy of blessing and love, regardless of the sultan's actions.

A third component essential to understanding Francis's view of mission in general and Sultan al-Kamil in particular is Francis's sense of the unity of creation, what Michael Blastic calls Francis's vision of "the cosmic fraternity of creation."[32] All of creation flows from God, so all creation, animal, mineral or vegetable, is one in God, especially all the human family. Artists portray Francis preaching to the birds as well as to the sultan in similar forms.[33] Both are emblems of his ministry to all creation. Francis's *Canticle of Creatures* is a clear expression of this unity of all reality. In it Francis calls upon the whole creation—Brother Sun, Sister Moon, Mother Earth and all her creatures, and even Sister Bodily Death—to join those forgiving persons who endure through sickness and trial in joyful praise of

29. Francis of Assisi, "The Earlier Rule," chap 15, v 5–7.

30. Ibid., chap 4, v 2.

31. Ibid., chap 22, v 1, 3, 4.

32. Blastic, "Franciscan Spirituality," 411.

33. Anonymous, *The Little Flowers of Saint Francis*, 26–27.

God. The Most High will crown those who "endure in peace."[34] The same equality of every person under God that called Francis to embrace the leper and become one with the poorest and most marginalized also would have led him to approach the powerful Sultan al-Kamil as a fellow child of God.

A fourth distinctive characteristic of Franciscan spirituality is the virtues of poverty and humility. These virtues shed light on the approach of St. Francis to al-Kamil. Francis preached and taught a radical humility expressed in absolute poverty, which made Franciscans vulnerable and dependent upon the generosity of others for survival. In a literal physical sense, Francis would have surrendered himself to the charity of the sultan in genuine humility. If the current pope's actions and words are any indication, it was these qualities of Francis that led the Jesuit Cardinal Bergoglio, who has reached out to literally wash the feet of Muslims, to choose the name Francis upon becoming pope.

These values and practices of Franciscan spirituality suggest Francis came to the sultan's tent to complete the unity of all creation he saw revealed in Christ's life. Nothing in Francis's history before or after suggests any lack of integrity in his humble, simple approach to all persons. Francis may have accepted at one level that the sultan was an enemy of the Church, but at a deeper level, he saw him first as a child of God worthy of respect and even love. Francis did not enter the sultan's tent as an enemy. He entered as a surrendered penitent to an unreconciled brother. His mission was conversion of a kind that would be more expressive of familial reconciliation than ideological victory over an evil and inferior faith.

We know less about the spirituality of Sultan al-Kamil than that of St. Francis, but we know he did not receive Francis and his companion monk as bitter enemies. He hosted them without violence. What we know of the Muslim leader's life suggests he may have appreciated Christian monks' piety and would have acted hospitably toward these two. Perhaps they reminded him of the Coptic monks of Egypt or the Sufi mystics of his native faith. Al-Kamil is known for ruling with justice and a willingness to listen to the viewpoints of others. The sultan allowed Francis and his companion to return to the Crusader camp unharmed. He later treated the captured army of the Fifth Crusade mercifully. A thirteenth-century Muslim poet wrote: "If they had conquered us, they would have spilled our blood. Now we have conquered them, and we have saved them."[35] Sultan al-Kamil eventually negotiated a

34. Francis of Assisi, "The Canticle of Creatures," v 11.

35 Johnson, "St. Francis and the Sultan," 58.

peace settlement on the Jerusalem issue that displeased many of his Muslim supporters, but provided an opportunity for future stability and peace.[36]

Francis returned from his contact with Islam clearly impressed by the faith and practices of those he had sought to convert. Numerous sources note the hints of Islamic spiritual practices in Francis's post-Egypt writings.[37] After experiencing the muezzin, the five times daily call to the ritual Muslim prayer, Francis gave the following suggestion to European civil authorities in order to "foster honor" to God: "every evening an announcement may be made by a messenger or some other sign that praise and thanksgiving may be given by all people to the all-powerful Lord God."[38] In a 1225 letter, he instructs that the people's response to hearing Jesus' name is to "adore his name with fear and reverence, prostrate on the ground."[39]

In conclusion, the meeting of Saint Francis and Sultan al-Kamil understood in historical context reveals a model of person-to-person contact infused with the spirituality of two world faiths potent with peacebuilding traditions. Such encounters provide a counterbalance to either faith's adherents stereotyping the "other" as an evil enemy who can only be dealt with by lethal force. It suggests the alternative power of human encounter rooted in genuine Christian and Muslim beliefs, a power to deepen one's own faith as in the case of Francis and to create political and military initiatives for justice and compromise, as in the case of al-Kamil.

The core of these possibilities for peacebuilding through personal encounter with those of another faith is not complex. They need little elaboration. The saint and the sultan came steeped in faiths calling for justice and peace. They met. They talked and listened. They parted as changed men who nudged humanity toward peace.

BIBLIOGRAPHY

Abu-Munshar, Maher Y. "Sultan Al-Kamil, Emperor Frederick II and the Submission of Jerusalem." *International Journal of Social Science and Humanity* 3 (2013) 443–47.

Acocella, Joan. "Rich Man, Poor Man: The Radical Visions of St. Francis." *New Yorker*, January 14, 2013. http://www.newyorker.com/magazine/2013/01/14/rich-man-poor-man.

36. See Abu-Manshar, "Sultan Al-Kamil."

37 See Rout, "St Francis of Assisi and Islam."

38. Francis of Assisi, "A Letter to the Rulers of the Peoples," 58–59l.

39. Francis of Assisi, "A Letter to the Entire Order," v 4.

Blastic, Michael. "Franciscan Spirituality." In *The New Dictionary of Catholic Spirituality*, edited by Michael Downey, 408–18. Collegeville, MN: Liturgical, 1993.

Cunningham, Lawrence. *Francis of Assisi: Performing the Gospel Life*. Grand Rapids: Eerdmans, 2004.

Dardess, George. *In the Spirit of St. Francis and the Sultan: Catholics and Muslims Working Together for the Common Good*. Kindle. Maryknoll, NY: Orbis, 2011.

Dennis, Marie, Joseph Nangle, Cynthia Moe-Lobeda, and Stuart Taylor. *St. Francis and the Foolishness of God*. Maryknoll, NY: Orbis, 1993.

Francis of Assisi. "The Canticle of Creatures." [1225]. *Francis and Clare of Assisi: Early Documents*. http://franciscantradition.org:8080/FAED/index.jsp?p= 114&workNum =21.

———. "The Earlier Rule." [1221]. *Francis and Clare of Assisi: Early Documents*. http:// franciscantradition.org:8080/FAED/index.jsp?workNum=12&p=63.

———. "A Letter to the Entire Order." [1225]. *Francis and Clare of Assisi: Early Documents*. http://franciscantradition.org:8080/FAED/index.jsp?workNum=23&p=116.

———. "A Letter to the Rulers of the Peoples." [1220]. *Francis and Clare of Assisi: Early Documents*. http://franciscantradition.org:8080/FAED/index.jsp?p=58&workNum =9.

———. "The Testament." [1226]. *Francis and Clare of Assisi: Early Documents*. http:// franciscantradition.org:8080/FAED/index.jsp?workNum=025¶g=001.

Ibrahim, Mahmood. "Francis Preaching to the Sultan: Art and Literature in the Hagiography of the Saint." In *Finding Saint Francis in Literature and Art*, edited by Cynthia Ho, Beth A. Mulvaney, and John K. Downey, 47–61. The New Middle Ages. New York: Palgrave Macmillan, 2009.

Johnson, Galen K. "St. Francis and the Sultan: An Historical and Critical Reassessment." *Mission Studies* 18 (2001) 146–64.

Ḳedar, B. Z. *Crusade and Mission: European Approaches toward the Muslims*. Princeton: Princeton University Press, 2014.

The Little Flowers of Saint Francis. [14th century]. Edited by Thomas Okey. Mineola, NY: Dover, 2003.

Moses, Paul. *The Saint and the Sultan: The Crusades, Islam, and Francis of Assisi's Mission of Peace*. New York: Doubleday, 2009.

Ratzinger, Joseph, Cardinal. "The Assissi Day of Prayer: The Splendor of the Peace of Francis." *30 Days* . Reprinted in *The Essential Pope Bendict XVI: His Central Writings and Speeches*, edited by John F. Thornton and Susan B. Varenne, 43–45. New York: HarperOne, 2007.

Rout, Paul. Al-Masaq. "St Francis of Assisi and Islam: A Theological Perspective on a Christian-Muslim Encounter." *Al-Masaq* 23 (2015) 205–15.

"St. Francis of Assisi." In *New Advent Catholic Encyclopedia*. http://home.newadvent.org / [14hcathen/06221a.htm.

Thomas of Celano. "The Life of Saint Francis (Thomas of Celano)." http://franciscantradition .org:8080/FAED/index.jsp?p=180&workNum=34.

Tolan, John V. *Saint Francis and the Sultan: The Curious Story of a Christian-Muslim Encounter*. New York: Oxford University Press, 2009.

Warren, Kathleen, and Joy Hart. *In the Footprints of Francis and the Sultan: A Model for Peacemaking*. NTSC. Cincinnati, OH: Franciscan Studio, 2012.

9

Roger Williams, Religious Freedom, and the Path to Peace

Robert N. Nash Jr.

In October of 1996 I attended a conference on religious diversity in Atlanta that was held at the Carter Center and sponsored by Emory University. As I recall, there were about 250–300 people of various religious stripes in attendance—Methodists, Muslims, Baptists, Buddhists, Presbyterians, Pentecostals, and many others. As part of the conference, we participated in a tolerance workshop in which we were asked to share with a partner the religious group against which we had the most prejudice.

I picked the International Society of Krishna Consciousness, not so much because I have huge prejudice against my Hare Krishna brothers and sisters, but mainly because a Hare Krishna sister had once approached me in the airport in Honolulu when I was about seventeen years old and informed me that she was handing out flowers to the most handsome men she could find. As a seventeen-year-old male, I automatically assumed that I fell into this category, so you can imagine my surprise when she asked for a donation and I realized that her interest in me had nothing to do with my looks!

My partner picked Roman Catholics. The leader then instructed us to repeat the name of our partner's religion to our partner ten times and our partner was to engage in word association with his or her religion. As my partner said the words, "Hare Krishna" to me, I responded with words like "airport," "flowers," "chants," and so forth. She then responded with words about Catholics, which seemed to focus primarily upon her sense that Catholics drank heavily and worshipped Mary.

We then returned to the large group and our leader asked all the persons who chose Catholics to stand. He invited them to shout out their words as he wrote them on the board. He then asked the Catholics to stand and respond. This went on for each religious group in the room.

Now what religious group do you think more people in that room had prejudice against than any other group? Exactly . . . Baptists! I don't recall the exact number of people who stood—but it seemed to me that only about ten people remained seated. They shared their words—racists, bigots, misogynists, rednecks . . . and on and on it went. The room seemed to have the impression that we Baptists were radicals and that we were generally radical about the wrong things.

And how many Baptists do you think attended a conference on religious diversity in Atlanta in 1996? Two! And we had found each other. The other Baptist was my partner. The entire room collapsed in laughter when the two of us stood. And we offered a very pathetic response to the words on the board. When the Hare Krishnas stood up, one gentleman among them simply looked at the words on the board and said, "It's all true!" And he sat down. And I wished I had had the sense to do the same thing when it came to responding to the words that described "Baptists."

I did not have time to voice it at that conference. But the truth of the matter is that as much good as bad can result from taking one's religion seriously. It all depends upon what one chooses to be radical about it. Yes, we Baptists are rather radical. When we embrace a theological idea, we embrace it fully. And we defend it passionately. And my hope is that there is something to be learned from a tradition which does this, particularly in a world in which religious radicalism is often viewed as the source of the violence rather than the solution to it. In the face of violence in the world, we are often encouraged to be moderate in expressing our views on our own religions. I would suggest in this essay that the way forward to peace in the world is through a more radical embrace of our own religious traditions rather than through the path of moderation.

So let me tell you a story about one Baptist who was so radically Baptist and so radically Christian for that matter that he pushed some of the most radical Christian ideas of his day to their most radical conclusions and, in the process, managed to articulate a defense of religious liberty and freedom based upon religious radicalism rather than tolerance. Honestly, there is some controversy as to just how Baptist he really was (he only remained one for about four to six months). Only God knows. But here is his story.

There once lived a Puritan and sometime Baptist who was among the most radical and extreme sectarian and ideological Puritans and Baptists who ever lived. His name was Roger Williams. What is so interesting about Williams is that his religious extremism led him to a surprisingly progressive position on religious liberty and the separation of church and state. Indeed, many historians and theologians consider him to be the founder of the American understanding and perspective on that separation and freedom. But Williams did not come to his position from the standpoint of enlightened thinking and the dignity of the individual person as did persons like James Madison and Thomas Jefferson; rather he came at it from deep theological and sectarian roots that emerged out of his Puritan and Calvinist embrace of the idea of the goodness and the sovereignty of God and, concomitantly, the notion of the total and utter depravity of humanity.

Roger Williams offers a way forward for us when it comes to fostering dialogue among all religions about nonviolence and about treating each other with dignity and respect, not because he calls us toward tolerance for the sake of tolerance, but rather because he calls us toward tolerance for the sake of our deepest convictions about our faith. It is possible to be so convinced of the rightness of one's own faith that it leads one to offer greater freedom to others rather than less. What I would like to do in this essay is to take Williams's radical and extremist position and push it even further than Williams did to the extent that, through a radical Christian position, we find a path away from violence and toward peace. Moreover, we find the same phenomenon within Judaism and Islam.

I will not take time to review Williams's biography here. Suffice it to say that he was born around 1603 in London, was educated at Cambridge where he studied theology and fell under the influence of Puritan Separatists, and that he immigrated to New England in about 1631. To be a Separatist in the 1630s was to take a step beyond simply that of the Puritans who sought to "purify" the church of some of the influences of the Church of England. To be a Separatist was to insist upon the removal of every element of Anglicanism and to repent of any association with the tradition. In time,

Williams's position was too radical and extreme even for his non-Separatist Puritan brothers and sisters and he was booted out of the Massachusetts Bay colony and sent out into the "howling wilderness" where he eventually founded the Rhode Island colony and helped to start the first Baptist church in America at Providence, Rhode Island.

Over the course of his life, Williams became increasingly convinced of the need to establish a "pure" church composed only of those persons who were among God's elect. One would assume that such a position would lead to a desire to establish a theocratic government on earth in which only the most pure of persons could rule. In fact, for Williams, the very opposite occurred. Even as he became convinced of the need for a pure church, he also became more convinced of the need for religious freedom and the separation of church and state as intrinsic foundations for every government. His theological perspective on this matter emerged from his Calvinist roots, which affirmed two realities: the absolute goodness and sovereignty of God and the absolute depravity and sinfulness of humanity. Taken together, these two doctrines led him to the conclusion that there could be no theocratic government prior to the return of Christ to earth and that there could be no true church until that same event.[1] By the time Williams was finished with his search for the true church, he was convinced only of the absolute theological purity of himself and of his wife. His church was a small one.

Williams presents his theological framework in a book entitled *The Bloudy Tenent of Persecution,* published in 1644 as a conversation between Truth and Peace. The book was not widely read in the seventeenth century (he dedicated it to Parliament and then Parliament ordered all copies burned), but it came to have a remarkable influence upon religious liberty and the separation of church and state, particularly in the United States. Even if he did not take his argument to its logical conclusion, it does, in fact, hold the key to religious liberty (if not the separation of church and state) in all forms of government, whether a democracy like the United States or a religious theocracy like Iran. One does not have to reside under a government in which religion and state are separate in order to champion religious liberty in a way that is in line with the deepest convictions of one's faith.

Williams could not tolerate compulsion in religious belief, saying it was tantamount to requiring "an unwilling Spouse . . . to enter into a forced

1. Morgan, *Roger Williams*, 49.

bed."[2] He detested the fact that people who did not believe in God were forced to take public oaths in the name of God. Williams freed God from the human mind as much as any other human being, and certainly more than most any Baptist. What Williams argued is that, as a sinful and fallible human being, he could not ultimately understand or grasp the mind of God and so therefore neither he nor any other human being could compel others to make any religious assertion about God. If he made such absolute statements, then he usurped the place of God, provided absolute proof of his own sinful state and, in the process, violated one of the most foundational theological assertions of his own religious tradition.

In the first introductory piece to his work, Williams offers twelve theses that he intends to defend. Numbers six and eight are directly related to religious freedom. Number six argues that "it is the will and command of God that . . . a permission of the most paganish, Jewish, Turkish, or anti-Christian consciences and worships be granted to all men in all nations and countries."[3] He eschews any sort of religious warfare, insisting that battle should be done only with the word of God or Scripture in order to convince others of the truth.

In the eighth thesis, he points out that God requires no uniformity of religion "to be enacted and enforced in any civil state" because such conformity leads to civil war, persecution, and violence in the name of religion.[4]

The starting point of Williams's argument appears to be his radical notion that Almighty God does not seek or demand the utilization of violence in order to accomplish his purposes in the world. Williams insisted that Jesus Christ himself had decreed that "the tares (or weeds) and the wheat . . . should be let alone in the world, and not plucked up until the harvest, which is the end of the world."[5] Jesus was so committed to this idea, Williams says, that he charged his disciple to be "so far from persecuting those that would not be of their religion that when they were persecuted they should pray (Matthew 5:44), when they were cursed, they should bless, etc."[6] He points out how often the tares become wheat and blasphemers and persecutors become faithful and idolaters become worshippers of God, if their salvation is left up to God and not left to a sinful humanity that

2. Williams, "Christenings," 38.

3. Williams, *Bloudy Tenent*, 3.

4. Ibid.

5. Ibid., 11.

6. Ibid.

is fully incapable of understanding the truth. He also points out just how often those who were persecuted by the church (like Jesus or John Wycliffe or Martin Luther) often turned out to have been promoting a truth that the church itself later embraced. He then warns in his own day

> of hundred thousands, men, women, children, fathers, mothers, husbands, wives, brothers, sisters, old and young, high and low, plundered, ravished, slaughtered, murdered, famished! And hence these cries [on the part of the religious power-holders], that men fling away the spiritual sword and spiritual artillery in spiritual and religious causes, and rather trust for the suppressing of each other's gods, conscience, and religion . . . to an arm of flesh and sword of steel.[7]

His point was that those who embraced the ways and teaching of Jesus ought to have faith and trust in God's power and ability to bring about God's purposes in the world and that no assistance was required from a sinful humanity except for its willingness to use the sword of the Spirit and of the Word of God as its weapon. Indeed, whenever the church sought to use swords of steel, it often killed the wheat at least as much as it destroyed the tares. This was why Jesus had insisted that the wheat and tares should be allowed to grow up together. Williams spoke powerfully to the folly of it all during the previous one hundred years in England:

> Henry VII leaves England under the slavish bondage of the pope's yoke. Henry VIII reforms all England to a new fashion, half papist, half Protestant. King Edward VI turns about the wheels of the state, and works the whole land to absolute Protestantism. Queen Mary, succeeding to the helm, steers a direct contrary course, breaks in pieces all Edward wrought, and brings forth an old edition of England's reformation all popish. Mary not living out half her days, as the prophet speaks of bloody persons, Elizabeth, like Joseph, advances from the prison to the palace, and from irons to the crown, she plucks up all her sister Mary's plants, and sounds a trumpet all Protestant.
>
> What sober man stands not amazed at these revolutions: And yet, like mother like daughter: and how zealous are we, their offspring, for a . . . better edition of a national Canaan, in imitation of Judah and Josiah, which, if attained, who knows how soon succeeding kings or parliaments will quite pull down and abrogate?[8]

7. Ibid., 32.

8. Ibid., 213–14.

Given this dismal history, it was his conviction that human beings ought to leave it all to God and embrace the conviction that "a false religion out of the church will not hurt the church, no more than weeds in the wilderness hurt the enclosed garden, or poison hurt the body when it is not touched or taken."[9] He also insisted that "a false religion and worship will not hurt the civil state in case the worshippers break no civil law." So false religion should be allowed to exist in the presence of both the church and the state and it should be left to God to inhibit its progress and not to a sinful humanity to attempt to do so.

The key theological idea upon which Williams established his convictions about religious freedom and the separation of church and state was his belief in the huge gap between God and humanity, a gap that could never be overcome through any human effort, including the fashioning of a theocratic government. Sinfulness and the total depravity of humanity would always blind human beings and keep them from being able to ascertain the will and purposes of God. He did not seek religious freedom for its own sake; rather, he sought it "because it was the only way to reach the true God."[10] Force, in his estimation, only advanced false religion; it never advanced the truth. And, left to its own path, truth would win out in the end. Left to the whims of a sinful humanity, truth would inevitably be lost and the purposes of God frustrated.

Roger Williams offers a perspective on religious freedom that might be embraced by the Abrahamic faiths of Judaism, Christianity, and Islam precisely because it emerges from this absolute conviction in the sovereignty of God and the sinfulness of humanity, concepts which are generally affirmed by all three faiths. Robert F. Shedinger points out that "given the way that Islam conceives of God, the world, and the purpose of human life, it should be clear that Islam will be fundamentally opposed to any form of government, be it secular liberal democracy or atheistic communist, that removes the sovereignty of God from its rightful place as guarantor of a just and egalitarian social, political, and economic order."[11] Williams's theological position actually affirms God's sovereignty as the basis for religious freedom in any government, whether it be a liberal democracy, a communist form of government, or an Islamic theocracy. For Williams, whatever the government (and he certainly preferred one in which church and state were

9. Ibid., 120.

10. Morgan, *Roger Williams,* 141.

11. Shedinger, "Roger Williams," 151.

separate), religious freedom should be protected for all because it is the only way to guarantee that God's truth emerges apart from contamination by human depravity and sin.

The truth of the matter is that no government, whether in a predominately Jewish, Muslim, Christian, Buddhist, Hindu, or any other context, has managed to rise above its own challenges to attain the highest levels of justice to which the principles of its dominant religious expression aspire. Such is the case in Israel where the Jewish ideal has suffered in the face of the plight of Palestinian peoples. It is the case with democracy in the United States or in Western Europe where Christianity has held sway in terms of the moral foundations of the nations and yet injustice runs rampant. And it is certainly the case in predominately Muslim nations in the world. No nation comes close to embodying the ideals of its own particular majority faith.

Roger Williams was not interested in defending democracies or theocracies, for that matter. He was interested in defending the truth about God. He was interested in creating contexts in which that truth was free to emerge apart from any effort on the part of a sinful humanity to restrict its emergence. For this reason, he did not argue for a particular form of government, though he did call for the separation of church and state. His simple insistence was that God's truth be allowed to grow up in the world without being restrained by human governments. He was against persecution in any form, whether brought by the state or a religious institution sanctioned by the state, toward any other religion. This was for him the only path to truth.

It is also the only path to peace—the only path. Williams was a creative thinker whose greatest gift was the ability to follow ideas through to their ultimate conclusions. He did not stop where others stopped; instead, he pushed on. In his context, he viewed the separation of the church and state as the only way to ensure that truth would ultimately prevail. Perhaps, though, even Williams stopped short of the implications of his own theological system. At the most foundational level, his notions about God's goodness and sovereignty and the depth of human depravity affirm a gap so wide that any government that emerges from a religious vision would do well to embrace them, no matter what system it seeks to implement and no matter whether it embraces the separation of church and state or not.

I argued just this point in a visit in January of 2014 to the Islamic Republic of Iran at the invitation of the Iranian government and in a meeting with the official "think tank" of the Iranian Foreign Ministry. I had been asked to talk about how we in the United States had created a mythology of our revolution that had enabled that revolution to stand the test of time. I pointed to Roger Williams and these very notions of God's sovereignty. I pointed out that religious freedom was not the sole province of democracy but rather that religious freedom was an idea that emerged from the conviction that only God could ultimately know the truth. Williams's ideas ensure a humility at the heart of human systems and a context in which all of us are free to argue our convictions and to worship the God that we embrace with the full conviction that that God, in the end, will work it all out to God's own glory.

Roger Williams articulated for all of us a theological conviction that nearly any Jewish, Christian, or Muslim person would embrace. He did it precisely because he was a radical, extreme person of faith who believed that his faith commitment was the absolute truth beyond any conceivable doubt. But he also recognized the limitations of his own sinfulness, something very few of us are usually willing to do, and it was this recognition that led him to articulate a doctrine of religious freedom based upon religious radicalism, that is, the notion that God does not require the help of a sinful humanity to accomplish God's purposes and that a forced conformity of the individual conscience is the greatest expression of that sinfulness.[12]

God affirms this, at least in the understanding of the People of the Book—for Jews, Christians, and Muslims alike. God is convinced that all of us will come to the truth if we are free to seek that truth without compulsion.

Surah al-Baqarah (2:255–56) states that

> 2:255. Allah—there is no God but He, the Ever-living, the Self-subsisting by Whom all subsist. Slumber overtakes Him not, nor sleep. To Him belongs whatever is in the heavens and whatever is in the earth. Who is he that can intercede with Him but by His permission? He knows what is before them and what is behind them. And they encompass nothing of His knowledge except what He pleases. His knowledge extends over the heavens and the earth, and the preservation of them both tires Him not. And He is the Most High, the Great.
>
> 2:256. There is no compulsion in religions—the right way is indeed clearly distinct from error. So whoever disbelieves in the devil and

12. Gaustad, *Roger Williams*, 94.

believes in Allah, he indeed lays hold on the firmest handle which shall never break. And Allah is Hearing, Knowing.[13]

The Hebrew Bible is equally clear. The prophet Isaiah writes in Isaiah 55:6–11:

> 6 Seek the LORD while he may be found,
> call upon him while he is near;
> 7 let the wicked forsake their way,
> and the unrighteous their thoughts;
> let them return to the Lord, that he may have mercy on them,
> and to our God, for he will abundantly pardon.
> 8 For my thoughts are not your thoughts,
> nor are your ways my ways, says the LORD
> 9 For as the heavens are higher than the earth,
> so are my ways higher than your ways
> and my thoughts than your thoughts.
>
> 10 For as the rain and the snow come down from heaven,
> and do not return there until they have watered the earth,
> making it bring forth and sprout,
> giving seed to the sower and bread to the eater,
> 11 so shall my word be that goes out from my mouth;
> it shall not return to me empty,
> but it shall accomplish that which I purpose,
> and succeed in the thing for which I sent it.[14]

And in the New Testament in Acts 17:22–28, Paul the Apostle visits in Athens where he recognizes the common search of all people for meaning and purpose:

> Then Paul stood in front of the Areopagus and said, "Athenians,
> I see how extremely religious you are in every way. 23 For as I
> went through the city and looked carefully at the objects of your
> worship, I found among them an altar with the inscription, 'To an
> unknown god.' What therefore you worship as unknown, this I
> proclaim to you. 24 The God who made the world and everything
> in it, he who is Lord of heaven and earth, does not live in shrines
> made by human hands, 25 nor is he served by human hands, as
> though he needed anything, since he himself gives to all mortals
> life and breath and all things. 26 From one ancestor he made all

13. *The Holy Qu'ran*, 115–16.

14. All biblical quotations are taken from the New Revised Standard Version of the Bible.

> nations to inhabit the whole earth, and he allotted the times of their existence and the boundaries of the places where they would live,
> 27 so that they would search for God and perhaps grope for him and find him—though indeed he is not far from each one of us.
> 28 For 'In him we live and move and have our being'; as even some of your own poets have said, 'For we too are his offspring.'"

Here are the affirmations made in each one of these sacred texts. They each affirm that human beings are on a quest to find meaning and purpose in life. They each affirm that it is God who offers that meaning and purpose. They each insist that, ultimately, God will prevail and the truth of God will win out. Our calling as human beings is to trust God to accomplish God's purposes in the world. It is not our calling to engage in violence and warfare with each other. It is our calling to affirm the sovereignty, power, and majesty of God who controls all of life and to whom we owe our ultimate allegiance. All of life should be given over to God's all-encompassing authority, love, and goodness. This is the fullest expression of the radical faith to which Roger Williams points us all. It is the only path to peace no matter what form of government a particular people might embrace.

There is a way to peace among the religions of the world that results, not from a moderation of our religious beliefs, but rather from a more radical embrace of them. Many conflicts in the world today are the products of religious difference—either between religions or within them. We often decry religious radicalism as the cause of such conflict and we seek to remove religion from the public square in order to maintain the peace.

The recent presidential election is a case in point. In his effort to win the election, Donald Trump issued a number of provocative statements about the religion of Islam, insisting that "Islam hates us" and equating the religion with violent extremists who twist its teachings and perspectives. A number of his cabinet appointments, including Lt. General Michael Flynn who briefly served as National Security Advisor and Stephen Bannon who will serve as an advisor to the new president, have referred to Islam as a "cancer" and as a dire threat to the United States.[15] These statements and perspectives assume that the only kind of radicalism that can emerge from Islam is the kind that is characterized by violence and extremism. They hope to purge the country of such violence by banning Muslim immigrants and perhaps eventually by banning the practice of the religion itself. They have identified religious extremists as the normative elements in the tradition.

15. Crowley and Toosi, "Trump Appointees."

But religious extremism and Islam are not one and the same. What is demanded from Islam as well as from Judaism and Christianity is the emergence of religious extremists who allow the highest values of the traditions to form and shape their lives. From Williams we learn that true peace and freedom in the world is far more likely to be accomplished when we follow the teachings of our religions through to their most radical conclusions rather than stopping short at the point of moderation—for it is in the radical forms of faith, properly expressed, that we find the largest measures of love, mercy, hope, and grace. If my Baptist brothers and sisters had actually listened to Williams, perhaps these words would have been the words offered up about us at a conference on religious diversity at the Carter Center in 1996. To put it another way, extremism is demanded in our day, but it is the form of extremism that emerges from the revolutionary embrace of the best values of a particular faith rather than from its most twisted ones.

BIBLIOGRAPHY

Crowley, Michael, and Nahal Toosi. "Trump Appointees Endorsed Link between Islam and Radicalism." http://www.politico.com/story/2016/11/trump-appointees-islam-radicalism-231647.

Gaustad, Edwin S. *Roger Williams: Lives and Legacies.* New York: Oxford University Press, 2005.

The Holy Qu'ran: Arabic Text with English Translation and Commentary. Translated by Maulana Muhammad Ali. Ohio: Ahmadiyya Anjuman Isha'at Islam Lahore, 2002.

Morgan, Edmund S. *Roger Williams: The Church and State.* New York: Harcourt, Brace and World, 1967.

Shedinger, Robert F. "Roger Williams Meets Sayyid Qutb: When the Quest for Religious Liberty Becomes a Force for Global Injustice." *Perspectives in Religious Studies* 32.2 (2005) 149–66.

Williams, Roger. *The Bloudy Tenent of Persecution for Cause of Conscience discussed in A Conference between Truth and Peace. Who, In all tender Affection, present to the high Court of Parliament, (as the result of their Discourse) these, (among other passages) of highest consideration.* 1644. Reprint, edited by Richard Groves. Macon, GA: Mercer University Press, 2001.

———. "Christenings Make not Christians, OR A Briefe Discourse concerning that name Heathen; commonly given to the Indians. As also concerning that great point of their Conversion." In *The Complete Writings of Roger Williams*, edited by Perry Miller, vol. 7, 26–41. 1645. Reprint, Eugene, OR: Wipf & Stock, 2007.

10

In the Steps of Pope John XXIII, the Reverend Doctor Martin Luther King Jr., and Archbishop Oscar Romero

James M. Dawsey and Adam Y. Wells

When first published during the course of the Second Vatican Council fifty-two years ago, Pope John XXIII's encyclical *Pacem in Terris* broke new ground in the attempt to build universal peace. While previous social encyclicals (including John XXIII's own *Mater et Magistra*, 1961) had been directed to the venerable brethren and faithful of the Catholic world, *Pacem in Terris* was addressed "to all men of good will." *Pacem in Terris* was not intended for Christian in-house discussion only. Peace is everyone's concern. Also, the encyclical was groundbreaking in insisting on a goal much greater than an absence of war. April 1963 was the time of the Cold War. Capitalism in the United States and Europe and communism in the Soviet Union battled for greater spheres of influence. And nuclear proliferation presented a threat to human survival. But, even given the tremendous world tension, humankind's goal must be greater than a simple lessening of conflict, John XXIII insisted. *Pacem in Terris* reminded that generation that the true subject of peacebuilders everywhere and of every stripe should be a deep and abiding peace on earth. And finally, *Pacem in Terris* affirmed that envisioning and describing such a peace, even a perfect peace, in itself is not sufficient. At most, it is a first step. Peacebuilding is always an activity, one in which individuals and states make choices. Our own actions and those actions of our governments can lead to continuing the status quo or to more enmity among us and our neighbors or to greater peace on earth. If true peace is to come, it is going to be by trudging forward, step by step.

IN THE FOOTSTEPS OF JOHN XXIII: JOINING HUMAN RIGHTS TO OBLIGATIONS

John XXIII claimed that peace was contingent on individuals and nations relating to one another as God intended. There was a social order established by the Creator. It was a moral order. It was an order that we can perceive in progress and change through reason and science. It was an order that we can harness for humankind's benefit. This order established how people should relate to each other and to the rest of creation and how states should relate one to another.

The right order of creation was knowable to everyone, Christians and non-Christians alike, John thought, through natural law. That is, human conscience revealed the Creator's intended moral social order to women and men and urged us to obey it. If structuring society as God intended, people and nations would be marked by justice, goodwill, charity, trust, freedom. And the world would know true peace.

John XXIII listed human rights that accompanied creation. Although significantly more extensive than the rights to life, liberty, and the pursuit of happiness of the American Declaration of Independence, John's list also was not comprehensive but instead offered examples. In other words, the encyclical gave insight into the types of rights that characterize human life when the world operates the way it should. The rights John XXIII listed included the right to preserve and develop life; the right to an education; the right to be respected; the right to freedom; the right to worship; the right to support when raising a family; the right to work; the right to ownership of property; the right to association; the right to travel; and the right to participate in public life.[1]

But, the freedom of one individual sometimes infringes upon the freedom of another. So, most helpful to our thinking, John XXIII's encyclical also reminded us of how each of these rights must be accompanied by corresponding duties. Individual rights walked hand in hand with

1. John XXIII, *Pacem in Terris*, §11–38.

corresponding obligations when building universal peace: "one man's natural right gives rise to a corresponding duty in other men; the duty, that is, of recognizing and respecting that right."[2] The most important of these duties, according to *Pacem in Terris*, was The Golden Rule: respecting the other.

The State played a role in preserving a balance between competing rights. Defense of an individual's rights cannot justify oppression, for instance, or the inaction of the State against clear injustice. The rights of minority populations need be protected. Also, States faced obligations toward other States, such as not pursuing their own development at the expense of injuring or oppressing others. Again, the overarching duty was respecting the other. And in case of disputes, these should be settled by general form of public authority—like the United Nations Organization with its Declaration on Human Rights.

Pacem in Terris connected human rights with individual obligations in a manner comfortable not only to Roman Catholics but to Protestants as well. In that regard, the encyclical was thoroughly ecumenical. At the beginning of the Protestant Reformation, the great Martin Luther framed the double affirmation of individual liberty and duties with these words: "A Christian man is a perfectly free lord of all, subject to no one else. And a Christian man is a perfectly free servant of all, subject to everyone."[3]

Freedom, for Luther, depended strictly on people's relation to the source of freedom. He argued that all people, not just Christians, were under the Creator's demand for justice.[4] The demand for justice was a natural law that applied universally. Although the demand for justice was clear in the Old and New Testaments, "both nature and love alike teach that I should act toward others as I would wish to be treated by them."[5]

My own religious background is United Methodist, and Methodist epistemology likewise affirms natural law.[6] John Wesley thought that there were a variety of ways of knowing God's truth. For Wesley, the historical life, ministry, and death of Jesus provided our clearest insight into the nature and will of God. The Gospels told about Jesus. But there were many paths to knowing our place in creation. The Word of God was present through

2 John XXIII, *Pacem in Terris*, §30

3. Luther, "Concerning Liberty Christian Liberty."

4. Luther, "Treatise on Good Works."

5. Luther, "On Secular Authority"

6. Outler, "The Wesleyan Quadrilateral in Wesley"; and Abraham, "The Wesleyan Quadrilateral in the American Methodist-Episcopal Tradition."

the Scriptures. Reason allowed insight, for as people's minds were created in the image and likeness of God, our thoughts (when thinking rationally) paralleled God's thoughts. This allowed for a natural understanding of good and evil, right and wrong, to all humans regardless of whether ever hearing of Christ or his teachings. The sciences allowed insight into the divine—as did the visual and performing arts, imagination, and beauty. The study of history helped us perceive God, for God is active in history. Also feelings—longings and yearnings, moments of joy, despair, hope, and trust—gave insight into the divine will.

Methodism emphasizes the free will of the believer. Wesley was Armenian in that he believed that while God knew the future, he did not control it. As with Luther, the individual was completely free to respond to or deny God's grace. But also the path to sanctification with Wesley presented a continual process of free choice. Every act, every moment provided an opportunity to love when not loving presented an equal possibility. The Christian's free will was such, in fact, that the individual's choices, when joined to the grace of God, could lead to perfect love.[7]

Freedom, for Wesley, carried over to the social sphere. In 1774, he wrote a tract attacking slavery that was widely read.[8] *Thoughts Upon Slavery* went through four editions in two years. In it, Wesley suggested the boycott of rum and sugar and followed up in 1887 by supporting the creation of the Society for the Abolition of the Slave Trade. Another writing, "Testimony Against Slavery," is even better remembered today:

> Give liberty to whom liberty is due, that is, to every child of man, to every partaker of human nature. Let none serve you but by his own act and deed, by his own voluntary action. Away with all whips, all chains, all compulsion. Be gentle toward all men; and see that you invariably do with every one as you would he should do unto you.[9]

Love manifested itself in service to humankind. Wesley not only fought against slavery. He opposed child labor, the working conditions of chimney sweeps and mine workers, the living conditions in tenements. He pushed for prison reform and better schooling for the poor. In one of his sermons based on the text of Matthew 25, "For I was hungry, and ye gave me meat: I was thirsty, and ye gave me drink: I was a stranger, and ye took

7. Wesley, "Sermon #40 on Christian Perfection."

8. Wesley, "Thoughts upon Slavery."

9. Long, *Pictures of Slavery*, 406–7.

me in: Naked, and ye clothed me: I was sick, and in prison and ye came unto me," Wesley referred to good works as "the perfection of religion."

> They are the highest part of that spiritual building whereof Jesus Christ is the foundation . . . The highest of all Christian graces . . . is properly and directly the love of our neighbor. And to him who attentively consider the whole tenor both of the Old and New Testament, it will be equally plain, that works springing from this love are the highest part of the religion therein revealed. Of these our Lord himself says, "Hereby is my Father glorified, that ye bring forth much fruit."[10]

Wesley referred to service to his fellow man as following in the Lord's footsteps. The Christian, he thought, was liberated in order to serve. Wesley was not opposed to making money but presented an interesting twist on capitalism by preaching that "having first, gained all you can, and, secondly saved all you can, then give all you can."[11] In a follow-up sermon, "the Causes of Inefficacy of Christianity,"[12] he decried that few Methodists kept his third dictum and urged his congregation to leave only half of their savings as inheritance to their children and to apply the other half in support of the poor in society. Wesley himself adopted the guide of keeping only ten percent of his earnings for himself while giving ninety percent for use of charity and evangelism.

The affirmation of radical freedom and radical responsibility to neighbor and community that we encounter in *Pacem in Terris*, Luther, and Wesley, of course has been the hallmark of Morehouse College. Founded as the Augusta Theological Institute in 1867 in the basement of the oldest independent African American church in the United States, the Springfield Baptist Church, the College's original purpose was to prepare black men (that is, former slaves and the sons of slaves) for ministry and teaching. From its inception, Morehouse held that all men were equal in that they were created equal. For Morehouse, that people were created in the image of God indicated a connection joining our rational minds and especially our ability to love to God Himself. And that humans were created in the likeness of God indicated that we could develop our minds, grow in love, and generally progress on our pilgrimage to heaven and in this life.[13]

10. Wesley, "Sermon #99 on the Reward of Righteousness."
11. Wesley, "Sermon #50 on the Use of Money."
12. Wesley, "Sermon #116 on the Causes of Inefficacy of Christianity."
13. Morehouse's is a radicalized view of equality that fits well with its Baptist and

But is the appeal to men and women of good will enough? Is persuasion enough? We applaud how *Pacem in Terris* answered Jesus's command to "love the Lord your God with all your heart, and with all your soul, and with all your mind"[14] by asking that we invest ourselves in others and in the world—in peacebuilding. The business world, the home, the schoolhouse are all proper places to glorify God. Christians and all people of good will are to engage their powers in labor towards Peace on Earth.

Behind John XXIII's conception of human rights rests the conviction that the Creator has provided a storehouse that would satisfy every physical need when used as intended. Creation is ordered and operated through discernible laws. Along with Luther, Wesley, and the Baptist founders of Morehouse, we may even expand John XXIII's thoughts and express them in our own words. People play a special role in creation: human labor transforms the raw gifts of nature, multiplying and increasing their benefit. Through creative imaginations and work, people participate with God in crafting a good world. People are also entrusted by the Creator to be stewards of creation, caring for everything in the world and making sure that this storehouse delighted and benefitted future generations.

Protestant roots. According to Albert Outler ("Some Concepts of Human Rights and Obligations in Classical Protestantism," 21–23), there were three specific ways Protestants extended the medieval view of equality: (1) The avowal of justification by faith through grace pushed the brotherhood and sisterhood of believers further by emphasizing how all are equally dependent on God for salvation. Justification occurred to individuals as they stood in the presence of God. The Holy Spirit could come to anyone, speak to anyone, touch anyone. No person's position before God was to be traced to birth, family name, or standing in society. (2) A leveling between people also occurred because Protestants emphasized the sinful nature of man. Luther used the image of men and women being like sows in the mud, while at same time being sons and daughters of God. Following the Apostle Paul and Augustine of Hippo, Protestants emphasized that all people are sinful. This does not mean that Protestants did not continue to recognize different degrees of conduct, holding for instance murder to be worse than gossip. But it did signify all equally needed God's grace. No one merited salvation. Man's sinfulness was such that all equally deserved death but were equally saved through faith. (3) And finally, by affirming the priesthood of all believers, Protestants extended equality between ministers (as they became titled) and laity. All Christians, according to the Protestant tradition, are "a royal priesthood and a holy nation" (1 Peter 2:9). Every Christian has a right and a responsibility to fulfill the duties of the priestly office. The need to mediate prayers and petitions, confessions of sin, and God's response disappeared. Laity and ministers were equally priests one to another. All became equally responsible for the congregation. When standing before God, there no longer existed any in-kind distinction between those who had been ordained and those who had not.

14. Matthew 22:37.

The purposes of the Creator in these regards are not a mystery. God revealed them through Her actions in history, through covenants, numerous spokespersons, and Sacred Writ. And since men and women are created in the image of God, beauty, intuition, and an innate sense of justice give clues as to human rights and responsibilities. Reason, especially, provides a natural understanding of men and women's place in creation. From this storehouse, creatures are intended to experience life in abundance. But because of greed or fear or rebellion or ignorance, people often do not use the Creator's gifts as intended. Social structures have become warped. In theological terms, sin has distorted the intent of creation. And the result is a world filled with unnecessary suffering, poverty, a deep divide between the haves and the have-nots. But social injustices can be rectified if people would only restructure society along the lines intended by the Creator.

But how exactly are we to bring about such conditions of true peace? How to build a society marked not only through the absence of war but by justice, by people who enjoy a full range of human rights and who assume corresponding duties, a society with less poverty, more education, greater economic equality, and a more equitable distribution of goods between individuals and nations? Here is where the prescriptions of *Pacem in Terris* fall short in our view. While the encyclical tremendously affected Catholic social teaching in a variety of ways, it is not clear that in itself it has moved our world much closer to the enduring peace visualized by the Pontiff. Critics sometimes point to John's idealized vision of individuals and community. Of greater concern, however, are the encyclical's suggestions (or lack thereof) for changing the structures of society to bring about this better community. After offering a few concrete recommendations (e.g., more pronounced activity by the United Nations; the illegitimacy of military force), *Pacem in Terris* falls back on the persuasive voice of the Church to bring about change. Like Luther, Wesley and so much of Christian moral theology, John XXIII falls back on the prescription of converting individuals, men of good will, to a new course of action. John eschews force and especially violence of any kind. But can nonviolent persuasion be effective in building a just society? In producing true peace?

IN THE STEPS OF MARTIN LUTHER KING JR.: A PROGRAM FOR CHANGING UNJUST SOCIAL STRUCTURES

When in December 1964 at Oslo, Morehouse College's most famous graduate, Dr. Martin Luther King Jr., accepted the Nobel Peace Prize, he sounded much of the optimism for true peace voiced by Pope John XXIII. "Sooner or later," he said, "all the people of the world will have to discover a way to live together in peace, and thereby transform this pending cosmic elegy into a creative psalm of brotherhood."[15] Dr. King refused "to accept the cynical notion" of an arms race. He believed that there was "still hope for a brighter tomorrow . . . that people everywhere can have three meals a day for their bodies, education and culture for their minds, and dignity, equality and freedom for their spirits; . . . [that] the lion and the lamb shall lie down together and every man sit under his own vine and fig tree and none shall be afraid; . . . that we shall overcome."[16]

Violence was no answer, he claimed, for while sometimes momentarily successful, violence never brought lasting peace. In fact "civilization and violence [were] antithetical concepts," to him. Dr. King's answer was love—a love that rejected all revenge, physical aggression, and retaliation.[17]

As we all know, Dr. King termed his alternative for building peace "nonviolent resistance." While being physically passive, the method was both active and aggressive spiritually. King wasn't "asking politely" for black equality. Nonviolent resistance asserted aggressively the rights and duties also enumerated in John's encyclical in order ultimately to effect justice: "We cannot be satisfied as long as a Negro in Mississippi cannot vote and a Negro in New York believes he has nothing for which to vote. No, no, we are not satisfied, and we will not be satisfied until 'justice rolls down like waters, and righteousness like a mighty stream.'"[18]

With characteristic humility, Dr. King credited the method of nonviolent resistance to India's great liberator Mohandas K. Gandhi—giving credit also to Morehouse's own Benjamin Elijah Mays for introducing him to it. But as there was something borrowed about Dr. King's method of nonviolent resistance, there was much new to it also.

15. King, "Nobel Prize Acceptance Speech," in *A Testament of Hope*, 224.

16. Ibid., 226.

17. Ibid., 225.

18. Ibid., 219.

Dr. King left us with a description of his nonviolent approach in his article "The Current Crisis in Race Relations."[19] He stressed five facts: (1) The method actively resists evil. It is not cowardly and is not passive. The "mind and the emotions are always active, constantly seeking to persuade the opponent that he is mistaken."[20] (2) The goal of nonviolent resistance is redemption, reconciliation, and the creation of a loving community. Thus, the method does not wish to humiliate or conquer the opponent but to win friendship and understanding. (3) The method seeks to defeat evil, rather than persons (even when they themselves are caught in that evil). The fight is against injustice and for justice—not against unjust individuals. (4) Nonviolent resistance not only avoids physical violence but avoids what Dr. King termed "violence of the spirit." He opposed hate campaigns or temptations to become bitter. The principle of love—loving the neighbor and one's enemies—was at the core of any resistance. And (5) the resister can accept suffering without retaliation because the creative forces of the universe are on the side of justice. In a final analysis, justice will win out.

In theological terms, Dr. King was concerned with structural sin. Sin is what dehumanizes us, making us different than the Creator intended. Sin cuts us off from God and thus from other people. So while Dr. King was concerned with individual sin, he was most concerned with those structures or building blocks of society that bring about injustice or allow it to happen. Clearly expressed in Dr. King's article is the importance he placed on changing the attitudes, views, and actions of both followers and opponents. In keeping with a main thrust of *Pacem in Terris*, peace on earth will only come when people think and act more lovingly one toward another—that is when we do unto others as we would have them do unto us. How to change attitudes, views, and actions? To that effect, we may include also the great attention Dr. King and his followers gave to news coverage of peacebuilding events. The newspaper and television coverage of the 1962 Birmingham confrontation with Bull Connor; the 1963 March on Washington; the 1964 voting rights Selma to Montgomery march with the "Bloody Sunday" confrontation at Pettus Bridge; and, the 1966 open-housing campaign in Chicago with the stoning of the marchers, etc., played a major role in tearing down racial segregation in this country. Dr. King's was a great effort in consciousness raising. Simply put, when white Americans saw themselves in these events, they did not like the people they saw. And when black men

19. King, "The Current Crisis in Race Relations," in *A Testament of Hope*, 85–90.

20. Ibid., 87.

and women saw themselves and read about themselves in these events, they took courage and became more determined in seeking a better tomorrow.

Again in theological terms, society's laws, justice system, monetary and banking regulations, economic organizations, wage and labor policies, tax codes, traditions of ownership and inheritance, cultural opinions, and even programs of education can be demonic in the sense that the structures may bring about injustice, which is fundamentally dehumanizing. Even more so, perhaps, than individual sin, unjust structures cause mass suffering. The sins are often hidden and even perpetrated by the "men (and women) of good will" to whom John XXIII's *Pacem in Terris* appealed. Because they often are hidden behind unrecognized privilege and good intentions, structural sins are harder to address than individual vices. And the Church itself sometimes participates unknowingly in such sinful structures.

Dr. King closely linked efforts of consciousness raising with aggressive attempts to change the laws and the enforcement of laws. To him, both thrusts were important to bringing greater justice in the United States. And all of us can recite some of the great Civil Rights victories that entailed the enforcement of court rulings and new legislation: Brown versus Board of Education of Topeka, Kansas (1954); the desegregation of the Montgomery City buses (1956); "the Little Rock Nine" (1957); James Meredith's enrollment at Ole Miss (1962); the passage (1962) and ratification (1964) of the 24th Amendment abolishing the poll tax; the Civil Rights Act of 1964; the Voting Rights Act of 1965; President Johnson's Executive Order 11246 enforcing affirmative action (1965); Loving versus Virginia (1967); the Civil Rights Act of 1968; etc.

In sum, while Dr. King joined John XXIII in saying that true peace would come when individuals and nations fully committed themselves to human rights, not only by affirming them but also by accepting the responsibilities that accompany liberty, he pushed beyond the Pontiff by offering concrete steps for changing unjust social structures. Dr. King's philosophy of nonviolent resistance, his activities raising awareness of how African Americans were treated, about America's War in Vietnam, and about the great divide in our society of rich and poor, and his appeal to the courts and legislative bodies for fair treatment for all people changed the social landscape of America.

IN THE STEPS OF ARCHBISHOP OSCAR ROMERO: BUILDING PEACE WHEN THERE ARE NO LEGAL AVENUES FOR JUSTICE

Dr. King's program of nonviolent resistance prevailed over time with the civil rights movement in the United States—at least to the extent that our society now provides greater opportunities for African Americans (and women) than before and in that we celebrate his birthday as a national holiday. But couldn't we argue that nonviolent resistance succeeded in the United States precisely because our nation was founded on an ideal of equality before the law? Isn't this a pattern peculiar to liberal societies such as our own? And further, isn't it fairly easy to imagine situations where the laws and their enforcement and public opinion are so controlled by purveyors of violence that Dr. King's approach might not have worked? Would his approach have worked, for instance, in Hitler's Germany? In Stalin's Soviet Union? In Kim Jong Un's North Korea? With ISIS? Do John XXIII and Martin Luther King Jr. provide directions for peacebuilding even when a given State's organs of justice themselves pervert human rights and when the newspapers, magazines, radio and television stations, and other instruments that form public opinion are overwhelmingly controlled by enemies of freedom? Yes. And the biography of San Salvador's Archbishop Oscar Romero helps us understand why.

The outline of Archbishop Romero's story is well known—a professorial bishop who in 1977 was thrust against his own wishes into a position of confrontation with the brutally repressive government of El Salvador, becoming "the voice of the voiceless" masses until assassinated in 1980.

Like the great sixteenth-century defender of Native Americans, Bartolomé de Las Casas, Romero found it necessary to appeal to a court that transcended local borders. As Las Casas had written about the Devastation of the Indies and taken his Defense of the Indians to Valladolid and King Charles V, Romero addressed universities (Georgetown and Louvain), the National Council of Churches in New York, and President Jimmy Carter. The motivation was similar: rogue States depend on the acquiescence of others when perpetrating atrocities. So, to redress injustices in El Salvador, Romero urged President Carter to shut off military aid to the Salvadoran government. He appealed to President Carter, as a Christian and a defender of human rights, to guarantee that America would "not intervene directly or indirectly, with military, economic, diplomatic, or other pressures in determining the destiny of the Salvadoran people."[21]

Following in the footsteps of *Pacem in Terris* and Martin Luther King Jr., Romero argued that the universe moved on the side of justice. And if El Salvador were left to its own designs, ultimately justice would win out over oppression. It was in fact the intervention of foreign interests, both political and economic, that allowed the repressive government of his country to remain in power. Instead of acquiescence, Romero petitioned people of good will from other countries to put public pressure on his own government to change its ways.

Peacebuilding seems always to come with great cost to participants. Morehouse College well remembers the martyrs of the American Civil Rights Movement of fifty years ago. Rosa Parks was arrested for refusing to give up her seat on the Montgomery city bus to a white passenger. So much violence and rioting accompanied James Meredith's enrollment at the University of Mississippi that President Kennedy sent five thousand federal troops into the state. Demonstrators were arrested in Birmingham, Alabama, for protesting segregation, and the nation was shocked by the images of brutality as the Commissioner of Public Safety used dogs and fire hoses against African Americans. Medgar Evers was murdered in Jackson, Mississippi. Four girls were killed in the bombing of the Sixteenth Street Baptist Church in Birmingham. Three young men who registered voters in Neshoba County, Mississippi, were murdered by the Ku Klux Klan. Fifty marchers were hospitalized at "Bloody Sunday." Dr. King was assassinated on the balcony of the Lorraine Motel in Memphis, Tennessee. And this list could be expanded manifold.

Archbishop Romero was assassinated in 1980 while celebrating Mass remembering the death of the mother of the publisher of *El Independiente*, one of the few remaining voices of justice and human rights in the country. From there, the Salvadoran government's violence escalated to the point that the government murdered approximately another 16,000 civilians the following year. In all, La Matanza (the Salvadoran government's death squads and campaign of terror against its own population) led to the massacre of 75,000 people and the displacement of close to 20 percent of El Salvador's population.[22]

21. Romero, "Letter to President Carter," 189.

22. Perhaps the most trustworthy numbers come from the 1993 Report of the UN Truth Commission (http://www .derechos.org/nizkor/salvador/informes/truth.html).

The homily Archbishop Romero was preaching, when killed, is eerily reminiscent of Dr. King's last speech in Memphis, 3 April 1968, on the eve of his assassination. Did both men have a presentiment that they would die? Martin Luther King Jr.'s concluding words are well known to us: "I've seen the promised land. I may not get there with you. But I want you to know tonight, that we, as a people will get to the promised land. And I'm happy, tonight. I'm not worried about anything. I'm not fearing any man. Mine eyes have seen the glory of the coming of the Lord."[23] What is so evident in Dr. King's words are his solidarity with others who have suffered and will suffer in pursuit of true peace, including Jesus himself hanging on the cross. The Christian's way of building peace can be no different than that of Christ crucified.

Here are Archbishop Romero's last words:

> We know that every effort to better society, especially when injustice and sin are so ingrained, is an effort that God blesses, that God wants, that God demands of us . . . We remember with gratitude this generous woman [Doña Sarita] who was able to sympathize with . . . all who work for a better world, and who added her own grain of wheat through her suffering . . . We know that no one can go on forever, but those who have put into their work a sense of very great faith, of love of God, of hope among human beings, find it all results in the splendors of a crown that is the sure reward of those who labor thus, cultivating truth, justice, love, and goodness on the earth . . .
>
> This holy mass, now, this Eucharist, is such an act of faith . . . May [Christ's] body immolated and this blood sacrificed for humans nourish us also, so that we may give our body and our blood to suffering and pain—like Christ, not for self, but to bring about justice and peace for our people.
>
> Let us join together, then, intimately in faith and hope at this moment of prayer for Doña Sarita and ourselves.[24]

While speaking this phrase, Oscar Romero was killed. He died in solidarity with Christ and all who suffer to build peace.

23. King, "I See the Promised Land," 286

24. Romero, "Last Homily of Archbishop Romero,"192–93.

CONCLUSION: THE LOGIC OF VIOLENCE AND THE THREAT OF NONVIOLENCE

While Pope John XXIII died of natural causes, both King and Romero were assassinated. The latter were, perhaps, more directly opposed to the prevailing social and political orders in their respective societies, which may explain why they met violent ends. Yet sociopolitical opposition does not suffice to explain why nonviolence so often breeds violent opposition. A crucial question remains: what is it that connects nonviolence to violence? Why is nonviolence so often perceived as a threat meriting violent (sometimes lethal) response?

Emmanuel Lévinas argues that our normal way of being in the world—i.e., our characteristic ways of perceiving, understanding, and ordering experience—privileges immanence. We take what is Other, what we do not understand, and make it ours. Yet by integrating the Other into our own horizons of experience, the Other is effectively stripped of its alterity; the transcendence of the Other is reduced to the immanence of the Same. As Levinas puts it, "When the Other enters into the horizon of knowledge, it already renounces alterity."[25] Hence, our normal ways of being mask a deeper violence toward the Other. Our drive to know, to comprehend, to order is nothing more than a drive to eliminate that which is Other.

Yet our totalizing impulses can be interrupted by an encounter with the absolutely Other—namely, that which resists our drive to integrate it into our horizons of experience. Such experiences "pull us up short," revealing the infinite depth of the Other, the limits of our finitude, as well as our ethical obligation to the Other. We encounter this Other not in the contemplation of God, but in the face of the human Other, whose "defenseless eyes" reveal an infinite depth that demands our response: "The epiphany of the Absolutely Other is a face by which the Other challenges and commands me through his nakedness, through his destitution. He challenges me from his humility and from his height."[26] This irruption of the Other into our horizons of experience obligates us, not in the sense of duty (for "duty" implies that there is a decision to be made about whether or not to fulfill the obligation), but in the sense of an immediate and inescapable call

25. Lévinas, *Basic Philosophical Writings*, 12.

26. Ibid., 18.

to responsibility—a responsibility that "empties the I of its imperialism and egoism," binding it inexorably to the Other.[27]

> Non-violent resistance forces an encounter with the absolutely Other. While violent resistance strives to negate otherness by simply defeating the opposition, non-violent resistance forces perpetrators of injustice to acknowledge the humanity of those who suffer. This encounter with the absolutely Other is not just a political threat, but an existential crisis that threatens to disrupt the totalizing gaze of the "I," creating an infinite responsibility to the Other. It is this crisis, I think, that often provokes a violent response. Yet, paradoxically, the assassinations of King and Romero did not lessen the scandal of their humanity, but broadcast it far and wide. As martyrs for peace, King and Romero force us all to acknowledge our responsibilities to the Other.[28]

BIBLIOGRAPHY

Abraham, W. J. "The Wesleyan Quadrilateral in the American Methodist-Episcopal Tradition." *Wesleyan Theological Journal* 20.1 (1985) 34–44.

John XXIII. *Mater et Magistra*. Boston: Daughters of St. Paul, 1961.

———. *Pacem in Terris*. Boston: Daughters of St. Paul, 1963.

King, Martin Luther Jr. *A Testament of Hope: The Essential Writings and Speeches of Martin Luther King, Jr.* Edited by James Melvin Washington. New York: Harper, 1986.

Lévinas, Emmanuel. "Transcendence and Height." In *Basic Philosophical Writings*, 149–60. Studies in Continental Thought. Bloomington: Indiana University Press, 1996.

Long, J. D. *Pictures of Slavery in Church and State; Including Personal Reminiscences, Biographical Sketches, Anecdotes, etc. etc. with an Appendix, Containing the Views of John Wesley and Richard Watson on Slavery*. Philadelphia: John Dixon Lang, 1857. http://docsouth.unc.edu/neh/long/long.html.

Luther, Martin. "Concerning Christian Liberty," 1520. Project Wittenberg, http://www.iclnet.org/pub/resources/text/wittenberg/luther/web/cclib-1.html.

———. "On Secular Authority: How Far Does the Obedience Owed it Extend?" 1523. http://home.roadrunner.com/~rickgardiner/texts/secauth.htm.

———. "A Treatise on Good Works." 1520. Project Wittenberg. http://www.iclnet.org/pub/resources/text/wittenberg/wittenberg-luthworks.html.

Outler, Albert C. "Some Concepts of Human Rights and Obligations in Classical Protestantism." In *Natural Law and Natural Right*, edited by A. L. Harding, 12–29. Studies in Jurisprudence. Dallas: Southern Methodist University Press, 1955.

———. "The Wesleyan Quadrilateral in Wesley." *Wesleyan Theological Journal* 20.1 (1985) 19–33.

27. Ibid.

28. Ibid.

Romero, Oscar. *Voice of the Voiceless: The Four Pastoral Letters and Other Statements.* Introductory Essays by Jon Sobrino and Ignacio Martin-Baró. Translated by Michael J. Walsh. Maryknoll, NY: Orbis, 1985.

UN Truth Commission. "Report of the Commission on the Truth for El Salvador." 1993. http://www.derechos.org/nizkor/salvador/informes/truth.html.

Wesley, John. "Sermon #40 on Christian Perfection." 1760. www.GodOnThe.Net/wesley

———. "Sermon #50 on the Use of Money." 1760. www.GodOnThe.Net/wesley.

———. "Sermon #99 on the Reward of Righteousness." 1760. www.GodOnThe.Net/wesley.

———. "Sermon #116 on the Causes of Inefficacy of Christianity." 1760. www. GodOnThe.Net /wesley.

———. "Thoughts upon Slavery." 1774. In *A Collection of Religious Tracts,* edited by Joseph Crukshank. Philadelphia: Lang, 1784. http://docsouth.unc.edu/church/wesley.html.

11

Reflections on Refugee and Asylum Policy in the United States and Germany

Bringing Peace to a Fractious World

Paul A. Harris and William E. Baker

The U.S. has always been of two minds about new immigrants. On the one hand, the country has historically been a refuge, a place of new beginnings, accepting and even recruiting new settlers to build the nation and its economy. On the other hand, the theme of protectionism has found recurrent expression in apprehension over the capacity of the culture and the economy to absorb newcomers, in the desire to limit labor market competition and assure minimal health standards, and even nativism in racist theories.

Charles Keely[1]

The world is experiencing a refugee crisis the likes of which have not been seen since the end of the Second World War. According to the United Nations High Commissioner for Refugees (UNHCR) there are an estimated

1. Keely, Speech before the Subcommittee on Immigration.

65.3 million persons who have been forced from their homes and of that number 21.3 million are refugees fleeing persecution, war, ethnic violence, or political chaos.[2] The number is staggering and it suggests that any hope for a long-term solution will require a truly global effort. Unfortunately, the current *Zeitgeist* throughout much of the developed world is one of pulling back on collective arrangements and pulling up the drawbridge to prevent entry to those who are seeking a better life for themselves and their families. The United States, a nation which is held out as the beacon of hope in a hopeless world, shows signs that it is abandoning its commitment to provide refuge and protection to the world's most vulnerable at a time when it is most needed. One of the first acts of the Donald Trump White House was to issue an Executive Order which suspended refugee resettlement to the United States on the grounds that refugees from Syria are a security risk. Though the total number of refugees resettling in the United States has for the past decade been capped at 80,000 per year, the symbolic effect of the United States closing its doors to "the homeless, tempest tossed"[3] is not lost on the rest of the world. In contrast to the US position, Germany has opened its doors to over one million refugees and asylum seekers since the late summer and early fall of 2015. Germany's commitment to providing refuge is enshrined in the constitution's Asylum Article (Article 16a) which provides the right of asylum as a fundamental right and it is the only fundamental right which is applicable only to foreigners.

The goal of this chapter is to help the reader gain a better understanding of the role in which refugee and asylum policy play in providing hope to a fractious world. As such, this chapter will trace both the United States' and Germany's postwar refugee and asylum policies highlighting both nations' historical commitment to providing shelter. Germany and the United States have historically played a central role in providing refuge and safe haven to those seeking shelter in the postwar years. Since the end of the Second World War, sustained wide-scale international immigration has transformed both Germany and the United States into magnet societies which have resettled millions of refugees and asylum seekers. However, with the onset of the wave of refugee and asylum seekers fleeing the violence in Syria, Iraq, Afghanistan, Somali, Libya, and the Sudan, we have seen an embrace and a rejection of those seeking relief. The embrace has come largely through the German government's granting of asylum to

2. United Nations High Commissioner for Refugees, "Figures at a Glance."

3. Lazarus, "The New Colossus."

nearly one million migrants arriving on its borders and train stations in the late summer and fall of 2015. The rejection can most clearly be seen in thirty-one US governors' refusing to resettle Syrian refugees and the recent US government ban on refugee resettlement. Germany's approach to refugee and asylum resettlement is humanitarian, whereas in the United States asylum and refugee policy are seen as matters of national security.

Nevertheless, for the past seventy years, the United States and Germany have served as havens for refugees, asylum seekers, and displaced persons and their acceptance of refugees and asylum seekers is largely dependent upon unique historical and ideological considerations. In the United States, the Cold War and the civil rights movement played a central role in the formation of a more expansive refugee and asylum regime. In Germany, the Cold War also played a role especially with regard to the millions of ethnic Germans who had lived in the Volga region of Russia since the sixteenth century, yet who were the target of Stalin's ethnic purges, suffering persecution and forcible resettlement to the Soviet Asian Republics in the fall of 1941. However, Germany's singular approach to refugee and asylum resettlement comes largely as a result of the country's war time past and the shame associated with the Third Reich based on what Markovits and Reich call "the politics of collective memory."[4] The politics of collective memory refers to the burden of German history as a result of the experiences of the Holocaust and the Second World War. For example, as the legal successor of the Third Reich, West Germany was obliged to offer citizenship to the eight million ethnic Germans who had been forcibly expelled from throughout Eastern Europe immediately after the war. In this case Article 116 of the German constitution conferred their citizenship:

> In the eyes of the constitution, everyone is a German who holds German citizenship or who, as a refugee or expellee of German *Volkszugehoerigkeit*, or as a spouse or descendant of such a person, has been admitted to the territory of the German Empire as it existed on December 31,1937.[5]

As Hoffman notes, "the admission of over eight million expellees, evacuees, and refugees by 1950 was thus understood as an act of solidarity and an attempt to deal justly with the consequence of the war."[6] This sad chap-

4. Markovitz and Reich, "Contemporary Power of Memory," 442 and *German Predicament*, 442.

5. Federal Republic of Germany, Basic Law, Article 116.

6. Hoffmann, "Immigration and Nationhood," 360.

ter of German history has largely been ignored and overshadowed by the enormity of the war crimes perpetuated against Nazi Germany's enemies. The politics of collective memory played a key role in the spring and fall of 1990 when a newly reunified Germany opened its doors to thousands of Russian-speaking Jews who sought refuge in the country.[7] Clearly, Germany's singular historical relationship with the Jewish people, coupled with a strong sense of moral obligation, are the core reasons for this policy. Germany in the immediate postwar years was an occupied land without an elected government and an infrastructure which did not function, a nation on the brink of starvation in which all major cities had been reduced to rubble with nearly 70 percent of all housing destroyed or inhabitable, and yet the temporary home to over eleven million non-German displaced persons of which 250,000 were Jews who survived the Holocaust. For these Jewish survivors, there was no home and, in most cases, no family to which they could return. An additional hardship faced by Europe's uprooted and homeless was the absence of any coordinated international humanitarian response with the notable exception of the United Nations Relief and Rehabilitation Administration (UNRRA). In late 1943, the UNRRA was established

> to plan, coordinate, administer or arrange for the administration of measures for the relief of victims of war in any area under the control of any of the United Nations through the provision of food, fuel, clothing, shelter and other basic necessities, medical and other essential services; and to facilitate in such areas, so far as necessary to the adequate provision of relief, the production and transportation of these articles and the furnishing of these services.[8]

The UNRRA operated Displaced Persons campus throughout allied occupied Germany (excluding the Soviet Zone) and was responsible for housing, feeding, providing medical care, education to and resettlement of some seven million non-Germans who had been moved to Germany during the war to work on farms and in the armament industry. Working closely with the occupation armies as well as the International Red Cross, by 1947, UNRRA was running over eight hundred camps and by the time it ended the agency, it resettled over nearly six million persons back to their

7. Harris, "Jüdische Einwanderung," 36.

8. United Nations Relief and Rehabilitation Administration, Administrative History.

home countries. Following on the heels of the UNRRA was the International Refugee Organization (IRO) and then with the passage of the 1951 Convention Relating to the Status of Refugees, the United Nations High Commissioner for Refugees (UNHCR) was established. Still in existence, the UNHCR leads and coordinates international action to protect refugees including internally displaced persons.

The idea of the United States as an asylum for the oppressed of the world has exerted a powerful influence on the hearts and minds of Americans. This sentiment is most clearly stated in Emma Lazarus' sonnet "The New Colossus" with the words, "Give me your tired, your poor, your huddled masses yearning to breathe free." Lazarus' famous lines have pulled at our national imagination and continue to inspire the way we think about freedom and immigration today. Over the years, the sonnet has become a part of American culture, serving as a call for immigrants' rights. As news of Nazi atrocities became publicized, President Truman issued a directive admitting the entrance of 40,000 war refugees. Partly as a result of the inflexibility of the national origins quota system, the government had to resort to temporary measures to meet emergency immigration situations. In 1948 the Displaced Persons Act was passed and authorized the entry of 415,000 persons to the United States by the end of 1952. Under this Act, refugee admission, for the first time in the nation's history, became a factor in US policy.[9]

The first major piece of postwar legislation came with the passage of the Immigration and Nationality Act of 1952 also known as the McCarran-Walter Act. The 1952 Act preserved the national origins quota and established a system of preferences for skilled workers. Furthermore, it also encouraged a strengthening of family ties by giving preference to US citizens. Throughout the Cold War, the issue of refugee and forced migration in the Northern and Western Hemisphere was largely kept in check as a result of the uneasy détente between the two global superpowers. US refugee policy came about as a result of this ideological divide. With the onset of the Cold War, additional refugee measures were enacted by Congress as allowed under the parole clause found in the 1952 Act which authorized the Attorney General to admit persons in emergency situations. The first of these came in the form of the 1953 Refugee Relief Act which admitted over 200,000 refugees outside of existing quotas. Legislation passed in 1957 permitted approximately 30,000 Hungarian "refugee-escapees" displaced

9. Ueda, *Postwar Immigrant America*, 36.

by the failed 1956 revolution to enter the United States—the 1957 Refugee Escapee Act. Under the new Act a refugee-escapee was defined as any alien who fled from any communist country because of persecution or fear of it. The parole clause also was used to admit more than 650,000 Cubans in the early 1960s; Czechoslovakians in the aftermath of the 1968 revolution; Chileans after 1973; and more than 400,000 Indochinese by the late 1970s following the fall of Saigon.

One of the most wide-sweeping changes in the history of US immigration policy came with the passage of the 1965 Immigration and Nationality Act. The 1965 Act introduced four basic policy changes which clearly reflected the Civil Rights era just as the 1952 Act reflected the Cold War era.

1) The abolition of the national origins quota system
2) The introduction of a new preference system based upon family reunification
3) The institution of individual labor clearance procedures based on economic skills
4) The introduction of a refugee policy.

The 1965 Act abolished the national origins system replacing it with an overall total of 160,000 with a 20,000-person limit per country for all nations outside the Western Hemisphere. Second, it capped immigration from Western Hemisphere countries at 120,000 without individual national limits. Immediately afterward President Johnson declared the United States would welcome any Cubans who wished to flee Castro's Communist state. Hundreds of thousands did so, leading Congress to pass the Cuban Adjustment Act of 1966.[10] Additionally, instead of "blanket revisions" special parole programs were implemented to handle Cuban, Vietnamese, and Soviet Jewish Refugees, many of which are still in practice.

During the 1980s concern over rising immigration from Latin America, the Caribbean Basin, and Asia; growing numbers of undocumented workers; and increased demand for entry by asylum seekers and refugees forced Congress and the White House to question immigration policy. Ultimately, between 1980 and 1990 seven changes were adopted, three in 1996 alone.

The Refugee Act of 1980 was the most wide-sweeping legislation of its kind ever enacted. Under the 1980 law, Congress benchmarked an annual

10. Martin, *A Nation of Immigrants*, 227–28.

refugee figure of 50,000. Hitherto, refugees were admitted on an ad hoc, emergency basis. The 1980 Act was significant in the area of a rights-based policy because it (a) established a national policy guaranteeing continued refugee admissions; (b) redefined the term "refugee" along the lines of the Geneva Convention, thus departing from the largely ideological, anti-communist grounds that had previously prevailed; (c) grounded the principle of asylum in US statutory law; and (d) permitted resettlement assistance for refugees.[11] The 1980 Act was the last major piece of legislation which specifically targeted refugees and asylum seekers. Passed during the height of the Cold War, the Act was established in response to the worldwide response to the two million Southeast Asian "boat people" who had escaped Vietnam, Cambodia, and Laos. Still in effect today, the Act has allowed for over three million refugees fleeing war and persecution an opportunity to create a new life for themselves and their families.

If we turn our attention to Germany, a cursory examination of German law might lead us to expect German immigration policies to be sharply restrictive and refugee policies to be exclusionary. Yet, in the past half century, immigration has been higher in Germany than in any other West European state, and Germany arguably has the most liberal refugee and asylum policy in Europe.[12] Despite a long history of absorbing migrants from East Central Europe, Germany lacks a "national model" around which to organize its immigration debate.[13] Unlike the United States, the only previous experience the country could draw upon was the incorporation of Polish laborers to the Ruhr industrial valley after World War I. The industrialization of Germany in the late nineteenth century transformed the Hohenzollern Empire into a country of immigration. The migration from East Central Europe came primarily in the form of seasonal workers and labor migrants from Russia, Poland, the Eastern parts of Prussia and Italy, who were recruited to perform manual labor in the growing industries on the Rhine, in Silesia, in the Ruhr, around Berlin, and to meet the agricultural demand for cheap labor.[14] Bade notes that by the outbreak of World War I the number of "foreign laborers" on German soil was around

11. Ibid.

12. Harris, "Jüdische Einwanderung," 39; Hollifield, *Immigrants, Markets and States*, 198–99.

13. Faist, "How to Define," 50; Kurthen, "Germany at Crossroads," 915–16.

14. Klessman, "Einwanderungsprobleme," 303–6.

1.2 million.[15] The majority of these were Poles from East Prussia followed by Russians from Galicia, then a part of the Austro-Hungarian Empire.

These migrants possessed little or no civil rights and were subject to questioning, internment, and deportation with little or no forewarning.[16] In addition, there were strict prohibitions against socializing and mixing with the indigenous German populace as well as against holding meetings and church services in their native tongue. Their status as foreign laborers allowed the authorities broad administrative and police powers which were designed to curb migrants' participation in nearly every aspect of their lives outside of work. Although labor migrants were subject to arbitrary deportation, there were some exceptions. The Ruhr-Poles enjoyed a "special legal status" in that they were considered East Prussian Citizens of Polish Descent. Although subject to intensive police scrutiny, their special legal status protected them from arbitrary deportation. In addition, they were permitted to organize their own clubs and societies and to establish their own press.[17] Their first union, the "Polish Professional Assembly," was formed shortly thereafter, along with numerous community and church related organizations. The Treaty of Versailles and the reestablishment of Poland gave the Ruhr-Poles the option of choosing either Polish or German citizenship and approximately a third of the roughly 350,000 decided to stay in the Ruhr Valley and become German citizens.[18]

The Ruhr-Polish "Germanization" notwithstanding, Germany fell far short of adopting an American or French style citizenship model. Indeed, despite its large foreign population, Germany continued to base citizenship on *jus sanguinis* (community of descent) as codified in its 1913 Citizenship Law rather than on *jus soli* (place of birth). The 1913 Law effectively permitted Germans living abroad (*Auslandsdeutsche*) to transmit citizenship to their descendants at birth. This has led several scholars to declare that German citizenship is inclusive to German emigrants but exclusive to immigrants in Germany.[19] However, since January 1, 2000, children born in Germany of foreign parents will receive citizenship, provided that one parent has legally resided in Germany for at least eight years. According

15. Bade, "Preussengaenger und Abwehrpolitik, 91–93; and Bade, "Billig und Willing, 311–12.

16. Klessman, "Einwanderungsprobleme," 305–6.

17. Ibid., 305.

18. Ibid, 308–9.

19. Brubaker, *Citizenship and Nationhood*, 169–70; Faist, "How to Define," 57–58.

to the so-called option model, the children have until their twenty-third birthday to decide which citizenship they wish to retain.

This ethno-cultural principle of citizenship is rooted in the conception of the nation as an organic cultural, linguistic, racial community. However, this seemingly exceptional or populist (*Volkisch*) view of German citizenship and German immigration policy is fallacious. Indeed, under the 1953 Federal Expellee and Refugee Law as amended in 1993 the continued migration, or return, of ethnic Germans living throughout the former Soviet Union to Germany made up a considerable portion of inflows into the Federal Republic and is based upon *Vertreibungsdruck* (expulsion pressure). However, this return migration should not be confused with a *volkisch character* of German citizenship. As Dietrich Thränhardt indicates:

> Germany is not the only country accepting ethnic migrants from Russia and other Commonwealth of Independent States (C.I.S.) states. All nations who feel that their co-ethnics live there are doing the same: Israel, Poland, Korea, Finland, Hungary, the Czech Republic and Greece. Moreover, Germany does not take in all ethnic Germans but only those who are considered as being under *Vertreibungsdruck* (expulsion pressure). Consequently, since the end of the Soviet empire, Germany only takes in ethnic Germans from C.I.S. countries on the assumption that the discrimination of Germans in the C.I.S. is continuing since they are not allowed to return to their historic settlements in the former Volga Republic. In contrast, ethnic Germans from Poland and Romania no longer have a right to immigrate after the end of the totalitarian regimes in these countries, unless they prove a special discrimination.[20]

To be certain, an estimated twelve million German citizens and ethnic Germans were "expelled" from Eastern Europe and resettled in the American, British, and Soviet zones of occupied Germany in the immediate aftermath of World War II, based upon their ethnicity alone. What many scholars and students of German immigration policy fail to see is that the victorious allied powers at the Potsdam Conference called for the resettlement of twelve million expellees within occupied Germany's new borders. As a result, the Allies enforced the resettlement of Germans and ethnic Germans alike to occupied Germany. The victorious Allies wanted integration of the German expellees from the East, to avoid any revisionist activity against the new

20. Thränhardt, "European Migration," 233.

borders in the East." In short, the policy of according citizenship to ethnic Germans was implemented by the US occupation authorities in Germany.

> You will require the persons of German extraction transferred to Germany be granted German nationality with full civil and political rights . . . You will take such measures as you may seem appropriate to assist the German authorities in effecting a program of resettlement.[21]

In one fell swoop, Article 116 of the Basic Law accorded these expellees full German citizenship. Subsequent claims of German citizenship by ethnic German repatriates from the former Soviet Union is guaranteed in the 1953 Federal Expellee and Refugee Law as amended in 1993 upon their legal resettlement or "return" to Germany. Those ethnic German repatriates who resettle in Germany are legally considered as Germans or co-ethnic returnees and counted as naturalized German citizens not as migrants.

Contemporary immigration and resettlement patterns to Germany can be better understood in light of traditional immigration movements since World War II. The first one lasting from 1945 to 1950 comprised the resettlement of ethnic German expellees and refugees during which time approximately eight million resettled in war-torn West Germany. The second, occurring from 1950 to 1961, brought large numbers of East Germans from the German Democratic Republic to the West. The third, covering the mid-1950s to 1973, was characterized by the importation of large numbers of foreign "guest workers" to work in various industries in West Germany. The fourth, lasting from 1973 to the late 1980s, saw the emergence of family member immigration resulting from the earlier recruitment of "guest workers" as well as a marked increase in asylum applicants. The fifth, occurring from the early 1980s to 1988, consisted of flows of ethnic Germans primarily from Eastern Europe (Poland, Romania) and a marked increase in asylum applicants. The sixth phase, in effect since 1989, has witnessed large numbers of ethnic German repatriates over 2.5 million, hundreds of thousands of asylum applicants, and approximately 250,000 Russian speaking Jews entering country since 1990.

Since 1989, Germany has become a haven where hundreds of thousands of newcomers comprised of asylum seekers, ethnic German repatriates, war refugees, Russian-speaking Jews and family members arrive yearly. By the end of 2016, over sixteen million people living in Germany had an

21. Cited in Thränhardt, "Germany an Ethnic Nation?" 10.

immigrant background and of that number, half did not have German citizenship. Germany like the United States is indeed a land of immigrants.[22]

The revolutionary changes which occurred throughout Eastern Europe and the Soviet Union since 1989 have ushered in the movement toward political pluralism and democratization. However, there also came a resurgent nationalism and jingoism at the expense of ethnic minorities living there. With a newfound freedom of expression, many nationalist and ultranationalist groups began to express openly their bigotry, intolerance, and hostility toward ethnic minorities. These expressions in some cases turned violent, as in the former Yugoslavia.

Coupled with the growing intolerance was a situation of economic disjuncture owing to the transition from centrally planned to free market economies. Economic uncertainty throughout the former Soviet Union and Eastern European states along with traditional "supply-push" factors further contributed to the desire and drive to emigrate. Many sought migration as a means to alleviate these desperate living conditions. Disregard of the rights of ethnic minorities or nationalities clearly has been one of the core causes for emigration. Indeed, the movement of Russian-speaking Jews and ethnic German repatriates to Germany can be directly linked to persecution at home. Since the end of the Cold War, Germany has had the tasks of managing reunification, substantial levels of ethnic German repatriate immigration, and soaring levels of asylum seekers.

As noted above, before the collapse of the Berlin Wall in 1989, migration came chiefly from the entrance of guest workers and their families. However, afterward and continuing up to the present there has been an increasing number of asylum seekers as well as war refugees fleeing wars in Afghanistan, Iraq, Syria as well as continued pressures from the war in the Balkans and now Ukraine. Germany continues to maintain Europe's most liberal asylum provisions. The country experienced the sharpest demand for asylum with 800,000 requests filed in 2015 and 322,599 in 2016.

Germany is unique among European Union member states in its immigration policies toward ethnic German repatriates and Jews from the former Soviet Union. Indeed, repatriated ethnic Germans migrants from the former Soviet Union comprise the largest state-assisted quota immigration in the world. Germany also is now the third principal country of immigration for Jews, following Israel and the United States, and the only West European state allowing their migration and permanent settlement.

22. Hunger, "Die Rolle von Migrantenselbstorganisationen," 44.

In addition to their legal status, both groups share similar postwar migration patterns and have traditionally used emigration as a "safety valve" in order to escape political and ethnic persecution at home.[23]

The face of immigration in Germany and the United States has undergone a demographic transformation in the past fifty years. With the adoption of the 1965 Immigration and Nationality Act in the United States, the national origins quota system was repealed thereby opening the door to places other than Europe. Indeed, the face of immigration has changed from European to Asian, Mexican, Caribbean, Central American and, to a lesser extent, African. As Vialet notes:

> [The 1965 Act] repealed the national origins quota system, which had regulated immigration to the United States since the 1920s. It replaced the quota system which was heavily weighted to favor immigrants from northern and western European countries, with a "preference system" which allotted immigrant visas on the basis of family relationships and needed skills.[24]

In the German case, liberal asylum provisions, as allowed under Article 16, coupled with the provision allowing ethnic German repatriate migration from the former Soviet Union, have helped to make Germany a true immigration country.

Historically, discrimination in both country's immigration regimes was the norm. Indeed, the 1952 McCarran-Walter Act in the United States upheld the national origins quota giving preference to Western and Northern Europeans as established originally in the 1924 Johnson-Reed Act. "Clearly racism, through slavery and the Jim Crow system was built into the American political system from the beginning."[25] "Most blacks were slaves, and free blacks were lumped together with slaves. Therefore [Supreme Court Justice Roger Taney] claimed, neither the Declaration of Independence nor the Constitution could have possibly meant to include blacks in their proclamations of rights."[26]

In the German case we observe a history of ethnic discrimination which predates the Third Reich. "The demand 'absolute exclusion of Russian-Polish workers from the German East' put forward by [Max] Weber and seized upon in more extreme forms by the political right with the

23. Harris, "Politics of Reparation and Return," 10.

24. Vialet, "Immigration," 3.

25. Hollifield, "Politics of International Migration, 167.

26. Smith, *Civic Ideals*, 267.

slogan 'Germany for Germans,' was greeted with approval far beyond the circles of pan-Germans in the late years of the Second Empire."[27] Oddly, the United States, a country with a rich history of immigration, imposed racial quotas in its first major postwar immigration legislation, whereas Germany did not. Despite utterances to the contrary, postwar Germany did not adopt racist immigration policies based on national origins.

Sustained immigration to the United States and Germany can best be explained in the context of the free market and in terms of the ongoing extension of rights to individuals who are not full members of the societies in which they reside. The attraction of markets and the protection given to aliens in rights-based regimes, taken together, explain the rise in immigration and its persistence in the face of economic crises, restrictive policies, and nationalist (anti-immigrant) political movements.[28] Immigration in postwar Germany and the United States was shaped by the social, economic, political, and historical forces to which they are closely tied. Indeed, the postwar immigration regimes of both Germany and the United States consist of a mix of inclusionary (expansive) and exclusionary (restrictive) policies.[29] This inclusionary tendency, argues Santel, is clearly evident in historically high levels of immigration and the granting of substantial civil, social, and political rights to legal permanent residents. The exclusionary tendency is manifested in strengthened border patrols, expedited deportations with limited due process, and the recent decision of the Trump administration to suspend refugee resettlement. The restrictions notwithstanding, the two countries continue to be powerful magnet societies for which war weary migrants desperately hope to gain entry.

Yet, it is just these expansive rights-based and citizenship policies which promote immigration and engage the capacity of advanced industrial democracies to control their borders. The central challenge of facing the United States and Germany, therefore, is to balance our international obligations and to do our "fair share" in refugee resettlement.

Indeed, the concept of refugee protection is itself inseparable from the notion of human rights. The right to seek asylum, for example, is enshrined in the United Nations Universal Declaration of Human Rights. The 1951 UN Refugee Convention requires international protection by providing refugees with fundamental rights and freedoms that a state normally

27. Herbert, *Foreign Labor in Germany*, 27–28.

28. Hollifield, *Immigrants, Markets and States*, 216.

29. Santel, *Migration*, 120.

reserves for its own citizens. What, then, are the limits to which states can affect control? Do the United States and Germany have a moral obligation to take in refugee and asylum seekers? Refugee and asylum policy has become a central issue of politics and public policy in Germany and the United States.

These myriad challenges have led scholars to focus their research on factors relating to state autonomy, sovereignty, and capacity in the control and regulation of international immigration. "State autonomy," Hollifield writes, "is the ability of governments to make or formulate policies without being subject to the excessive demands of special interests."[30] Therefore, policy effectiveness, that is, the extent to which the state is capable of directly influencing migration flows through policy change, is taken as one measure of state strength.

The commonly held view that liberal democracies such as Germany and the United States cannot control unwanted migration is unwarranted, despite the intensification of migration pressures in recent years.[31] A review of the experiences of Germany and the United States reveals considerable regulating capacity: "This capacity is certainly growing, not declining, over time, that some states possess more capacity than others, that the control capacities of particular states vary substantially across the four areas, and that these capacities fluctuate periodically in conjunction with contingent cycles of salience and effort."[32] Regarding refugee admissions in Germany and the United States, we observe clear instances where state capacity to control immigration and resettlement inflows can be controlled. German and US policy makers have instituted particular approaches designed to mediate and control refugee flows and resettlement, allowing policy makers, in turn, to institute control measures based upon cultural, historical, humanitarian concerns and foreign policy considerations. Clearly this is the case in the United States regarding Cubans, South East Asians, and Jews and Evangelical Christians from the former Soviet Union. In the German case, this is most evident in their treatment of ethnic German, Soviet Jewish migrants and asylum seekers. Yet, these constraints do not represent a weakening of state capacity per se: "Rather it does mean that individuals or groups may be admitted for raisons d'etat who would otherwise have been denied. States will from time to time find themselves confronted with

30. Hollifield, "Immigration and the French State," 58.

31. Freeman, "Can Liberal States Control," 17–20.

32. Ibid., 17.

an urgent situation that more or less compels operating outside normal channels."[33] Rather, when applied to admission criteria, the sovereignty of Germany and the United States to decide who enters and who becomes a member of the political community is largely determined by the shared understanding of its citizens and policy makers.

The elusive search for peace in a fractious world coupled with the search for improved economic, social, and political conditions is the defining challenge of advanced industrial democracies such as the United States and Germany today. Therefore, the regulation of refugee and asylum admissions is, and will be for some time, one of the major challenges of immigration control for the magnet societies of Germany and the United States. As we have pointed out, the liberalization and—now restriction—of refugee and asylum policy in Germany and the United States has occurred as a result of both international events, i.e., the Cold War, the Syrian Civil War, and the Balkan War (push factors) as well as national policies which allow for the permanent resettlement of refugees and asylum seekers (pull factors).

First a word about push factors. Push factors that drive the ever-growing number of immigrants to the advanced industrial democracies include persecution on the basis of national origin, race, religion, or political ideology such as occurred during decolonization, and more recently following the breakup of the Soviet Union. Push factors emanate from regions with a number of countries in which violence and brutality impel large numbers of people to cross international borders in search of security, these "bad neighborhoods," as Myron Weiner notes, included the successor states to Yugoslavia, portions of the former Soviet Union, much of sub-Saharan Africa, Vietnam, Cambodia, Laos, Central America, Haiti, Cuba—and since 2011—Syria and other parts of the Middle East as a result of the Syrian Civil War and unrest in the region.[34]

Pull factors, have come about through the liberalizing politics of Germany and the United States, which have brought about the rise of a new rights-based politics and rights-based liberalism.[35] In other words, Germany and the United States are democracies and that is part of their attraction for asylum seekers and refugees. Current refugee and asylum policy has become one of the most intractable issues on the policy agenda

33. Ibid., 27.

34. Weiner, "Bad Neighbors," 208–9.

35. Hollifield, *Immigrants, Markets and States*, 4–17.

in Germany and the United States. Despite their limited ability to predict the consequences of their respective immigration policies—such as the current refugee crisis as a result of the Syrian Civil War—this should not equate with a loss of sovereignty or regulatory power in either Germany or the United States. Virtually all major immigration events in Germany and the United States within the past fifty years have been the result of changing international conditions, i.e., war, ethnic, religious, and political persecution, or domestic forces, i.e., nationalist and nativist movements, whose outcomes and consequences have been virtually impossible to predict. As Haas notes, "Most political actors are incapable of long-range purposive behavior because they stumble from one set of decisions into the next as a result of not having been able to foresee many of the implications and consequences of earlier decisions."[36]

Refugee and asylum seekers are neither confined to one nation nor to a single geographic region. Most policy makers and political leaders have recognized that independent national policies will be insufficient to confront a humanitarian crisis that continues to place great demands on advanced industrial democracies. The challenge then is to continue to build upon those areas in which policy can address the problems of negative spill-over such as was advanced with the signing of the 1951 U.N. Convention and Protocol Relating to the Status of Refugees, the Maastricht Treaty in 1992, or the Amsterdam Treaty in 1997. Yet, each member state still retains its own legislation regarding the status of foreigners as well as its own laws with respect to naturalization and immigrant rights.

Yet, our examination of postwar Germany and the United States departs somewhat from this transnational globalization thesis with respect to refugee and asylum seekers. We realize that the true burden sharing among all nations can better be effected through international communitarian efforts, *Gemeinschaftsaufgabe,* via closer integration, tighter institutional networks, and greater involvement of policy makers, communities of faith, nongovernmental organizations, and individual citizens. Both Germany and the United States have shown and continue to show great resolve in crafting refugee and asylum policies with regard to their respective histories and political cultures as they come to terms with issues such as conditions of entry and residence, unanticipated influxes of asylum seekers and refugees, the rising tide of illegal entry, and the process of naturalization. This stresses the singular historical (moral) claims of nation states and

36. Haas, "Study of Regional Integration," 627.

argues that openness on part of the receiving society must be moderated with a willingness to care for the newcomers. When applied to refugee and asylum this view upholds the claims of both Germany and the United States to wide-ranging control over who enters and becomes a member of the political community. Viewed in this light we call to mind the words of Charles Taylor: "In an irremediably pluralistic society, a state that identifies with a certain conception of life will favor some people at the expense of others."[37]

Up until the 9/11 attacks, the postwar trend in the United States was to advance, emphasize, and legitimize the rights of people seeking refuge. Since then refugee and asylum seekers are now seen as possible threats to national security rather than as a humanitarian issue. In 2003, the Immigration and Naturalization Service was merged with the newly created Department of Homeland Security (DHS) and is now known as the US Citizenship and Immigration Services (USCIS). The USCIS is now the principal federal agency responsible for border control to include adjudicating refugee and asylum claims.

In 2005 the US Commission on International Religious Freedom (USCIRF) presented a report to Congress which found a disturbing trend in asylum practice. The report found that US asylum policy routinely detains and houses asylum seekers with convicted felons until their application has undergone a full range of security checks. Depending on the applicant, this process can last several months, even if the asylum seeker has established a credible fear of persecution, has family ties in this country, and poses no security risk. At present, the Immigration and Customs Enforcement Agency (ICE) within the Department of Homeland Security (DHS) houses asylum seekers in jail and jail-like facilities.[38] ICE also has instituted a project in which 10,000 asylum seekers not even accused of a crime are now wearing electronic anklets to monitor their whereabouts. Clearly, this is inappropriate for noncriminal asylum seekers.[39] And, if this were not enough, one of the first acts of the Trump administration was to suspend all refugee resettlement, ordering the Secretary of State to "determine what additional procedures should be taken to ensure that those approved for refugee admission do not pose a threat to the security and welfare of the United States."[40]

37. Taylor, *Reconciling the Solitudes,* 125.

38. U.S. Commission on International Religious Freedom, "Special Report."

39. National Public Radio, "Morning Edition."

40. Executive Order No. 13769.

In contrast, Germany has adopted a more humanitarian view of the crisis as described in the words of *The New York Times* columnist, Roger Cohen. "There's a new can-do nation. It's called Germany. The United States, fear ridden, has passed the torch."[41] And Germany has done its part; however, no nation however strong can go it alone. Today Germany along with a small handful of European Union nations—notably Greece, Italy, Austria, and the Netherlands—are carrying the lion's share of the burden in providing refuge and asylum to the hundreds of thousands of migrants who are seeking relief. Yet, there are growing signs of resettlement fatigue taking hold in the country. For example, the far right Alternative for Germany (known by the German acronym AfD) has made headway in the fall 2017 national elections. In both Germany and the United States, the major challenge will be to address the sustained demand for entry concomitant to universal principles of human rights and a sincere resolve to hope against all hope and work to bring peace to a fractious world.

BIBLIOGRAPHY

Bade, Klaus J. "'Billig und willig'—die ausländischen Wanderarbeiter im kaiserlichen Deutschland." In *Deutsche im Ausland. Fremde in Deutschland: Migration in Geschichte und Gegenwart*, edited by Klaus J. Bade, 311–24. Munich: Beck, 1993.

———. "Preussengaenger und Abwehrpolitik: Auslaenderbeschaeftigung, Auslaenderpolitik, und Auslaenderkontrolle auf dem Arbeitsmaket in Preussen vor dem Ersten Weltkrieg." *Archiv fuer Sozialgeschicte* 24 (1984) 91–162.

Brubaker, Rogers. *Citizenship and Nationhood in France and Germany*. Cambridge: Harvard University Press, 1992.

Cohen, Roger. "Germany, Refugee Nation." *New York Times*, December 21, 2015.

Executive Order No. 13769. Executive Order Protecting The Nation From Foreign Terrorist Entry Into The United States. *Weekly Compilation of Presidential Documents*, Friday, January 27, 2017. https://www.gpo.gov/fdsys/browse/collection.

Faist, Thomas. "How to Define a Foreigner? The Symbolic Politics of Immigration in German Partisan Discourse, 1978–1992." *West European Politics* 18 (Spring 1995) 50–71.

Federal Republic of Germany. 1949. Basic Law of the Federal Republic. Article 116.

Freeman, Gary P. "Can Liberal States Control Unwanted Migration?" *The Annals of the American Academy of Political and Social Science* 534 (1994) 17–30.

Haas, Ernst B. "The Study of Regional Integration: Reflections on the Joy and Anguish of Pre-Theorizing." *International Organization* 24 (1970) 607–46.

Harris, Paul A. "Jüdische Einwanderung nach Deutschland. Politische Debatte und administrative Umsetzung." *Zeitschrift für Migration und Soziale Arbeit* 1 (1997) 36–39.

41. Cohen, "Germany, Refugee Nation."

———. "The Politics of Reparation and Return: Soviet Jewish and Ethnic German Migration to the New Germany." PhD diss., Auburn University, 1997.

———. "An Unexpected, Yet Welcome Development: Jewish Migration to Germany and the Rebirth of a Community." In *Einwanderung in Erklärten und Unerklärten Einwanderungsländern: Analyse und Vergleich*, edited by Uwe Hunger et al., 121–48. Studien zur Politikwissenschaft B/93. Münster: Lit, 2001.

Herbert, Ulrich. *A History of Foreign Labor in Germany, 1880–1980: Seasonal Workers, Forced Laborers, Guest Workers.* Ann Arbor: University of Michigan Press, 1990.

Hoffmann, Christhard. "Immigration and Nationhood in the Federal Republic of Germany." In *The Postwar Transformation of Germany: Democracy, Prosperity, and Nationhood*, edited by John S. Brady et al., 357–77. Ann Arbor: University of Michigan Press, 1999.

Hollifield, James F. *Immigrants, Markets and States. The Political Economy of Postwar Europe.* Cambridge: Harvard University Press, 1992.

———. "Immigration and the French State." *Comparative Political Studies* 23 (1990) 56–79.

———. "The Politics of International Migration: How Can We 'Bring the State Back In?'" In *Migration Theory: Talking across Disciplines*, edited by Caroline B. Brettell and James F. Hollifeld, 137–85. New York: Routledge, 2000.

Hunger, Uwe. "Die Rolle von Migrantenselbstorganisationen im Integrationsprozess: Ein demokratietheoretischer Ansatz." In *Herausforderung Migration—Perspektiven der vergleichenden Politikwissenschaft: Festschrift für Dietrich Thränhardt*, edited by Sigrid Baringhorst et al., 33–51. Studien zur Politikwissenschaft. Abteilung B, Forschungberichte und Dissertationen 97. Berlin: Lit, 2006.

Keely, Charles. Speech. U.S. Senate Committee on the Judiciary, Subcommittee on Immigration and Refugee Policy, 97th Congress, 1st Session, 1981.

Klessman, Christoph. "Einwanderungsprobleme im Auswanderungsland: das Beispiel der 'Ruhrpolen.'" In *Deutsche im Ausland. Fremde in Deutschland: Migration in Geschichte und Gegenwart*, edited by Klaus J. Bade, 303–10. Munich: Beck, 1993.

Kurthen, Hermann. "Germany at the Crossroads: National Identity and the Challenges of Immigration." *International Migration Review* 29.4 (1995) 914–38.

Lazarus, Emma. "The New Colossus." Liberty State Park, 1883.

Markovits, Andrei S., and Simon Reich. "The Contemporary Power of Memory: The Dilemmas for German Foreign Policy." In *The Postwar Transformation of Germany: Democracy, Prosperity, and Nationhood*, edited by John S. Brady et al., 439–72. Ann Arbor: University of Michigan Press, 1997.

———. *The German Predicament: Memory and Power in the New Europe.* Ithaca, NY: Cornell University Press, 1997.

Martin, Susan F. *A Nation of Immigrants.* Cambridge: Cambridge University Press, 2011.

National Public Radio, Morning Edition. "As Asylum Seekers Swap Prison Beds for Ankle Bracelets, Same Firm Profits." November 13, 2015.

Santel, Bernhard. *Migration in und nach Europa: Erfahrungen, Strukturen, Politik.* Opladen: Leske & Budrich, 1995.

Smith, Rogers. *Civic Ideals: Conflicting Visions of Citizenship in U.S. History.* New Haven: Yale University Press, 1997.

Taylor, Charles. *Reconciling the Solitudes: Essays on Canadian Federalism and Nationalism.* Montreal: McGill-Queens University Press, 1993.

Thränhardt, Dietrich. "European Migration from East to West: Present Patterns and Future Directions." *New Community* 22.2 (1996) 227–42.

———. "Is Germany an Ethnic Nation?" Paper prepared for discussion at the Magnet Societies Workshop: Immigration in Postwar Germany and the United States, Evangelische Akademie Loccum, FRG, June 14–18, 2000.

Ueda, Reed. *Postwar Immigrant America: A Social History.* Boston: St. Martin's, 1994.

United Nations High Commissioner for Refugees (UNHCR) 2017. Figures at a Glance. Accessed on 2/20/2017. http://www.unhcr.org/en-us/figures-at-a-glance.html.

United Nations Relief and Rehabilitation Administration, Administrative History (UNRRA). 1943. https://archives.un.org/sites/archives.un.org/files/files/Finding%20Aids /2015_Finding_Aids/AG-018.pdf.

U.S. Commission on International Religious Freedom (USCIRF). Special Report: Assessing the U.S. Government's Detention of Asylum Seekers, 2013.

Vialet, Joyce C. "Immigration: Reasons for Growth, 1981–1995." Congressional Research Service Report. Washington, DC: The Committee for the National Institute for the Environment, 1997.

Weiner, Myron. "Bad Neighbors, Bad Neighborhoods: An Inquiry into the Causes of Refugee Flows, 1969–1992." In *Migrants, Refugees, and Foreign Policy: U.S. and German Policies toward Countries of Origin,* edited by Rainer Muenz and Myron Weiner, 183–22. Providence, RI: Berghahn, 1997.

Contributors

Wm. Loyd Allen received his training for Christian ministry at the Southern Baptist Theological Seminary in Louisville, Kentucky, where he was awarded the MDiv (1978) and PhD (1984) degrees. After graduation, Dr. Allen took a position as a religion professor and campus minister at Brewton-Parker College in South Georgia for five years before moving back to Louisville for three years on the church history faculty of Southern Seminary. In 1992, Mississippi College called him to become the head of its Christianity department. He left Mississippi after three years to become professor of church history and spiritual formation on the founding faculty of the McAfee School of Theology where he currently holds the Sylvan Hills Chair of Baptist Heritage.

William E. Baker is the Executive Director of the A. L. Burruss Institute of Public Service and Research, and Assistant Professor of Public Administration at Kennesaw State University. Prior to his academic appointments, he worked in local government as an administrator and as a practicing management consultant to cities and counties in the South. His research has focused on local government policy issues, and he has published several book chapters and articles. Most recently, his main focus has been the local government response to immigration. He teaches in the Master of Public Administration program in management, policy analysis, and evaluation at Kennesaw State University.

Donal Carbaugh is Professor of Communication at the University of Massachusetts, Amherst. He is recipient of the Samuel F. Conti Faculty Research Fellow, which is the highest award for research at his university; he is also the recipient of teaching awards including that as a finalist for the university's campus-wide outstanding teaching award. From 2005 to 2010, he was a member of the Research Advisory Group for the Security Needs Assessment Project of the United Nations Institute for Disarmament Research in Geneva. He is author of *Cultures in Conversation*, which was awarded the Outstanding Book of the Year in International and Intercultural Communication by the National Communication Association.

James M. Dawsey is the Wolfe Chair and Professor of Religious Studies at Emory & Henry College, Virginia. He arrived in southwest Virginia from Auburn University in Alabama, where he served as a chaired professor in the Religion Department. His main scholarly interests are in the areas of New Testament studies, especially the gospels; the formation of Christian societies; and Christian missionary activities in South America. He is an ordained minister in the South Carolina Annual Conference of the United Methodist Church. Dawsey has been married to Dixie Marie since 1971.

Paul A. Harris is a Professor in the Department of Political Science and Associate Director of the Honors College at Auburn University. He has nearly two decades full-time teaching experience, having taught for ten years (August 1998–July 2008) at Augusta State University in Augusta, Georgia, and for one year as a Friedrich Ebert Foundation Post-Doctoral Fellow at the Westfälische Wilhelms Universität Münster, Germany (September 1997–July 1998). Dr. Harris's research specialization is comparative immigration policy on which topic he has published widely in English and in German.

Abdelwahab Hechiche is a member of the School of Interdisciplinary Global Studies at the University of South Florida. His post-graduate studies were at the University of Tunis, at the University of Paris: Sorbonne, and at the Institute of Advanced International Relations of the faculty of Law-Pantheon. His doctoral dissertation dealt with The Palestine Question and Israeli-Jordanian Relations. He is a Laureate of the Foundation de la Vocation. He was a Fellow at the Harvard Center for Middle Eastern Studies, and a Dean Rusk Fellow at the Center of International Studies in Atlanta. In 2015, he was inducted into Dr. M.L.K Jr.'s College of Scholars at Morehouse College in Atlanta.

Robert N. Nash Jr. serves as the Arnall-Mann-Thomasson Professor of Missions and World Religions and Associate Dean for the Doctor of Ministry Program at McAfee School of Theology at Mercer University. He received his PhD degree in Church History (1989) and his MDiv degree (1985) from The Southern Baptist Theological Seminary in Louisville, Kentucky. In addition, he completed both his MA (History) and BA degrees at Georgia College and State University in Milledgeville, Georgia. Prior to coming to McAfee, Dr. Nash served as Global Missions Coordinator at the Cooperative Baptist Fellowship (2006–2012) and as a professor in the religion departments at both Shorter College in Rome, Georgia (1994–2006) and at Judson College in Marion, Alabama (1992–1994).

Richard Penaskovic is Emeritus Professor at Auburn University, where he was Professor of Religious Studies for the past thirty years. He has written several books and published over 100 articles, 25 in peer-reviewed journals such as *Theological Studies, Heythrop Journal* (London), *Louvain Studies* (Belgium), *The New Blackfriars Journal* (Great Britain), *Scholarly Publishing* (Toronto), *Augustinian Studies*, and *Horizons*. His book, *Critical Thinking and the Academic Study of Religion* is available from Duke University Press. He presently serves as Associate Editor of the journal, *Philosophy & Theology: Marquette University Journal* in which capacity he edits the Karl Rahner Papers.

Mustafa Şahin (Ph.D., Florida International University) is a Lecturer at Sam Nunn School of International Affairs at Georgia Tech where he teaches courses on the Middle East Relations. Previously he was a Visiting Assistant Professor at the University of South Florida and the Director of Academic Affairs at the Atlantic Institute. His research areas are Turkish Foreign Policy, Political Islam, Islamic spirituality and Islamic movements in Turkey. His most recent publications include "Spirituality and Social Justice in Islam" in Wiley-Blackwell Companion to Islamic Spirituality (forthcoming), and "Said Nursi and the Nur Movement in Turkey: An Atomistic Approach," in Digest of Middle East Studies."

Ori Z. Soltes teaches at Georgetown University across a range of disciplines, from art history and theology to philosophy and political history. He is the former Director and Curator of the B'nai B'rith Klutznick National Jewish Museum. He is also the author of scores of books, articles, exhibition catalogues, and essays on a range of topics. Recent books include *Our Sacred Signs: How Jewish, Christian, and Muslim Art Draw from the Same Source*; *Searching for Oneness: Mysticism in Judaism, Christianity, and*

Islam; and *Embracing the World: Fethullah Gülen's Thought and Its Relationship to Jalaluddin Rumi and Others*.

Jason R. Tatlock is an Associate Professor at Armstrong State University and the former chair of the Middle East Council of the University System of Georgia. He received his PhD in Near Eastern Studies from the University of Michigan and previously conducted graduate work at Jerusalem University College. He specializes in the history and religions of the Levant with a focus on the region of Israel/Palestine. His publications center on the ancient Near East and the modern Israeli-Palestinian conflict, emphasizing the role played by the United Nations. He is the editor of *The Middle East: Its History and Culture* (2012).

John A. Tures is a Professor of Political Science at LaGrange College. Before that, he worked for Evidence Based Research Inc. in the Washington DC suburbs from 2000 to 2002 and taught at the University of Delaware from 1999 to 2000. He received his PhD in political science in 2000 from Florida State University in Tallahassee, Florida. He has published in the *International Studies Quarterly*, the *Journal of Peace Research*, the *Middle East Journal*, the *Digest of Middle East Studies*, the *Arab Reform Bulletin*, and other journals. He is married to Elizabeth, and they have two children, Valerie and Zach.

Adam Y. Wells is an Assistant Professor of Religious Studies at Emory & Henry College. He received his PhD in Religion from the University of Virginia (2012), his MAR in Biblical Studies from Yale Divinity School (2007), and his BA in Philosophy (with honors) from Wake Forest University (2001). Dr. Wells's main scholarly interests are the theological and philosophical traditions of Christianity, Judaism, and Islam. His current work examines the kenosis hymn (Philippians 2: 5–11) as a foundation for theological and philosophical reflection about the nature of creation and incarnation. He is also interested in theoretical issues surrounding interreligious dialogue.

Index